ENABLING

KNOWLEDGE

CREATION

ENABLING

KNOWLEDGE

CREATION

How to Unlock the Mystery of Tacit Knowledge
and Release the Power of Innovation

GEORG VON KROGH

KAZUO ICHIJO

IKUJIRO NONAKA

OXFORD
UNIVERSITY PRESS
2000

OXFORD
UNIVERSITY PRESS

Oxford   New York
Athens   Auckland   Bangkok   Bogotá   Buenos Aires
Calcutta   Cape Town   Chennai   Dar es Salaam   Delhi   Florence
Hong Kong   Istanbul   Karachi   Kuala Lumpur   Madrid   Melbourne
Mexico City   Mumbai   Nairobi   Paris   São Paulo   Singapore
Taipei   Tokyo   Toronto   Warsaw

and associated companies
Berlin   Ibadan

Copyright © 2000 by Oxford University Press, Inc.

Published by Oxford University Press, Inc.
198 Madison Avenue, New York, New York 10016

Oxford is a registered trademark of Oxford University Press

Library of Congress Cataloging-in-Publication Data

Von Krogh, Georg.
Enabling knowledge creation / Georg von Krogh, Kazuo Ichijo, Ikujiro Nonaka.
p.   cm.
Includes bibliographical references and index.
ISBN 0–19–512616–5
1. Creativity ability in business. 2. Organizational learning. 3. Communication
in management. 4. Knowledge management. I. Ichijo, Kazuo, 1958–
II. Nonaka, Ikujiro, 1935–   III. Title
HD53.V63 2000
658.4'038–dc21   00–020291

3 5 7 9 8 6 4 2

Printed in the United States of America
on acid-free paper

CONTENTS

PREFACE

This is a book about knowledge enabling. It is our strong conviction that knowledge cannot be managed, only enabled. Since the publication of *The Knowledge-Creating Company* by Nonaka and Takeuchi in 1995, the concept of knowledge as competitive advantage of a firm has been drawing considerable attention from the corporate world and management academics. However, in many organizations, a legitimate interest in knowledge creation has been reduced to an overemphasis on information technology or measurement tools. Knowledge management rather than knowledge creation has been frequently discussed in business. However, the term *management* implies control of processes that may be inherently uncontrollable or, at least, stifled by heavy-handed direction.

From our perspective, managers need to support knowledge creation rather than control it, and the specifics of how and why they should do so form the core of the book. We call this knowledge enabling—the overall set of organizational activities that positively affect knowledge creation— and will emphasize throughout *Enabling Knowledge Creation* why such a concept can help managers grapple with the real difficulties involved in building a knowledge-creating company consistently and systematically.

This book provides new concepts about how knowledge in organizations can be created and used for competitive advantage by describing knowledge-enabling conditions. In *Enabling Knowledge Creation*, we move beyond the current limitations of knowledge management and knowledge-creation theory to discuss practical approaches to the amorphous, constantly evolving human realm of knowledge. The reason we have decided to write this book is twofold. First, *The Knowledge-Creating Company*, one of the predecessors of this book, focused on the process of knowledge creation. As a result, it was not as helpful as it might have been in telling readers how to go about actually creating knowledge. *Enabling Knowledge Creation* provides more practical guidance about knowledge creation. Second, we want to add stronger validity to our argument by describing many vivid new examples of companies worldwide that have successfully created knowledge-enabling organizations, proving that it can be done and that it works.

The Knowledge-Creating Company might have succeeded in formaliz-
ing the generic model of knowledge creation and demonstrating that
Japanese companies had become successful, especially in the 1980s,
because of their skills and expertise at organizational knowledge creation.
Since then, Japanese companies have been faced with the longest and
most severe recession in recent history. This could undermine the importance of organizational knowledge creation. We contend, however, that
the recent setback of many Japanese companies was due to their limited
attention to enabling conditions for organizational knowledge creation. As
a result, they have failed in creating organizational knowledge consistently. *Enabling Knowledge Creation* elaborates the reasons and the practical ways to support knowledge creation so that firms can create
organizational knowledge consistently and systematically.

This book is the product of knowledge enabling. The initial idea was
generated while Georg von Krogh was at Hitotsubashi University as a visiting professor in the summer of 1996. Until then, Nonaka and Ichijo had
been intensively studying Maekawa Seisakujo and Shiseido, two Japanese
knowledge-enabling companies highlighted in the book, and gradually
realized the necessity for describing more practical approaches to organizational knowledge creation, which was also one of von Krogh's research
focuses. The three had many intensive meetings at Hitotsubashi
University and developed a vision of writing a new book about knowledge
enabling. We stimulated our ideas through various communication mechanisms. E-mail helped us a lot, as we were often geographically separated.
At the same time, we tried to have as many face-to-face meetings as possible, in Tokyo, Phoenix, Zurich, Saint Gallen, Cologne, and Onsen, a spa
resort (hot springs) in Kanazawa, Japan. All five knowledge enablers
described in *Enabling Knowledge Creation*—(1) instill a knowledge
vision, (2) manage conversation, (3) mobilize knowledge activists, (4) create the right context, and (5) globalize local knowledge—played a crucial
role in our work.

There are many acknowledgments due when a book is the result of
research that has been conducted on a global basis. We would like to start,
however, with a special thanks to the person who helped us find our words
and worked so hard to bring them to life on the written page. Martha
Nichols carefully read our draft and provided valuable comments and
excellent editing. She stimulated our thinking, gave us support and heart-
warming encouragement, and helped us articulate our ideas. Her partnership has been invaluable to us.

A book like this required tremendous cooperation from all the companies that participated in our research. We learned a lot from the executives and managers we interviewed, who were forthcoming, candid, and

generous with their time. The people who were excited by our ideas and supportive of our efforts helped us immeasurably. There are too many to name, but we owe special thanks to Yoshiharu Fukuhara, chairman of Shiseido; Nobuyki Idei, co-CEO of Sony; and Masao Maekawa, chairman of Maekawa Seisakujo, who ignited our concept of knowledge enabling through intensive dialogue. There are also numerous managers who have contributed to this book. They are Leif Edvinsson of Skandia; Satoshi Hotta of General Electric Japan; Yukiko Ishikawa of Ayura Laboratories; Yoshio Iwasaki, Shun Murakami, and Junko Shinozaki of Maekawa Seisakujo; Oka Komiyama and Toru Hiroshima of Toshiba; Carla Kriwet of Boston Consulting Group; Hiroyuki Morimoto and Naoto Terakawa of Sony; Andreas Rihs of Phonak; Bernd-Michael Rumpf and Pierre Hessler of Gemini Consulting; Helmut Volkmann and Michael Mirow of Siemens AG; and Wouter de Vries and Manfred Aben of Unilever. We especially want to thank Carla Kriwet, who participated in writing the Adtrantz story, as well as Bernd-Michael Rumpf, who participated in writing the Gemini story.

Our academic debts are large. Hirotaka Takeuchi has been a great influence on our thinking about knowledge enabling, along with Yaichi Aoshima, Andrea Back, Philippe Byosiere, Michael D. Cohen, Michael Cusumano, Daniel R. Denison, Jane Dutton, Peter Gomez, Robert Grant, Hiroyuki Itami, Tadao Kagono, Toshihiro Kanai, Noboru Konno, Marjorie Lyles, Iwao Nakatani, Tsuyoshi Numagami, Günter Müller-Stewens, Akihito Okumura, Robert E. Quinn, Johannes Rüegg-Stürm, Kiyonori Sakakibara, Yoshiya Teramoto, David J. Teece, Noel M. Tichy, Markus Venzin, and Seiichiro Yonekura.

Our colleagues who directly worked on this book were unbelievably committed, professional, and tolerant of our pace and style. We thank them for hanging in there on this project. In Saint Gallen, a group of research associates played an important role in researching and drafting elements for various stories: Pablo Erat for the Gemini story, Dirk Kleine for the Volkmann story, and Philipp Käser for the Gemini story as well as for the Phonak and Skandia story. Marija Köhne, also a research associate, as well as Philipp Käser provided invaluable and highly professional editorial assistance. In Japan, Ryoko Toyama, Dai Seno, and Yuki Matsuda were indispensable in finalizing the book. Noriko Morimoto has provided excellent administrative work and kept all the pieces together.

It was wonderful to have a helpful and enthusiastic editor who is a knowledge caretaker himself. Herb Addison of Oxford University Press believed in the concept, in us, and in the project. He kept us on track while encouraging us to fully explore the complexities and practical implications of the material. He provided very valuable comments and advice to us, especially in the final stage of book writing. We are grateful to Herb Addison for being enthusiastic about our concept and for his close involvement as our study evolved and proceded.

Last, we want to say "Thank you" to our families and friends for letting us concentrate on this book while having less time with them. We thank them for allowing us to complete this book and for giving us a reason to hurry up and get it done.

St. Gallen and Tokyo, June 1999   Georg von Krogh
                                                            Kazuo Ichijo
                                                          Ikujiro Nonaka

ENABLING

KNOWLEDGE

CREATION

· 1 ·

FROM MANAGING
TO ENABLING KNOWLEDGE

*In a knowledge-based economy, the new coin of the realm
is learning.*

—Robert Reich

S ince the early 1990s, knowledge management has become a hot
issue. Business researchers, consultants, and media pundits from all
over the map have exhorted today's companies to consider knowledge creation a source of competitive advantage, to focus on the needs of
knowledge workers—the growing professional corps of engineers, scientists, medical doctors, writers, software designers, and other creative
thinkers—and to build a learning environment that will meet the demands
of the postindustrial information economy. Robert Reich, former U.S. sec-
retary of labor, is just one of many political commentators to emphasize
the importance of knowledge and learning for both top managers and individual workers. As Reich notes in "The Company of the Future,"

> Want to build a business that can outlive its first good idea? Create a cul-
> ture that values learning. Want to build a career that allows you to grow
> into new responsibilities? Maintain your hunger to learn—and join an
> organization where you'll be given the chance to learn continuously.[1]

It is hard to argue with such advice. Pioneering companies like Dow
Chemical, Skandia, Siemens, Chevron, and Nokia have not only boosted
interest in knowledge management through their successes but have also
significantly changed the ways in which they operate. Indeed, much of
our own research has been devoted to the study of knowledge in organizations, and the work in our previous books and a number of articles certainly underpins this volume.[2]

3

Yet while it is easy to say "create a culture that values learning" or to discuss the knowledge-based economy in general terms, the human processes involved—creativity, conversation, judgment, teaching, and learning—are difficult to quantify. Based on what we now know about companies that have struggled with these issues, we believe the concept of knowledge management itself is limited. In many organizations, a legitimate interest in knowledge creation has been reduced to an overemphasis on information technology or other measurement tools. In fact, the term *management* implies control of processes that may be inherently uncontrollable or, at the least, stifled by heavy-handed direction.

From our perspective, managers need to support knowledge creation rather than control it, and the specifics of how and why they should do so form the core of this book. We call this *knowledge enabling*—the overall set of organizational activities that positively affect knowledge creation—and will emphasize throughout why such a concept can help managers grapple with the real difficulties involved in building a knowledge-creating company. Knowledge enabling includes facilitating relationships and conversations as well as sharing local knowledge across an organization or beyond geographic and cultural borders. At a deeper level, however, it relies on a new sense of emotional knowledge and care in the organization, one that highlights how people treat each other and encourages creativity—even playfulness.

Consider Helmut Volkmann, senior director of corporate research and development at the Siemens corporation in Germany. His office, which he calls an "atelier for innovators," is a mix of multimedia exhibition, control desk, church, and postmodern dining room. A dozen computer terminals; slide projectors; a model of "Xenia, the knowledge city"; a set of colored chairs; and a fanciful picture of knowledge islands, cities, routes, and ships titled "Departure to the Continent of Solutions" make this a futuristic work environment. But beyond these physical details is the attitude of Volkmann himself. In a recent interview, he noted,

> People use various terms to describe me—"boundary-breaker," although this is not really on target; a "corporate philosopher," but this seems overly sophisticated; a "futurist," but that sounds faddish to me. Journalists like snappy terms, and in their newspaper articles I have been called "bird of paradise," "court jester," "clown," "crank," or even "the spinner." Personally, I would just like to be called a "thought-maker"—somebody who thinks and reflects. That's what I really am.[3]

In our terms, Volkmann is an extreme form of a *knowledge activist*—a manager with broad social and intellectual vision as well as experience in nitty-gritty business operations, someone who connects external and internal knowledge initiatives and mobilizes workers throughout the organization to use knowledge more effectively. But even if Volkmann may seem like an ambitious dreamer, other top companies have innovative executives who fit the bill of knowledge activist. These include Skandia's Leif Edvinsson, Shiseido's Yoshinaru Fukuhara, and General Electric's Jack Welch.

In *Enabling Knowledge Creation*, we move beyond the current limitations of knowledge-management theory to discuss practical approaches to the amorphous, constantly evolving, human realm of knowledge. We identify five *knowledge enablers*—(1) instill a knowledge vision, (2) manage conversations, (3) mobilize knowledge activists, (4) create the right context, and (5) globalize local knowledge—weaving in detailed stories from Siemens, Skandia, Shiseido, Sony, Phonak, Adtranz, General Electric, and other companies. We consider the crucial role of strategy in light of this enabling framework, along with "the sand in the machinery"—the most common individual and organizational barriers to knowledge creation. We also stress the importance of *microcommunities of knowledge*, the small groups within an organization whose members share what they know as well as common values and goals.

The ultimate success of knowledge creation depends on how these and other organizational members relate through the different steps of the process. Although this may seem obvious, few companies to date have made relationships a priority; they may discuss their commitment to a "caring" workplace in a mission statement, but most do not practice what they preach, often because the language of caring, relating, and enabling sounds so foreign in a business context. No one can deny that the contemporary global arena is more competitive than ever. But ironically, a company may need to flip some of that cutthroat attitude on its head in order to remain competitive over the long haul. Knowledge workers cannot be bullied into creativity or information sharing; and the traditional forms of compensation and organizational hierarchy do not motivate people sufficiently for them to develop the strong relationships required for knowledge creation on a continuing basis.

In other words, it is time that managers put care on their agendas. After a heavy period of downsizing and restructuring, most corporations need to revitalize their human side. They need to revitalize the fragile processes of knowledge creation, setting up company homes or "ateliers for innovators" that generate new sources of knowledge. They can start by fostering care in organizational relationships—the very essence of knowledge enabling.

KNOWLEDGE IN ORGANIZATIONS: SOME BASIC DEFINITIONS

Knowledge is one of those concepts that is extremely meaningful, positive, promising, and hard to pin down. If you ask a group of cognitive scientists what it is, they will probably agree that knowledge involves cognitive structures that represent a given reality. But if one of these scientists brings up knowledge in an after-dinner conversation with an interested manager, he will quickly realize that no definition cuts across all disciplines, professional levels, and organizations. The manager is much more likely to associate knowledge with specific situations and "know-how": For example, an engineer schedules her maintenance activities by listening carefully to the sound of an engine and thereby estimating the approximate time to engine failure. Both the scientist and the manager are right, of course. Knowledge is often in the eye of the beholder, and you give meaning to the concept through the way you use it (Wittgenstein, 1958).

Many researchers have defined various kinds of knowledge in organizations, the interplay between individual and organizational knowledge, organizational learning models, and so on.[4] This book does not cover our own past work in detail or conduct an extensive review of the literature. But we begin by summarizing several basic ideas that are integral to knowledge enabling. These ideas appear throughout *Enabling Knowledge Creation* and are examined from different angles as the chapters proceed. Knowledge itself is mutable, after all, and can take on many faces in an organization.

First, *knowledge is justified true belief*.[5] An individual justifies the truthfulness of his or her beliefs based on observations of the world; these observations, in turn, depend on a unique viewpoint, personal sensibility, and individual experience.[6] Therefore, when somebody creates knowledge, he or she makes sense out of a new situation by holding justified beliefs and committing to them. Under this definition, knowledge is a construction of reality rather than something that is true in any abstract or universal way.[7] The creation of knowledge is not simply a compilation of facts but a uniquely human process that cannot be reduced or easily replicated. It can involve feelings and belief systems of which one may not even be conscious, which brings us to the next point.

Second, *knowledge is both explicit and tacit*. Some knowledge can be put on paper, formulated in sentences, or captured in drawings. An engineer, for example, conveys her knowledge of a product design through drawings and specifications, making what she knows explicit. Yet other kinds of knowledge are tied to the senses, skills in bodily movement, individual perception, physical experiences, rules of thumb, and intuition. Such tacit knowledge is often very difficult to describe to others.[8] Putting together the pieces of a high-precision luxury watch, for instance, or interpreting a complex seismic readout of an oil reservoir demands knowledge that cannot be found in a manual or easily conveyed to a novice. While the idea of tacit knowledge makes sense intuitively to most people, managers often have a hard time coming to grips with it on a practical level. Recognizing the value of tacit knowledge and figuring out how to use it is the key challenge in a knowledge-creating company, one that requires extended conversations and good personal relationships—that is, knowledge enabling. Tacit knowledge may seem too mysterious to be usefully or consistently applied in a business situation, but this shifting, context-specific quality is precisely what makes it a powerful tool for innovation. The challenge comes in enabling such a creative source, rather than ignoring or muzzling it.

Therefore, we come to our third point: *effective knowledge creation depends on an enabling context*. What we mean by enabling context is a shared space that fosters emerging relationships. Based on the Japanese idea of *ba* (or "place"), such an organizational context can be physical, virtual, mental, or—more likely—all three. This definition of context is connected to our first two points: knowledge is dynamic, relational, and based on human action; it depends on the situation and people involved rather than on absolute truth or hard facts. The essential thing for managers to remember is that all knowledge, as opposed to information or data, depends on its context. You might say that knowledge is embedded in *ba*, and that supporting the whole process of knowledge creation requires the necessary context or "knowledge space."

Last but not least, *organizational knowledge creation involves five main steps*. If such a big concept is not broken down into different subprocesses, managers and workers alike may find the whole endeavor too daunting; at worst, executive discussion of knowledge creation or organizational learning will seem meaningless. The five knowledge-creation steps we emphasize here are (1) sharing tacit knowledge, (2) creating concepts, (3) justifying concepts, (4) building a prototype, and (5) cross-leveling knowledge.[9] These steps or phases are analyzed more thoroughly in subsequent chapters. For now, we describe them generally by referring to how a team might create a new product.

The process starts when team members meet to share their knowledge of a given product area, much of which is tacit and can include insights into customer needs, information about new technologies, and the personal skills required to perform complex tasks. Based on its ability to share such tacit knowledge, the team creates a new product concept. At this stage, the concept may be a specification of functionality, an algorithm, a manufacturing-process description, drawings, and so on. In the next phase, the team, often involving outside participants, justifies the concept. Members use market studies, benchmarking, customer focus groups, trend studies, the company's expressed vision and strategy, and whatever else it takes to build arguments for or against the concept. After such careful scrutiny, a concept that is chosen for further development is transformed into a prototype. In this example, that means a prototype of the product, although other knowledge-creation efforts may yield a draft of a new marketing campaign, a description of a new financial service, or something else that is not a physical representation. The general goal is to create a tangible manifestation of the team's knowledge. Finally, the team assumes responsibility for sharing its knowledge with the organization at large, including additional manufacturing and marketing/sales groups that can offer feedback about the new product.

As these ideas indicate, knowledge creation is a social as well as an individual process. Sharing tacit knowledge requires individuals to share their personal beliefs about a situation with other team members. At that point, justification becomes public. Each individual is faced with the tremendous challenge of justifying his or her true beliefs in front of others—and it is this need for justification, explanation, persuasion, and human connectedness that makes knowledge creation a highly fragile process.[10]

THE LINKS BETWEEN KNOWLEDGE ENABLING AND CREATION

Indeed, the fragility of knowledge creation means that it must be carefully supported by a number of activities that enable it to happen in spite of the obstacles. Knowledge enabling encompasses this set of organizational activities, as we have already noted; by this we refer primarily to activities that occur within an organizational context, but customers, suppliers, or other partners may also be part of the process. For example, when a company is developing a vision of future knowledge that it needs, managers may have to consult outside experts like suppliers, universities, or research laboratories. We also want to emphasize that knowledge enabling involves both deliberate activities—those that can be planned and directed by management—and emergent ones—the unintended consequences of intended actions, or discovery after the fact that a particular activity promotes knowledge creation.

Overall, knowledge enabling should be thought of in a circular manner; it is always aimed at enhancing the knowledge-creating potential of the company. Of course, it is useful to break up these various organizational processes, deliberate or otherwise, into separate categories. We believe the five knowledge enablers at the heart of this book are the most important ones: (1) instill a knowledge vision, (2) manage conversations, (3) mobilize knowledge activists, (4) create the right context, and (5) globalize local knowledge. Chapters 5 through 9 examine each of them in detail. Table 1.1 shows when and to what degree each enabler affects knowledge creation.

Two obvious links between knowledge creation and enabling are revealed by the table's 5 x 5 grid. First, all five enablers have a strong

Table 1.1. Knowledge Enabling: The 5 x 5 Grid

KNOWLEDGE-CREATION STEPS

KNOWLEDGE ENABLERS	Sharing Tacit Knowledge	Creating a Concept	Justifying a Concept	Building a Prototype	Cross-Leveling Knowledge
Instill a Vision		√	√√	√	√√
Manage Conversations	√√	√√	√√	√√	√√
Mobilize Activists		√	√	√	√√
Create the Right Context	√	√	√√	√	√√
Globalize Local Knowledge					√√

influence on cross-leveling of knowledge: They help to increase dissemination of information throughout an organization and to dismantle the
barriers to communication. Second, the enabler connected most closely
with relationships and care in the organization—*manage conversations*—
strongly affects all five knowledge-creation steps.

The latter is a key insight from our perspective. For any given project,
knowledge creation has to happen in a caring atmosphere, one in which
organizational members take an active interest in applying the insights
provided by others. Regardless of the phase of knowledge creation, good
relations purge the process of distrust and fear, and break down personal
and organizational barriers. Effective conversations allow for higher creativity; stimulate the sharing of tacit knowledge, concept creation, and
justification; are essential for developing a powerful prototype; and lubri-
cate the flow of knowledge across various organizational levels. The
multinational consumer-products company Unilever, for example, has
recognized that innovation requires well-functioning, interdisciplinary
teams. When team members take a lenient and helping attitude toward
one another, new ideas flow easily, and even radically different knowledge
can be created. At Unilever, this approach has resulted in a number of
successful culinary products. The company supports such caring relationships through incentives for excellent team performance in product
development and carefully arranged social events.[11] Its corporate purpose
states, "Our long-term success requires total commitment . . . to working
together effectively and a willingness to embrace new ideas and learn
continuously."[12]

As for the other enablers, *instill a knowledge vision* legitimizes
knowledge-creation initiatives throughout the company. This enabler has
a relatively low impact on tacit-knowledge sharing, since the social

interplay among community members matters more in this context. A clearly formulated vision, however, may help the community to articulate more effectively the concepts they create; and it is of great importance in the concept-justification phase, because concepts must be selected that eventually help the company achieve its knowledge vision. Instilling a vision will also encourage better utilization of knowledge and help to legitimize the knowledge-transfer process itself.

The third enabler, *mobilize knowledge activists*, emphasizes the people who trigger and coordinate knowledge-creation processes. Such mobilization helps achieve broader participation in concept justification and prototype building, where the microcommunity of knowledge is supplemented with various types of expertise (manufacturing, marketing, legal). This enabler also influences concept creation, because knowledge activists can inspire the microcommunities involved, as well as coordinate the knowledge-creation processes of several communities or teams. The activist can spot potential redundancies and/or synergies in the explicit knowledge created, thereby helping each community to better align its work with the overall vision.

The fourth enabler, *create the right context*, is closely tied to a company's structure, since the ways project teams are formed and interact within the larger confines of a multinational organization determine the extent to which knowledge is valued. An enabling context or *ba* must be founded on care in the organization. In fact, establishing the right context is what knowledge enabling is all about, especially when it is based on a supportive organizational structure and aligned with strategy. Creating the right context affects all five knowledge-creation steps, particularly concept justification and cross-leveling of knowledge.

Finally, *globalize local knowledge* emphasizes dissemination across many organizational levels. Although members of a team or microcommunity must share tacit knowledge and engage in concept creation, justification, and prototype building, these steps are not essential to getting existing knowledge to the right people or groups. The fifth enabler matters most when knowledge creation and utilization are separated in time and space, and it is instrumental in bringing about organizational knowledge.

THE NEW KNOWLEDGE PLAYERS:
ACTIVISTS, CARING EXPERTS, EPISTEMOLOGISTS

The emergent aspects of knowledge enabling match the fluid nature of knowledge creation, as they do any kind of complex human activity. For many managers, however, accustomed as they are to rational decision making and clear lines of authority, this approach may sound confusing and even threatening. Let us reiterate that there are solid, practical reasons for a knowledge-enabling perspective. Because knowledge enabling emphasizes human relationships and good communication, it can have a positive impact on the quality of new knowledge; the speed with which that new knowledge is created; employee satisfaction; corporate image; and relations with customers, suppliers, and other strategic partners. Such results are harder to measure than margins or inventory; yet these intangible improvements can create a sustainable competitive advantage and ultimately influence the bottom line.

The Shiseido Company, for example, found itself in an increasingly harsh external environment by the late 1980s. A leading cosmetics manufacturer both in Japan and globally, Shiseido is known for its sophisticated products; the concept for them, based on modern pharmaceutical research and Western medical practices, originated with founder Yushin Fukuhara in the last century. More than a hundred years later, however, Shiseido confronted different customer expectations—new skin conditions and ideas about health—and competition—expensive, well-known foreign brands or alternative companies selling "natural" products. Once Yoshiharu Fukuhara, the founder's grandson, became president in 1987, he embarked on developing a new Shiseido brand, one that would take advantage of the company's mix of Eastern and Western philosophies and result in a postmodern cosmetic concept. These efforts involved a cross-divisional "cabinet," whose members actively debated the merits of natural therapy and "life-force cosmetics," as well as new project teams. By 1995, Shiseido had launched its successful Ayura brand, named after the Hindu word for life.[13]

While many companies have embraced knowledge initiatives of some sort—and this in itself represents a marked improvement over more traditional business approaches—few have transformed their product concepts or operations as Shiseido has. In part, these initiatives have been constrained by the rhetoric of knowledge management. A large number of firms now employ "knowledge officers," have established staff functions for knowledge management, or renamed previous positions to include terms like knowledge or intellectual capital. Knowledge officers sometimes consider themselves "corporate intellectuals" who have an omnipotent say in all dealings with knowledge. In some cases, giving an executive explicit responsibility for knowledge has been a positive change. Because of time constraints, knowledge officers may be the only ones charged with formulating a company's knowledge vision, and at least they can judge the relevance of various forms and sources. But the fact that just one manager is assigned to such an unwieldy task points up the limits of the approach, as does the hierarchical label of "officer."

Similarly, knowledge management often focuses on knowledge workers rather than the human processes involved. Drucker (1994) and

Toffler (1990) both suggest that knowledge is an important source of power held by a very few. For such commentators, knowledge workers can be anything from a lawyer to a systems analyst to a corporate planner; the point is not the specific type of professional work but the multiple talents this new worker must have. He or she needs to be a thinker, a team player, a team leader, a critic, an autonomous decision maker—adaptable, responsible, and so on. The goal of knowledge management, then, is to stimulate individual professionals to do an excellent job while capturing their knowledge and transforming it into something the company can use—new routines, new customer insights, new product concepts.

Such characterizations of the generic knowledge worker are illuminating and may eventually make top executives more sensitive to the challenges facing a changing workforce. In our opinion, however, the key quality of knowledge workers is their humanness. Only through being human can they become knowledge workers. Restricting the knowledge-worker category to certain types of professional employees will stifle a company's capacity to unleash the full potential of its human resources. Knowledge creation might occur in the close interaction between an untrained salesperson and a new customer, for example, or when a service technician together with his team finds a new solution for manufacturing a product, or a young assistant with a computer hobby might propose new ways to present the company on the World Wide Web. In other words, knowledge work is a human condition, not a privileged one.

To be sure, managers and professionals still play essential roles in any knowledge-creating company. But to be effective, they may need to adjust how they define themselves, as well as the ways in which they relate with other people at all levels in the organization. A knowledge activist like Helmut Volkmann considers himself a thought-maker; we would also call him a merchant of foresight, an executive who not only looks beyond each quarterly report but actively sells his vision of the future to other knowledge players. In addition, managers, along with individual workers, might be called caring experts, psychologists, or futurizers.

They might even be corporate epistemologists—executives who focus on the theory of knowledge itself. Yoshinaru Fukuhara, for instance, notes that Shiseido's challenge lies in "integrating 'current' or 'postmodern' cultural capital with modern industrial developments."[14] Masao Maekawa of the Maekawa Manufacturing Company talks openly about encouraging *ba* at his company and the use of tacit knowledge.[15] But unlike Fukuhara, Maekawa, and Volkmann, many businesspeople believe that such a theory is too abstract or academic to have practical value.

We recently attended a large international conference in which academics, managers, and consultants gathered to present their ideas about knowledge management. Looking through the program, we found too many presentations had titles like "Knowledge Mining," "Knowledge Management: The New Frontier of Business Process Reengineering," or "Knowledge: What's in It for Me?" Finally, we spotted one session that piqued our interest and decided to attend. Hearing this speech, we were convinced that some of the speaker's ideas were new and quite exotic. Afterward, we went for coffee and sat down at a table with some managers. One of them had attended the same lecture, and his verdict was very different: "rambling," "cloudy," "obfuscating," "not at all related to practice," and "nothing I could take home" were some of the phrases he used to describe what we had found so exciting. Had we missed the point?

Perhaps there will always be a difference between what academics and practitioners find fascinating, but in this instance we believe the manager's response reflects the basic problem with the knowledge-management movement. It has been set in motion and continues onward without any substantial theoretical reason to be. Practitioners of knowledge management are quick to dismiss the fundamental theories of knowledge, but imagine a bunch of medical doctors dismissing the theories of biochemistry. Companies engaged in knowledge creation should spend considerable time figuring out what knowledge means in their organizations and how to apply the concept practically. As the cognitive scientist and manager we described earlier had discovered, knowledge can mean different things to different people. Yet multiple perspectives are not a confusing mess to be feared but a source of creative potential.

Terms like *merchant of foresight* and *conversation manager* may not work as official job titles, but this playful use of language indicates the many roles executives need to take on in the contemporary workplace. As Leif Edvinsson, a vice president of Skandia's Assurance and Financial Services business unit, said:

> The visualization of knowledge is crucial, because if people see it, they have a conversation about it and might also be tempted to act. They decide to become part of the wave, internalizing it and using it for themselves.[16]

The wave is a metaphor for the generation, growth, and transfer of ideas. Although Edvinsson is referring to a particular "futurizing" initiative here, he covers a lot of enabling ground—as all knowledge activists, caring experts, and epistemologists do.

MICROCOMMUNITIES OF KNOWLEDGE

Beyond the efforts of individual players, people work together in groups to create knowledge. Forming productive work communities, based as they are on social processes, is the final piece of our knowledge-enabling framework. Thus far, we have spoken quite generally of teams, but we believe referring to such groups as microcommunities of knowledge[17] extends the concept in a useful way. The bottleneck in knowledge creation usually occurs when individual members know nothing or very little—namely, before they have shared their tacit knowledge. Larger communities of knowledge can share certain practices, routines, and languages, but for new tacit knowledge to emerge through socialization the group must be small: five to seven people. Yet these microcommunities are still communities, involving the dense network of relationships the term implies.

In some ways, using the team as the basic unit of knowledge creation is limited. A microcommunity of knowledge has more potential to evolve over time rather than being project- or deadline-driven; as such, it will develop its own rituals, languages, practices, norms, and values. Microcommunities are characterized by face-to-face interactions, and gradually members get to know more about each other's personalities, fields of interest, possible agendas, and the corresponding forms of behavior that may or may not seem acceptable to the rest of the group (Schutz, 1967; Wenger, 1998).

Look closely at the evolution of microcommunities. They can be formed from the outside by a department head, a research and development (R&D) manager, or an engineer who is responsible for developing a product. In this case, the community's assignment, membership, benefits of membership, and distinctiveness are based on other initiatives in the company, and it operates more like a team. But microcommunities of knowledge can also form in a self-organized manner, as described by Jean-Paul Sartre (1976). At first, members may be part of a loose gathering, in which they share a common location in time and space, physically or electronically. For example, they happen to end up on the same special-interest site on the company's intranet, or sit at the same table during lunch; they may meet by chance at the company's football club or a local pub.

At this stage, knowledge is individual. But as these members start interacting more intensely, they form reciprocal relationships, talk about general issues, perhaps fix a number of future meetings—that is, they form a more coherent group. Once they become a "fused group," in Sartre's terms, members recognize their common interests, individual needs, and different areas of expertise. For example, one group member indicates that she sees a great business opportunity in combining Liquid Crystal Display (LCD) technology with the development of self-repairing metals. Another member has expertise in the area of LCD technology and becomes interested in the venture. Above all, a fused group is driven by a kind of shared curiosity about what other members know and what the group might eventually accomplish if they continue to explore their interests and skills. At this stage, social knowledge is largely explicit; it can easily be described to others.

When common interests have been identified, a fused group may become a "pledged group." In this case, the group organizes members' rights and duties according to a pledge or charter. The explicit knowledge of the group is supplemented with knowledge of the pledge as well as some additional tacit knowledge of the passion, commitment, and positive emotions felt by group members. What we call a microcommunity transforms a pledged group into action; it starts to engage in knowledge creation. Engaging in knowledge creation and having a pledge gives this community an identity of its own, not one imposed from outside by the company. A microcommunity also fosters internal coherence by emphasizing the benefits of membership—fun, joy, or future rewards.

Who are the natural members of these microcommunities of knowledge? They can be engineers, marketers, lawyers, controllers, scientists, front-line personnel, sales executives, and so forth. Members can be drawn from various businesses, functional areas, and departments; they may even be customers, suppliers, or other partners. As with project teams and other more traditional work groups, diverse membership benefits the entire unit in the sharing of tacit knowledge, concept creation, and concept justification.

More important, the evolution of a gathering into a microcommunity will be part of its collective memory. Participating in the evolution of the group, each member knows the down-and-dirty details of community relations: why a certain line of argument is unproductive; why certain members with particular knowledge were brought in at one time; why it is considered rude to interrupt while others are talking; why its composition inhibited the group in investigating a certain type of technology. This kind of shared tacit knowledge enables members to carry on relationships over time, handle the exit of team members, and assimilate new participants. As such knowledge is made explicit, the group gradually gains its identity. But a microcommunity also continuously searches for and refines its identity; by breaking individual and shared knowledge boundaries, and by replacing individuals, it is in a constant state of becoming.

Once a microcommunity is broken up or disbands, of course, much of its tacit knowledge is lost, especially the kind that involves relations among community members. The capacity to regenerate social relations over time disappears, which is why maintaining microcommunities is so essential to knowledge enabling. Tacit knowledge cannot be captured and regained in documents, not even videos that show the interactions among community members. The only way to regain such organizational capital is to recreate the unique conditions of that microcommunity of knowledge—a difficult, if not impossible chore, considering how emergent and serendipitous social relations are.

HOW THIS BOOK IS ORGANIZED

Because relationships and communication processes are so hard to pin down, much of the research that informs *Enabling Knowledge Creation* is based on ten companies that we have observed or worked with closely in recent years. We present many of these company stories in full, emphasizing a whole array of factors that can determine successful knowledge enabling. Much as we might like to organize and describe the knowledge enablers neatly, organizational life is too complex to quantify in this fashion. The stories often exemplify more than one enabler in action. And because each company has its own culture, business situation, and mix of people, our analysis is necessarily qualitative, depending as much on how the knowledge players involved conceptualize or describe a particular process as on sales figures and business history.

After this introductory chapter, Chapter 2, "The Limits of Knowledge Management: Why So Many Barriers Still Exist," examines the pitfalls of a knowledge-management approach in more detail and discusses both individual and organizational barriers to knowledge creation. We present the three foundational premises of knowledge enabling, as well as the story of the Phonak Company. Chapter 3, "Care in the Organization: Why an Enabling Context Matters," presents more background on this important issue, along with managerial strategies for fostering care in the workplace and examples from Narvesen, Unilever, and Shiseido. Chapter 4, "Strategy and Knowledge Creation: Ensuring Survival in the Present and Advancement in the Future," underscores how strategic considerations of knowledge can better serve a company. Skandia's "Future Center" is described in this regard.

The book's five central chapters focus on each of the knowledge enablers. Chapter 5, "Enabler 1: Instill a Knowledge Vision," moves from the mechanics of business strategy to the importance of creating an overall vision of knowledge in any organization. We analyze Shiseido's development of a new product vision in more depth here. Chapter 6, "Enabler 2: Manage Conversations," looks at how organizational members talk with one another. It lays out plans for facilitating conversations and relationship building, as well as comparing specific initiatives at Maekawa and General Electric. Chapter 7, "Enabler 3: Mobilize Knowledge Activists," discusses what active organizational change agents can do to spark knowledge creation, returning to Helmut Volkmann at Siemens. Chapter 8, "Enabler 4: Create the Right Context," examines the close connections among organizational structure, strategy, and knowledge enabling as exemplified by Sony, Maekawa, and Toshiba. Chapter 9, "Enabler 5: Globalize Local Knowledge," considers the complicated issue of knowledge dissemination and includes an extended discussion of an Indian technology-transfer project at Adtranz, which at the time was itself a joint venture of Asea Brown Boveri and Daimler Benz.

The book concludes with the story of a management consulting firm, Chapter 10, "Knowledge Enabling in Action: Dismantling Barriers at Gemini Consulting," and "Chapter 11, Epilogue: The Knowledge-Enabling Journey." The Gemini story, based on a firm whose primary business depends on knowledge creation, is a fitting example of the many challenges managers face. Our last chapter nods to the long journey ahead but offers some practical tips for how to proceed.

Knowledge enabling involves a mix of deliberate decisions and going with the flow. Although managers can certainly influence the process, they may need to reassess their own work style and social interactions. But there *is* a payoff—long-term growth, sustainable competitive advantage, and the kind of culture of innovation that can ensure a company's future—and we propose specific approaches to what may seem to be a thorny, complicated task. Recognizing the need to exploit the knowledge potential in their organizations, companies like Siemens and 3M allow individual workers to participate in knowledge-creation projects and to care for their own personal knowledge development. At 3M, engineers can spend up to 15 percent of their time working on ideas and innovative projects that they choose for themselves. While not every employee makes use of this "slack time," the company's management signals that it allowed, even desirable, for employees to explore themes that go beyond the conventional.[18]

The real point is that while you may be able to manage related organizational processes like community building and knowledge exchange, you cannot manage knowledge itself. Those who try to control knowledge creation do so at their peril, often putting up barriers or falling into the pitfalls described in the next chapter.

· 2 ·

THE LIMITS
OF KNOWLEDGE MANAGEMENT

Why So Many Barriers Still Exist

For your people to be innovative and motivated, you need to consider human needs. If you feel good and appreciated, you are much more open to many things than if you always need to defend yourself.

—Andreas Rihs, CEO, Phonak

Many managers today would readily admit that knowledge creation matters to their companies, especially if they work for high-technology firms that depend on innovation. They might even say their companies have made knowledge creation a priority through special workshops, new procedures, the assignment of a knowledge officer, extensive deployment of information technology, and so on. But supporting and sustaining knowledge creation is much harder than it sounds and can often turn into a source of tension within an organization. Whether executives become frustrated with or cynical about knowledge-management efforts, they often end up at a loss.

As we emphasized in the first chapter, knowledge creation is a fragile process, one that is not amenable to traditional management techniques. Individuals may be reluctant or even unable to accept new lessons, insights, ideas, or observations. Moreover, organizations can be challenging arenas for creating new knowledge. Their members may have to overcome severe barriers to sharing knowledge with others, including the disapproval of a boss or other executives if they express an unpopular opinion. There are essentially two types of barriers: individual and organizational. The two are different yet interrelated, and companies need integrated mechanisms to dismantle both of them.

Many barriers to knowledge creation crop up regardless of managerial style, simply because the process depends so much on the vagaries of human relationships and differing intellectual capabilities; knowledge-enabling managers recognize these basic human factors rather than ignore them, turning the challenges of human interaction into new strengths. But some barriers are created or reinforced by a limited management approach. After we describe individual and organizational barriers to knowledge creation, we summarize the pitfalls of knowledge management—the approach found in many current companies—and lay out the three counter premises of knowledge enabling. The chapter concludes with a detailed discussion of how the Swiss company Phonak has confronted its knowledge barriers, moving toward a vision in which, according to co-founder Andreas Rihs, "management is often expected to act like psychologists."[1]

INDIVIDUAL BARRIERS TO KNOWLEDGE CREATION

Knowledge creation at the individual level involves the ability to deal with new situations, events, information, and contexts. Executives who want to integrate knowledge management into their overall plans for business renewal often have a very optimistic view of how well people handle new experiences. Consider the following statement by a manager; he is speaking of a program intended to transform the company for which he works into a learning organization:

> [Our program] is about taking the whole organization through a process of renewal from the old ways of doing things to the new. Its success lies in its ability to galvanize an entire workforce to create a new future, not just for themselves, but for the organization as a whole. It is releasing the unexplored capabilities of the people to sustain major growth without added costs. (Matthews, 1997, p. 130)

Similar descriptions can be heard in other firms; these optimistic managers assume organizations are quite proactive. And in this rosy scenario, individual workers are fully capable of dealing with new situations—hence the claim that these "unexplored capabilities" will incur no "added costs." Based on our observations, however, many companies find it difficult to overcome individual knowledge barriers. Often their proposed success programs lead only to increased personal insecurity.

Why is it so hard for individuals to accept or integrate new knowledge? We believe at least two individual barriers—limited accommodation and threat to self-image—can wreak havoc with managerial good intentions.

First, recall our initial definition of knowledge as justified true belief. Human beings constantly justify their beliefs about what is true against their own experiences (Varela, Thompson, and Rosch, 1992). Over the course of a lifetime, an individual's beliefs are gained through upbringing and integration into a family; education and training; social expectations; emotional states and turning points; job-related tasks; and tastes and preferences grounded in many experiments.[2] Every time someone is confronted with new sensory input—whether it is a colleague's statement, a plant tour, an e-mail message, or a musical tune—that person approaches the new stimulus with his or her experiences and beliefs about the world (Maturana and Varela, 1987).

To use the terminology of the well-known developmental psychologist Jean Piaget (1960), people deal with sensory input through the twin processes of assimilation and accommodation. The human brain is "hungry" for input from the environment, and assimilation is the process by which an individual integrates this data into his or her existing experiences.[3] In other words, individuals make sense of and comprehend the world through assimilation. For example, in an automated plant, when a control panel indicates overheating of a machine, the experienced engineer assimilates this signal. Her response comes from years of training and results in a routine performance.

In other cases, individuals encounter new situations for which they have developed no clear responses or routines. Accommodation is the process by which people give meaning to new input signals, distinguishing them as something that lies beyond what they already know. If a response is called for, they have to try new actions in these new situations. For example, a student of business strategy can use past case studies to interpret elements of a new case. But if a case does not match his experience, he will have to account for new elements like industry factors, technology, or a changing customer base to devise a proper decision for management—that is, he will have to accommodate these new elements into his experience of learning business strategy.

When accommodation becomes too challenging, individual barriers to new knowledge result. A worker might be confronted with a new situation in which her past experience is not sufficient, such as a very complex task, a set of technical terms, or an emotional outburst from a colleague. She might be exposed to a new set of customer requirements beyond her worst nightmare, or a technological development that has been sprung on her with no warning and no training. Under such circumstances, individuals can feel trapped, an emotional response that creates a strong mental barrier to new knowledge. An individual's justified beliefs normally build up through a chain of events, but in a radically new and different situation the justification process may break down (Goldman, 1992). The harder an individual finds accommodation to be, the more stressed and anxious he feels (Harvey and Brown, 1992). In some instances, he will lose interest in the new situation entirely or turn away to other more acceptable tasks and impressions.

New knowledge can also pose a threat to self-image. In order to accommodate, people must make changes in themselves—existential changes

(Polanyi, 1958).[4] In the age of voice-controlled word-processing, a stenographer has to reconsider his profession quite seriously. He may have to accommodate new routines and technical requirements associated with another line of work. For most of us, such changes in work and profession involve a major shift in who we are. Indeed, what we know—and how that affects what we do—is often at the root of personal identity. Because knowledge is so intimately tied to self-image, people often resist anything new. Breaking away from known habits can feel very risky. When the CEO expects everybody to use Lotus Notes effectively, for instance, many respond by evoking their self-image: "You know, I'm not the computer type," or "I'd rather talk to somebody than use all that high-tech stuff." These may be excuses, but the beliefs about self that underlie them can be powerful inhibitors.

When executives present a new vision of future knowledge creation in a company, similar barriers are likely to emerge. Some people will see the need to accommodate new knowledge, leading to deep existential changes; others will just find it threatening. A new organizational structure may allow individuals to work directly on knowledge-creation tasks, often in teams—the transformative wave of the future, according to many business pundits—yet it will also put people into situations in which they have to accommodate very different experiences and knowledge. Marketers may have to cooperate with manufacturing workers; salespeople may have to work with scientists. Although there is good reason to believe this kind of cross-leveling is necessary for knowledge creation, managers should not assume it will happen without a hitch.

In all such social encounters, people are likely to present themselves to others through stories or personal narratives. They tell the stories of their lives, careers, dreams, wishes, hopes, and turning points. Occasionally they try to impress their listeners by emphasizing certain moments and downplaying others.[5] They tell such stories to console themselves, to justify their behavior, to communicate their values and beliefs, and to look competent and able—not to look incompetent in their colleagues' eyes.[6] In particular, people produce well-crafted stories about their expertise. What co-workers know about your expertise will help them to draw on your knowledge whenever it is needed; what a manager knows of your performance record will allow him or her to assign you to the right tasks. Still, these stories also represent individual barriers to new knowledge. People are loath to accommodate new knowledge that undermines or runs counter to their stories, especially if that knowledge is conveyed by other group participants with different backgrounds. A trained engineer will have a difficult time admitting that he does not know the new technological developments that a young sales representative enthusiastically discusses with him. In this way, variety in group members' knowledge, the very source of creativity and successful task completion, can be a major barrier to effective group work.[7]

Maintaining a serious self-image as well as self-respect can be tough when participation in organizational knowledge work dramatically changes the basis for personal narratives. ("Before I joined this team, I was considered a competent guy.") Such workers may withdraw or reduce their collaboration to a minimum. Here we are talking about mental rather than physical withdrawal from participation in workshops, teams, or microcommunities; nevertheless, mentally "checking out" in this fashion is a serious obstacle to knowledge creation in a group setting. By gradually withdrawing, the individual interferes with the communal process of sharing knowledge. He or she makes a silent statement that something is wrong.

ORGANIZATIONAL BARRIERS: THE PROBLEM WITH COMPANY PARADIGMS

Each member of a community has unique, personal knowledge, at least part of which is tacit and not easily explained to others. When managers bring workers together for a project, the challenge for everyone is discovering how to utilize this potential, leveraging it into more than just the sum of what individual members know. Whenever individuals share their knowledge in a group, they must publicly justify what they believe. We have already noted that this can be quite difficult—fraught with self-doubt, fear of going against community norms or ruining established relationships, and the overall need to stand up for one's own ideas. In fact, the crucial part justification plays in knowledge creation is what makes it such a highly fragile process.

In any organization, there are four severe barriers to justification in a group setting: (1) the need for a legitimate language, (2) organizational stories, (3) procedures, and (4) company paradigms.[8] Like individual knowledge barriers, organizational barriers often arise because of natural human tendencies. But these barriers can also be strengthened because of the wrong managerial attitude toward knowledge, particularly when it comes to procedures and the acceptance of limited company paradigms.

First, language is key to individual learning and reflection. For the purpose of sharing what one knows, however, tacit knowledge has to be made explicit through a common language that is acceptable to other community members and the company at large. The sticking point is that some personal knowledge can be expressed only by using words that may be unfamiliar to other organizational members. Indeed, recognition of new business opportunities might require an innovative vocabulary that includes words like *neutraceuticals, infotainment, edutainment,* or *cybershopping*.

Once such innovative words are recognized, they quickly become part of a company's working vocabulary. But legitimizing the right language matters for other reasons as well. Knowledge and distinction making are closely tied, and the articulation of new knowledge requires a process in which people move from broad distinctions to increasingly fine ones (von Krogh and Roos, 1995a). If the fine distinctions are lost, you might be deprived of new knowledge. For the pharmaceutical industry, for instance—which relies on finding plants from which to extract substances that may become new products—the rapid disintegration of many South American native languages is problematic. Such languages, traditionally spoken by groups who live in the rain forest or other botanically rich environments, make very fine distinctions in naming families of plants with different genetic structures. To the untrained eye, these plants may seem just slightly different from plants within the same family. Pharmaceutical researchers may not have the time or patience to make such fine distinctions; yet if their native informants no longer speak the old language, a valuable source of knowledge has been lost.

On the other hand, if distinctions are too fine, larger issues may be ignored—that is, the people involved "may not see the forest for the trees." The legitimate push for rational thinking in a community can become a major obstacle to new knowledge creation and broader distinction making (Weick and Westley, 1996). Imagine a community of engineers in a typewriter company. On the agenda is the competitive advantages to be found in technological solutions. Knowing the industry and the technologies possible, the team leader pushes for precision and rational arguments. The group makes fine distinctions, isolating for discussion the ball-head of their company and the arm-hammer systems of a competitor. Yet such high precision obscures the competitive reality: namely, that the whole typewriter industry is about to vanish. When communities descend into increasingly picky discussions about terminology, it can be difficult for individuals to justify their personal beliefs about what is really happening. Who wants to tell these devoted engineers that they will be out of work in a couple of years?

As for the second barrier, all organizations have stories of various kinds. They constitute organizational memory or a commonsense understanding of how things work that allows individuals to regulate their own behavior. Such stories help people orient themselves both in terms of bonding with others (whom to bond with and when) and in understanding the organization's value system (Kreps, 1989).[9] Yet stories are another barrier to new knowledge creation, since they make it difficult for individuals to express contradictory ideas. Sometimes the stories that circulate are largely negative; they describe failed entrepreneurs, failed marketing campaigns, failed attempts at implementing technology. Consider an engineer who

wants to convince his group to develop new software for steering a production line. He might be told, "Don't you remember that guy Finch, the
one who tried to do stuff like that himself? Well, *he's* not with us anymore."

Organizational stories and company myths can polarize new knowledge and direct attention elsewhere. Stories might highlight the differences between new knowledge and knowledge that already exists, thereby
making the new seem less legitimate. For example, during the early 1970s
in some European pharmaceutical companies, chemical engineers with
an interest in biotechnology must have had a hard time. Stories circulated
then about other companies (such as Monsanto in the United States) that
had spent millions of dollars in biotechnology development without any
tangible results. In effect, this organizational "common sense" isolated
biotechnological knowledge from other research about the natural extrac-
tion of hormones, chemical synthesis, purification of natural substances,
and so forth, discouraging young engineers and redirecting their attention
toward traditional pharmaceutical processes.

The third knowledge barrier involves procedures, the double-edged
sword of knowledge management. On the one hand, a procedure represents embedded experiences and successful solutions to complex tasks, as
well as coordination of solutions among various tasks in the organization.
It makes the organization more effective and efficient in current operations. On the other hand, by directing communication, defining planning
steps, and setting performance measures for control, it can work against
public justification of beliefs.[10] The creation of new knowledge that
resulted in Sharp's pocket organizer, for instance, required engineering
staffs from at least three distinct technical milieus and groups. Any knowledge-creation and innovation process also requires budgets that are beyond
the control of each microcommunity involved. Yet in most companies,
the procedures in place do not allow for crossing disciplinary or functional
lines in this manner. Nor do they allow individuals to spend sufficient
time or resources on new knowledge-creation projects. Employees are
rarely motivated to fight an ineffective procedure because they know that
the more diligently they follow it, the less likely they are to experience the
negative consequences of bucking the system—such as acquiring a bad
reputation, receiving fewer financial incentives, or weakening their career
prospects (Barnes, 1988).

Moreover, personal knowledge that questions an organization's procedures is hard to share because it runs counter to the very mechanism
believed to make the firm effective—the procedures themselves, which
often appear in a technical blueprint or set of explicit guidelines. At Xerox,
for example, Brown and Duguid (1991) found that service technicians
often had to go beyond the technical manuals to repair copy machines
successfully. By sharing knowledge among themselves—via an unofficial

microcommunity—they developed a major route to solving highly complex problems. Legitimizing such approaches and allowing workers to put manuals aside is part of the process of making the public justification process easier.

The last major organizational barrier to knowledge creation is the most fundamental and all-encompassing: company paradigms. A company's strategic intent, vision or mission statements, and core values constitute its paradigm or worldview. Paradigms become ingrained in any organization; they define the themes talked about in management meetings, the language used, the key stories told, and the routines followed. Paradigms even influence what data and information employees are likely to search for (such as competitor information, customer surveys, or supplier studies) as well as how they should interpret that data (Schwandt, 1997; Prahalad and Bettis, 1986).

In general, paradigms socialize new organizational members, getting them to line up behind the current thinking of the company. To remain coherent at all, any organization requires shared goals, values, and norms; again, much of this is a natural part of socialization and the ways human beings operate in groups. However, as executives and consultants increasingly emphasize overarching company visions, linked business strategies, and corporate cultures, it should be clear that such paradigms have the power to make or break knowledge creation. Our own discussions of knowledge strategy and vision in later chapters indicate the positive role they can play. But paradigms also determine the legitimacy of personal knowledge within an organization. Personal knowledge that conforms with the paradigm will be quickly embraced by colleagues; nonconformist attempts to justify personal beliefs are often met with skepticism.

When any or all of the four organizational barriers exist, individual insights may never make it through the whole process of knowledge creation. Great ideas, great arguments, great concepts are killed and never transformed into successful products or services. Tacit knowledge cannot be shared because nobody else in the firm will accept new, innovative language; alternatively, other organizational members may be paralyzed by stories of past failure. Having beaten their heads against the proverbial brick wall, individuals often decide to stop contributing new ideas. They join the large class of passive participants in many of today's companies. Or the best employees get tired and leave—only to compete with the company from outside.

WHAT'S WRONG WITH KNOWLEDGE MANAGEMENT?

The current popularity of knowledge-management initiatives might lead one to believe that many firms are constructively addressing the barriers to knowledge creation. Yet, it is much easier to talk about knowledge than to "walk the talk." In addition, knowledge management as it is practiced in most firms represents a constricting paradigm rather than a transformative one. The emphasis on quantifying ever smaller pieces of information, an obsession with measurement tools, the use of terminology that may limit the free flow of ideas, the rigid procedures established—and the overarching assumption that knowledge can be controlled—all reinforce many of the barriers discussed above instead of dismantling them.

Indeed, based on our work, we have found that the whole concept of knowledge management is associated with a number of pitfalls. In this section, we present three of the main ones. Note that they are rather broad, gathered from our observations of various knowledge-management initiatives. Our intention here is not to cast a shadow on many of the positive knowledge-management ideas surfacing today. By pointing out possible limitations, we hope to guide managers who have already accepted the importance of knowledge creation toward an approach that is more flexible and realistic.

Pitfall 1: Knowledge management relies on easily detectable, quantifiable information. Typically, knowledge-management efforts break information into smaller chunks that can be detected throughout the company, stored for later use, manipulated by being combined with other chunks, and transferred where they are needed. Information under this rubric covers a range of items: documents, policies, databases, procedures. The ultimate goal of knowledge management is to get the right information to the right people at the right pace—and it depends on information technology.

This is not a new approach, nor is it trivial. Information management is certainly needed in all organizations, and careful handling and storage of information can result in tremendously positive outcomes for business organizations. Starting in 1987, for example, Sun Microsystems invested heavily in building an information network that distributed more accurate information about inventories to managers, which allowed them to make better logistical and purchasing decisions. Over a six-year period, Sun's annual inventory turnover increased from four to about eleven times. The system was also expanded to include the company's customers and suppliers so that accurate and timely information now flows along the whole value chain. During the same period, the time that elapsed between registering an order and logging revenue was reduced from about 275 days to 135 (Hof, 1995b).

If knowledge equals information, much of contemporary knowledge management makes sense. Information technology such as that implemented by Sun becomes the key enabler, and heavy investments in these systems can be justified. Information systems coupled with video and teleconferencing, for example, go beyond classic groupware solutions like Lotus Notes, helping to leverage knowledge throughout a company. Three-dimensional computer aided design/computer aided manufacturing (CAD-CAM) systems can aid the development of concepts and prototypes in knowledge creation. An electronic list of experts along with their areas of expertise can help in assembling a microcommunity of knowledge.

The issue here is not one of relevance but of categorization. In many knowledge-management approaches, information and knowledge are equated. Therefore, knowledge management has been myopically inter-preted as simply information management. The cognitivist research tra-dition has also contributed to the confusion between information and knowledge. Since the early 1950s, well-known scientists like Warren McCulloch, Herbert Simon, and Marvin Minsky have developed formal models of human cognition that resemble a machine for information pro-cessing.[11] To the cognitivist, knowledge is explicit, can be encoded and stored, and is easy to transmit to others.[12]

Many knowledge-management initiatives are based on the same assumptions. But they fail to make the fundamental distinction between information and knowledge, or to account for the different management styles and activities required. Information is data put in context; it is related to other pieces of data. As Gregory Bateson notes, "Information is a dif-ference, which makes difference."[13] An individual, for example, notices differences when he or she reads a new document, comparing it to past documents. Information is about meaning, and it forms the basis for knowledge. Yet knowledge goes one step farther: It encompasses the beliefs of groups or individuals, and it is intimately tied to action. Beliefs, com-mitments, and actions cannot be captured and represented in the same manner as information. Nor is knowledge always detectable; it is created spontaneously, often unpredictably. Therefore, storing knowledge and transferring it electronically from one part of the company to another is difficult.

To be sure, information technology is helpful, perhaps indispensable, in the modern corporation. But information systems are of limited use-fulness in facilitating a group's commitment to a concept, sharing emo-tions tied to tacit experience, or embodying the knowledge related to a certain task. The human skills that drive knowledge creation have much more to do with relationships and community-building than databases, and companies need to invest in training that emphasizes emotional knowledge and social interaction. Investments in information technology alone cannot make the knowledge-creating company happen.

Pitfall 2: Knowledge management is devoted to the manufacture of tools. Of the knowledge-management approaches that have come to our atten-tion, many are obsessed with tools and instruments. Yet the architects of these tools seldom stop to reflect on their fundamental impact on the organization. Because knowledge-management initiatives are aimed at producing business results, such tools normally have to be made as explicit and general as possible. Some tools set out to identify the knowledge that exists in a group of organizational members, a unit, or the whole company. Once identified, other tools are used to assess the business impact of that knowledge. Still more tools find new ways to connect existing knowledge with existing value-creating tasks of the company. Some measure the quality of knowledge. Others prepare the organization for retaining the knowledge of employees who leave.

While tools may allow companies to get started with knowledge creation, they should slide off to the background once the effort is underway. When tools and methods are overemphasized, they not only guide the awareness of individual organizational members but also constrain it. Most important, sometimes applying the tools correctly ends up outweighing the results of knowledge creation. For example, a large organization implemented electronic "yellow pages," a system in which the relevant skills of employees can be identified. At first, the system allowed people great freedom in describing their skills, and some used this opportunity to market and sell themselves. The system manager found this less than satisfying and pushed for more coherence and consistency in the categorization of skills. As a result, people felt that the system became too constraining and did not describe what they knew, and commitment to and interest in it gradually subsided throughout the organization.

What the process gains in structure, logic, and speed, it loses in creativity, insights, and the forging of necessary social links. In some of our research (Lyles, Aadne, and von Krogh, 1998), we have empirically studied knowledge transfer between companies involved in East-West joint ventures, identifying conditions that enhance this process. There is strong evidence that a climate that fosters trust, care, and personal networks among employees is one of the most important conditions for spreading technical and administrative knowledge effectively.

Consider the following analogy. The toolbox is secondary to the carpenter. His toolbox is full of many tools that do many things, but he has to select the *right* tool for a given job, which requires a broad understanding of the whole construction process. The same can be said of knowledge creation. Tools should be selected, adapted, or even created on the fly to fulfill the particular needs of a given microcommunity; they should not be imposed or enforced. For example, in the customer-focus program at Asea Brown Boveri, cross-functional teams of development and manufacturing engineers, sales representatives, and technicians solve practical problems in areas ranging from manufacturing to customer service. At their disposal they have a little booklet, or "toolbox," that describes some techniques for group problem solving. The teams then select their own tools to fit their particular needs (Baumgartner, 1995).

Pitfall 3: Knowledge management depends on a knowledge officer. When companies embark on knowledge-management initiatives, many give a knowledge officer—usually a fairly high-ranking executive—responsibility for the results. Such executives have a variety of duties: They can craft a company's knowledge vision, establish knowledge-management systems, implement information-technology platforms to help build "knowledge networks," establish the value of the firm's intellectual capital, and design compensation systems that will push the development of expertise. Effective knowledge officers depend on knowledge or intellectual capital reports that are filled out and handed in by business areas or departments. They will suggest actions to take when these reports show a possible weakness. For example, indicators like turnover of employees annually, the level of computer illiteracy, and the average employee level of education may reveal alarming patterns; the knowledge officer is responsible for inquiring into the matter and bringing knowledge management back to an even keel.

This conception of the knowledge officer can yield useful information, but it is also limited. First, knowledge is generally created close to the marketplace. In a staff position, the knowledge officer will find it difficult to keep up with knowledge creation occurring in various business operations. It would be hard, for instance, to keep track of a product improvement initiated by a customer and executed by a small team of service engineers and salespeople. Instead of focusing on direction setting, planning, and control of this process, a more sensible approach is to facilitate the conditions that enable knowledge creation—such as encouraging regular feedback from customers. Rather than being passive analysts and controllers, knowledge officers should think of themselves as knowledge activists.

In addition, knowledge should not be thought of as an "asset" in a classical sense, subject to a bureaucratic administration and isolated in a separate staff function; knowledge creation is a dynamic process that can involve contributions from hundreds of people in an organization. Because it is vital for sustainable business performance, it should be considered a general management responsibility, one that originates at the top of the company and is distributed through middle management to all operational levels. A knowledge activist, as opposed to a staff officer, can connect various line management activities and bring these together under a common vision.

Another problem with the knowledge officer role has to do with resource allocation and decisions about what knowledge is important to the company. Since executives in the knowledge officer position often have little to do with day-to-day business operations, they may not understand or may neglect knowledge about a new product, material, manufacturing technology, or market trend. In the early stages, they may even block attempts in the firm to experiment with such novel solutions. Knowledge officers may favor exploitation of existing knowledge over new initiatives, hindering the exploration of new knowledge that could eventually lead to successful innovations. In our view, resource allocation for knowledge creation is the responsibility of line managers much closer to the source.

Finally, knowledge creation should be without boundaries, involving multiple disciplines, multiple functions, and organizational members with different experiences. It should also cross organizational boundaries, extending to suppliers, customers, even competitors. However, in order to justify their existence, knowledge staffs (like most organizational units) tend to build up their own boundaries, practices, values, and codes of conduct, often creating arcane or overly technical terminology so that others cannot participate in what they do. In this case, identity hinges on difference. Establishing such boundaries runs counter to the workings of a true knowledge-creating company and reinforces the organizational barriers that already exist.[14]

HOW KNOWLEDGE ENABLING AVOIDS THE PITFALLS: THREE PREMISES

Of course, for so many executives and consultants to be obsessed with tools, information technology, and staff boundaries is understandable. Expensive as some information systems are, at least they have a definite price tag; it is easier to make a business case for them and to point to proposed investments and predicted outcomes. Executives who have gone this route are not foolish, careless, or uninformed, but sometimes they may be shortsighted. To focus on what can be easily described is natural; unfortunately, productive and sustained knowledge creation requires more. The good news is that knowledge enabling is founded on basic human skills. All managers have the potential to be effective, caring experts and activists, if they allow themselves to be, and the three premises that follow indicate why this is so.

Premise 1: Knowledge is justified true belief, individual and social, tacit and explicit. Knowledge is closely attached to human emotions, aspirations, hopes, and intentions. This book's ideas are based on a constructionist perspective rather than the machine logic of a cognitivist. Humberto Maturana and Francesco Varela (1987), two Chilean biologists, have suggested that cognition is a creative act of bringing forth a world. Because knowledge is embodied, closely tied to the senses and previous experiences, people create the world in ways that are unique to them. Both the constructionist and cognitivist perspectives on knowledge have influenced management theory and practice,[15] but the exciting thing about constructionist studies is that they pay attention to the tacit aspects of knowledge in addition to its explicit forms.

Groups of people as well as individuals, hold tacit and explicit knowledge which allows for competent collective action. In a company, members might share explicit social knowledge embedded and routinized, sometimes formalized in organizational procedures for solving a task. Yet even explicit social knowledge cannot all be captured in writing or turned into routines; some might be shared orally or by example, such as when to use the procedure, and the possible limits and exceptions to it. More to the point, much of social knowledge is also tacit: It involves shared beliefs about a situation that are justified but not explicit. Such tacit knowledge can be task-specific—how to de-bone a salmon while keeping the flesh intact, selecting and working with the materials for high-quality furniture, how to ride a bicycle without falling off—but more general issues such as how to relate in a group, deal with a stressful situation, or handle leadership are also part of a community's social tacit knowledge.

What this means is that knowledge is not simply information, especially when it is tacit and shared with other community members. When companies put information and knowledge into the same category, they neglect the very particular nature of knowledge and its creation; at worst, their elaborate information systems and measurement tools may leave out the creative aspect of knowledge. The real managerial challenge is enabling knowledge creation; capturing its by-product, information, is the easy part.

Premise 2: Knowledge depends on your perspective. Despite efforts to come up with general measurement tools that apply across many situations, knowledge is scalable (von Krogh and Roos, 1995a). It depends on an individual's perspective and a given context. In fact, everything known is attached to a particular scale of observation; change the scale, and knowledge of a phenomenon also changes. For example, you can describe your immediate surroundings—the room you are sitting in, your desk, and the view from the window. From a helicopter outside, however, you would see the building from above as well as the surrounding countryside, the roads leading to and passing by the building, and other people on the streets. The helicopter view offers a better understanding of your overall context.

At the other extreme, a researcher uses an electron microscope to tighten the scale of observation, going inward, investigating the molecular structure of the table where she is sitting. In studying any subject, a student starts with a general overview, then delves into detailed themes belonging to that subject. As part of the learning process, she might also scale up, trying to find links between that subject and others. This upward and downward scaling are both important ways of knowing a phenomenon better, and changing perspectives is a natural function of human cognition. In a business organization, acknowledging a range of perspectives is essential, even if general tools can help define what kinds of knowledge are most relevant to the company.

Premise 3: Knowledge creation is a craft, not a science. Knowledge activists and microcommunities share in the craft of knowledge creation; it is not the responsibility of one staff officer. The organizational members involved are aware of the knowledge visions, structures, and processes that can enable knowledge creation; they discuss the concrete application to their own context and develop their own practice. Knowledge activists catalyze and coordinate knowledge creation, as well as instill a sense of vision for the communities engaged in it. Most important, in their active engagement with various communities, they come to share some of the best knowledge creation practices throughout an organization. In many cases, this is a far cry from what most knowledge officers do; it gives the people responsible for knowledge creation both more power and less.

Managers may long for clear responsibilities and tasks—or a scientific analysis of what happens when—but the ebb and flow of knowledge in any company requires a more expansive approach. Individual and organizational barriers are inherent to knowledge creation: lack of understanding, lack of agreement, lack of a common language, company myths, failure stories, and rigid procedures. Yet even if an overly scientific attitude contributes to these barriers, we do not mean that knowledge creation happens by default; it has to be carefully enabled through an aware and sensitive management practice.

Is this hard to achieve from scratch? Yes. Is this an impossible goal? No—especially if boundary-breaking managers are in place. The rest of this chapter focuses on Phonak, a company that has emphasized dismantling the usual boundaries between management and line workers, researchers, and functions. Although this firm had visionary founders, it has experienced its share of individual and organizational knowledge barriers. As with all knowledge-creating companies, Phonak's ability to transcend the barriers began with a recognition that they do, in fact, exist.

PHONAK: BREAKING THE BOUNDARIES OF KNOWLEDGE

Located in Stäfa/Zurich, Switzerland, Phonak is one of the world's leaders in advanced hearing systems.[16] It was founded in 1964 by Beda Diethelm, an engineer by training; marketer Andreas (Andy) Rihs joined

Diethelm's one-man company in 1966 to reorganize its sales activities. Thirty years later, Rihs is now CEO, and Phonak has 1115 employees from more than 30 nations, 464 of whom work in Switzerland. Most of its production (96 percent) is exported to 80 other countries, which generated a turnover of approximately 166 million U.S. $ during 1998/99—an 18 percent increase on the previous year's figure. During the same period, net profit increased by 28 percent, reaching 19 million U.S. $.[17] Each year, Phonak reinvests 8 to 9 percent of the turnover in research and development. After Siemens, U.S.-based Starkey, and Danish Oticon, Phonak ranks as the world's fourth largest developer and manufacturer of high-tech hearing computers.

The development of hearing instruments is an interdisciplinary task, drawing on fields like microelectronics, micromechanics, medicine, audiology, psychoacoustics, physics, and psychology. Because of the specialized requirements of Phonak's products, which involve miniature components and state-of-the-art electronics, the company has not been able to profit from synergies with other industry branches or technologies. To create truly superior hearing systems, it has been forced to find independent solutions, developing and producing everything in-house. That means Phonak's products have been characterized by long life cycles, a situation that has lessened the company's exposure to intense technological competition and given it time to develop new products from scratch.

Its superior hearing systems have set many industrial standards: In 1978, Phonak's SuperFront was the first high-power hearing aid. With amplification of 70 to 80 decibels and sound pressure of more than 140 decibels, it can be fitted to hearing-impaired children from the age of three months on. The company produced this superlative hearing aid for twenty years. Another more recent product, AudioZoom, is now based on a dual-microphone technology for clear hearing and understanding even in noisy environments. By enabling users to switch between "wide-angle" and "zoom" modes, the product allows them to pick up all sounds equally or to focus on a desired speech signal—a technology that, as of this writing, is still unique to AudioZoom.

As for the company's other products, PiCS (Personal integrated Communication System) is a digitally programmable hearing computer. It led to Phonak's first large-scale success in 1994/95, resulting in a sales increase of 26 percent. It was one of the first hearing instruments to offer three different signal-processing strategies: one standard program (considered audiologically correct for the wearer) and two "comfort" programs that are individually programmable and selectable by remote control. Phonak's MicroLink, the world's smallest radio receiver, transforms hearing instruments into genuine communication systems. A wireless microphone ensures high-quality transmission of speech and sound over long distances or in noisy surroundings. (As a pioneer in wireless technology, Phonak has even provided its competitors with these technologies to a certain extent.) In 1999, the company plans to launch a fully digital hearing computer. It will behave similar to the inner ear and go far beyond the capabilities of other fully digital hearing instruments on the market.

Beyond Phonak's success, the hearing-instrument market itself has been characterized by marked and sustainable growth. According to some estimates, 10 percent of the population of industrialized nations suffers from some kind of hearing problem, yet only between 1 and 2 percent use hearing instruments. While market expansion in Europe has been limited to date by governmental and social-insurance restrictions, markets in regions like Asia, Latin America, Africa, and Eastern Europe are largely undeveloped and have enormous growth potential.

Valuing People: Dismantling Personal and Organizational Barriers

Phonak's success is partly based on expanding markets and savvy business decisions. But this company has been particularly innovative and growth driven because of the attention it paid to breaking down knowledge barriers. This story illustrates not only how personal and organizational barriers to communication and knowledge sharing can be dismantled, but also how Phonak's boundary-breaking culture has been physically manifested in the architecture of its buildings; how its expanding organization has become a coherent "macrocommunity"; and how it has achieved the necessary balance between creative chaos and managerial order.

Most important, Phonak's people are considered crucial to its long-term success. Its corporate culture is characterized by direct interaction and a policy of openness without hiding what one knows, creating the space — or overall enabling context — necessary for creativity and spontaneity. Although this may seem to be a natural element of any high-tech company, even Phonak has found this a challenge. As Christian Berg, head of research and development, notes, "We have specialists dwelling in their own fields of interest. A typical engineer doesn't look to the left or to the right. This is 'engineer syndrome' par excellence."

At Phonak, direct interaction and openness are mainly based on three factors: interdisciplinarity via a "classless society," personal assertiveness, and total involvement. These factors, which are detailed below, originated with the values of founders Diethelm and Rihs; but they are also connected to Phonak's core business: the peculiarity of developing hearing instruments. Indeed, this company — whose strategy depends on technical improvements in hearing — is good at listening on a variety of levels.

A Classless Society

Beda Diethelm and Andy Rihs joined forces because they knew neither could develop and sell such complex products on his own. Andy Rihs says, "We knew we had to share. Nobody knows everything because of this interdisciplinarity." From the beginning, both men were very creative and unconventional. Sometimes they had a "crazy" dialogue, in which Rihs's market ideas and Diethelm's technological suggestions were blended. Hierarchy was never an issue because the focus was always on the product. Authority was based on competence. Diethelm maintained responsibility for engineering products, but he supported Rihs in marketing. Although Diethelm is still a member of Phonak's board of directors, he withdrew from his operational role in 1997.

Because Phonak had to develop its own technological solutions in-house, a classless society evolved. For the equipment needed to mold synthetic material, "when we presented our concepts to companies specialized in this area, we were told that this would never work. We had to develop it on our own," explains Rolf Schweizer, director of production and logistics. As a result, Phonak ended up with fewer management levels than traditional engineering companies; none of the engineers had senior or junior ranks, and promotion was based on demonstrated skill and creativity rather than seniority. Communication was and is of a high density, direct and very fast. Conflicts were resolved early on to prevent any turf battles. Phonak had to go its own way, strengthening the cohesion and identity of its corporate society.

Personal Assertiveness

At Phonak, employees must accept each other, whether they are from different departments or nations. If a person is unable to work in a team, even a very competent employee may be asked to leave. Rolf Schweizer says, "We have people from thirty-two nations, but we would never accept any political bias. This is politically neutral territory—this is Phonak. You need to set an example by showing that everybody is a valued colleague independent of skin color, political origin, or religion. The Phonak employee is a human being who should feel comfortable in every respect." The annual barbecue on the roof of the Phonak building and the meals Asian employees cook together nurture this friendly togetherness. Community spirit is reflected in the company's language: the word *they* is banned. According to Christian Berg: "*We* are doing it, so if something goes wrong, *we* did it."

Beyond mutual acceptance, Phonak workers are encouraged to speak their minds. When there are too many unspoken laws in a company, employees get defensive, fearing they might make a mistake. If most people in an organization think, "I have to be careful about what I say," inno-vation, creative ideas, and alternative solutions are suppressed. Managers should also avoid scaring employees by setting impossible standards or seeming god-like. For open, direct, and constructive communication to take place, all status symbols and class levels should be removed. At Phonak, management conveys the attitude that not everything must be profound or serious. A certain easygoing style is cultivated—a coopera-tive way of speaking. Andy Rihs points out,

> It is very important that management leads in a way that people feel we really are not perfect. That's our number-one thing: We know we are not perfect. But we can try to do better, and that's what we are doing.

Managers do not walk around the whole day frowning; factual prob-lems are not confused with personnel issues. In general, organizational leaders need to kindle the entrepreneurial flame within employees, allowing them to experiment (even if they make mistakes along the way), to become enthusiastically committed (even if a project is not entirely realistic), and to express their ideas publicly (even if they do not conform to the conventional wisdom). Such personal assertiveness is crucial for innovation.

Total Involvement

According to Rihs, "Employees are our most important assets. We can't afford to lose our most important assets. We have to utilize the knowledge of every single employee. Everybody has to understand the importance of their work for us, and they have to be personally responsible to a great extent."

When organizational members play such a decisive role, they want and need to be taken seriously. They want total involvement. From the first stages of new product development at Phonak, for instance, even the solderer is included in the process. Based on her knowledge of how she holds the soldering equipment, she can give feedback about product design so that she is able to do work of the highest quality. To ensure this free flow of information, everybody is allowed to talk to everyone else. In this kind of company, people want to understand why a suggestion has been rejected because they have to live with the decision. Within such a creative, innovative, and classless society, managers cannot simply impose decisions from on high. However, when an agreement has been reached by everyone involved, tasks will be carried out quickly and smoothly.

Maintaining this culture costs time, money, and energy, of course. It is much easier and less time-consuming merely to dictate what has to be done. But when a new employee enters Phonak, he or she is provided with a mentor (at least) for the first few weeks, as well as with personal and technical training. Managers talk directly to people who behave in an unconstructive way, whether they are affecting somebody else's work or interfering with a team's efforts. Because the company has to adapt continually to new products and market opportunities, employees at all levels need to be able to adapt as well, letting go of well-adjusted routines. To launch the digital hearing instrument, for example, many employees will have to change their mind-sets. In production, they will have to concentrate on fewer products at the same time they are learning to change production lines. Once again, everybody involved, from the solderer up, needs to be totally involved in new products and strategies from the beginning.

Managers also put in more time explaining negative decisions objectively; that way, these do not seem like a personal defeat for the employee. Rolf Schweizer says, "By marking people's individual career paths with clear goals, we aim to develop people so that they can do what they do best, not what they would like to do most. Otherwise, you would end up with just top managers." As a consequence, managers often cannot be recognized as such. Rather than acting authoritarian, they are simply people with natural authority. On average, workers are relatively young, and they hold positions based on suitability, not seniority. There are no hierarchies in the traditional sense, and the right people take on the right responsibilities. Andy Rihs, for example, is CEO because of his excellent skills in motivating and leading people, and his profound knowledge of the hearing-systems business.

Boundary-Breaking Architecture

The "Phonak House," Beda Diethelm's brainchild, is a visual representation of the company's boundary-breaking culture. The original House, which was built in 1987, was extended with a new building in 1997, more than tripling the company's production capacity. But the entrance of the square, three-storey traditional building is still decorated with a bas-relief made from the impressions of many employee hands, symbolizing how Phonak's current strength has been achieved only through the combined knowledge and skills of its workers. Inside, one hears a babble of voices; communication is perceptible. Outstanding features like the glass-roofed atrium (open on all floors) and the free-standing staircase, which includes decorative waterfalls, marble steps, and mirror-fronted balustrades, emphasize a mix of many levels and elements yet also create an aura of intimacy (see Figure 2.1).

In the building that links the old Phonak House with the new, a gallery of mirrors, designed by Phonak staff, again expresses the value attached to people. The connecting part is characterized by light-flooded passages.

Figure 2.1. Interior of the Phonak House.

Two restaurants, one on the first floor and a smaller one on the top, are places to relax, providing plenty of room to wind down with colleagues. The first-floor restaurant is a large, open space in which people meet and talk; a winding steel staircase stretches from the entrance to the roof. With its big windows, the round structure forms the heart of the entire complex. The new building has the same architecture as the original Phonak House. Transparency, light, and contrasting designs contribute to an inspiring work environment—that is, this physical space reinforces the company's enabling context.

At Phonak, walls are considered physical manifestations of mental barriers. Therefore, the House features a minimum of dividing walls in order to maximize personal contacts. Employees work in open areas, although it is possible to find private space. In fact, only people who feel at ease in an open and sometimes noisy work environment do well here. It is also true that everybody, whether in routine production or basic research, has to take personal responsibility for his or her job. For that reason, Phonak House cannot serve as a simple blueprint for other companies or countries. Nonetheless, its basic ideas do apply to workplaces around the world.

For example, the idea of replacing office space with an open atrium reflects the new logic of knowledge-intensive companies. The quality of the work environment is decisive, rather than the number or size of individual offices. Because of the atrium, voices from all areas of the House can be heard in any given spot, and people can be seen circulating throughout while working; the entire building is full of light and recognized as a unified entity. The architecture encourages people to meet, interact, and communicate. Nobody can work there without being exposed daily to the full range of company operations. There are not many conference rooms; the restaurants are meeting places where people do not have to reserve a room, they just meet there. And every day at 9:30, the whole company, management included, gathers on the first floor for a coffee break.

There is no separate floor for the directors. Phonak's top managers are located on the ground floor in order to be visible and accessible to every employee. In addition, people who benefit from each other's work are located side by side. For example, research, systems design, product development, electroacoustics, and software—all the departments that cooperate in the innovative phases of product development—are located on the top floor, close to the restaurant there. Yet the location of the departments is also flexible. If a new product line requires it, anything can be changed. The launch of the fully digital hearing computer, for example, required a new conceptualization of manufacturing procedures, including significant alterations to the production floor plan to accomplish the change from the lot to line production.

Scaling Up: Creating a Macrocommunity

While the Phonak House helps eliminate barriers to knowledge sharing on its physical site, the company is also growing and expanding far beyond its original buildings. In the future, not all Phonak employees will be able to work in close physical proximity; even people focused on the same project may be located in different countries. The question for this and other knowledge-creating companies is, how can the right enabling context be maintained during a growth phase, when people no longer sit next to each other, and direct personal communication is not always possible?

At Phonak, the company's strategic focus remains on the product—its quality, design, competitiveness—so that a growing organization and proliferating procedures do not hinder expansion. The company has begun building a coherent macrocommunity through structural changes to the organization. Even in 1992, it launched a spin-off, Phonak Communications, to provide its communication technology division with an independent identity. That way, Phonak Communications is not constantly in conflict with other divisions and does not have to adhere to unnecessary organizational priorities.

On a larger scale, to prepare the launch of its new digital hearing instrument, Phonak introduced a new organization in the spring of 1998. Because top managers believe this product will initiate another growth phase, they have divided tasks into strategic and operative categories. Even while operations were becoming increasingly time-consuming, new strategic challenges kept cropping up. Hence, groupwide key personnel are involed in both strategy and operational tasks. Group management and group functions are organized within the Phonak Holding, which is responsible for strategic marketing—building up the worldwide distribution network, finance, and control of subsidiaries. Operational activities are mainly carried out by Phonak AG and Phonak Communications AG, companies within the holding. They consist of product development, manufacturing, logistics, and sales support.

One advantage of the new organization is that it helps break down geographic knowledge boundaries. With the regionalization of Phonak's subsidiaries, country-specific aspects can be leveraged for the whole company. Whereas companies in Latin countries have strong skills in public relations, for example, they can learn from the precision and thoroughness that German manufacturers are known for. In addition, regionalization and decentralization paradoxically lead to a higher degree of integration. Every country has its own standards, which often hinder innovation. Phonak's managers want its employees all over the world to stand behind the company by changing regional standards that have become barriers. Even the company's product designs need to be globally discussed and the essential aspects regionally adapted. Andy Rihs notes, "The market impact would be much different if Americans said, 'That's a European design.' On the other hand, we need to ensure that there *is* a European design."

In fact, the organizational structure represents figuratively, on a larger scale, what Phonak House does physically: People are obliged to talk with each other, but this happens naturally, not hierarchically. They are either connected by the same task—such as the design of a new product, in which experts from product development cooperate with the staff of regional sales subsidiaries—or they come together because they belong to the same team. For example, the R&D leadership team consists of researchers from Phonak AG and Phonak Communications. Team members are not located on the same physical site, but the team consists of people from the same geographic region: from Phonak House (in the central part of Switzerland) and from Phonak Communications (in the western part of Switzerland).

On an even more "macro" scale, Phonak's growth has been supported by marketing and promotion strategies that position its brand worldwide. This brand position is linked to the company's vision—the idea being that if people are looking for superior hearing instruments, there is just one product they will turn to: a Phonak. Global branding serves as an integrator in many respects and is reflected in corporate management and culture. Employees do not work for Andy Rihs; they work for Phonak. Communication is oriented toward the outside—customers, suppliers, other research groups—across geographic boundaries via the entire Phonak macrocommunity implied by the brand, and based on the common language the company uses to break down individual and organizational boundaries. Otherwise, some people might feel abandoned, as if they had been left to fend for themselves.

Balancing Chaos and Order

If everything remains confidential, the accumulation and distribution of knowledge is impossible. CEO Rihs uses the metaphor of a snowball to explain the logic of knowledge creation: "If you want to receive a letter, write a letter first. The more you give, the more you get. If Phonak wants to receive input from outside, it has to share and give knowledge outside first."

While this company's culture and structure may be open, that does not mean management is completely hands off. Phonak executives do set guidelines and limits under which, as on a highway, individual managers or workers can develop their own driving styles. From a procedural perspective, work is fairly unstructured at an early stage but becomes increasingly "funnneled" as a product develops. The main point is that even people working on a highly structured process at the end of the funnel know about activities at the top and can contribute to the less-structured phases. Structure speeds up the production process and ensures quality at the same time that it reinforces the snowball principle. This is possible only because the structure does not dominate the interaction of people but supports it—a good example of knowledge enabling. Hierarchical authority helps organize activities but is not imposed for its own sake.

The following four steps give a rough overview of the phases of product development at Phonak. Marketing and distribution proceed in parallel lines, peaking in the last two phases. Toward the end of these phases, more and more people become involved. They start functioning as teams and cooperating, as in a game of rugby.

1. *Basic Research*: The development of a new hearing instrument starts with the research team's goal of improving solutions for a given hearing problem. The team defines what technical objective should be achieved, and a technical solution is presented. For the digital hearing instrument, for example, the goal is to make it perform like an artificial inner ear.
2. *Concept Creation*: Engineers from the systems-design group join the

research team in this phase. The challenge here is to design a technical solution that can become an actual hearing instrument. Building blocks for technology systems, such as microelectronic chips, are developed. These may be used for several products.

3. *Product Development:* The product-development group becomes involved at this stage, cooperating with systems design. Several concepts are combined to form a product. Product development considers many different standards, depending on the countries and regional companies involved. Time pressure increases.

4. *Manufacturing:* This final phase is tightly structured to ensure quality and quantity of products within the shortest possible time frame. Clear goals are set, and working procedures are constantly repeated. Total involvement is crucial.

Given this complex process, how does the company balance chaos and order? In fact, successful innovations generally take place in an open, even slightly chaotic environment. A few years ago, Phonak attempted to structure product innovation in a pilot department; managers wanted to speed up development projects so that they would be ready for production at an earlier stage. However, this was a great mistake because too much knowledge was either lost or incorrectly applied. Technical solutions were presented without either careful consideration of how easy they would be to manufacture or attention paid to country-specific product standards. To create a viable new product, R&D needs to be in touch with every discipline. These workers need to cooperate with the production department to ensure that products will be of the highest quality. Researchers, systems designers, and product developers must not remain in an upper class of their own; an employee on the production line may contribute as much to a new product as they do.

The basic research phase is especially difficult to plan. Sometimes it takes two years, sometimes ten, to come up with a solution. Researchers work with external institutions and partners like universities, medical doctors, psychologists, and physicists, all of which add an element of uncertainty. Basic research, as well as concept development, often seems rather chaotic, consisting of a fluid dialogue among the research team, marketing experts, and systems designers. At Phonak, there is room for both open-minded thinkers and the detail-oriented. Herbert Bächler, manager of the research team, cites the freedom to act intuitively as essential for creativity. The interdisciplinarity of teams and individuals also contributes to innovation: Sometimes engineers spend up to 40 percent of their work time acting as marketing experts, interacting with customers.

Depending on the phase of the product-development process, the means of communication will differ. In the first two phases, communication mainly consists of dialogues or conversations. Such dialogue is structured through some arranged meetings. Every first and third Monday afternoon of the month, the leaders of all departments gather for interdisciplinary information sharing. Operating and financial issues are discussed, following a standardized agenda. Every second Monday afternoon, company management (and every fourth Monday, all managers) assemble to share information on company business, statistics, and politics. Once a month, engineers and marketers gather to coordinate their activities.

After a concept has been developed, written communication and other forms of explicit knowledge become increasingly important. Reports, demonstrations, prototypes, and videos are used to spread knowledge. For example, production by contractors is much easier if the processes are clearly documented. Documentation was much improved by ISO certification, which involves a dated document and signature.[18] Reports may block creativity at the early stages, but they are necessary for the problem-solving process. One can verify when and why the wrong decisions were taken. At Phonak, a phase-review document prevents things from being done twice: The phases are finished in the appropriate sequence and debriefed.

Debriefing raises the question of how to handle failures. Phonak managers distinguish between failures in explicit knowledge and those that involve tacit knowledge. If someone is doing a task for the first time, in a risky area, he or she is allowed to make mistakes; otherwise, innovation would be impossible. But when tasks are supposed to be familiar, mistakes are a problem. In this instance, managers must practice discipline, care, and honest communication.

At a company like Phonak, the farther down the funnel you go, the fewer mistakes are acceptable—the goal being to attain a 90 percent success rate by the time the manufacturing stage is reached. For technical reasons, the process becomes highly structured then. Since the 1980s, materials handling has been completely integrated and computerized. Manufacturing processes are graphically illustrated, and production capacity and work plans must match specified goals. Because the processes are so complex, team leaders are responsible for ensuring that they are carried out with great precision.

THE PHONAK LESSON: OPEN-ENDED CONTROL

In essence, management lays down guidelines that provide an optimal work environment.[19] At Phonak, "optimal" means an enabling context that dispenses with hierarchical formality, breaks down knowledge barriers, and allows employees much more freedom than in traditional organizations. But in order for any R&D project to be successful, it must be given the highest priority. People will dedicate themselves only when they know that what they are doing matters to the company. This does not indicate laziness or lack of commitment, but a kind of natural "conservation of energy" that will be practiced by any employee who wants to remain with an organization. Phonak's priorities are set by a community that represents top management and all operating divisions. The company has a rolling five-year plan that sets targets for the long run based on a variety of competitive scenarios; this rolling plan provides some strategic control but also enough flexibility to shift and adapt to new conditions.

If such open-ended control seems like a managerial paradox, you are right. But the constantly shifting demands of today's knowledge economy and the marketplace—be it local, regional, or global—are full of such paradoxes. At this and other companies, setting standards and constant growth are possible only because knowledge flows freely. Phonak House's physical space reflects its culture, in which employees are considered the company's most important assets. Participation in a decentralized macro-community reinforces this culture on a larger scale. But breaking all the boundaries is not enough: Management guidelines help maintain a productive equilibrium between chaos and order.

It is in this balancing act—supporting creativity and unhindered communication, yet shaping it to serve the organization's goals—that managerial "psychologists" or caring experts come into their own. And as the next chapter emphasizes, fostering care in the organization is an essential part of knowledge enabling.

· 3 ·

CARE IN THE ORGANIZATION

Why an Enabling Context Matters

*To care for another person, in the most significant sense,
is to help him grow and actualize himself.*
— Milton Mayeroff

Knowledge creation puts particular demands on organizational relationships. In order to share personal knowledge, individuals must rely on others to listen and react to their ideas. Constructive and helpful relations enable people to share their insights and freely discuss their concerns. They also enable microcommunities, the origin of knowledge creation in companies, to form and self-organize. Good relationships purge a knowledge-creation process of distrust, fear, and dissatisfaction, and allow organizational members to feel safe enough to explore the unknown territories of new markets, new customers, new products, and new manufacturing technologies.

At a more basic level, the ways in which people interact—cooperative sharing versus competitive hoarding, "join us" versus "not at my table"—strongly affect the distribution of tacit knowledge. The sharing of tacit knowledge is especially susceptible to the barriers mentioned in the last chapter, and it requires careful nurturing. Since knowledge is often equated with power and influence in a firm, knowledge "shielding" tactics can become daily practice (Pfeffer, 1992). This hoarding of knowledge is one of the fundamental issues of modern business organizations, and it is why the concept of care has such relevance for today's companies.

The importance of relationships in a business setting may seem obvious, necessary, and almost not worth mentioning. Yet as all managers know, difficulties often arise precisely because of "people problems." When productive knowledge creation—the very engine of innovation in

45

many contemporary organizations—is threatened, the bottom line can suffer. Beyond sharing of tacit knowledge, high or low levels of care affect the other four steps of the knowledge-creation process. The creation and justification of concepts is influenced by the strength of relationships and the extent to which organizational members feel they can suggest new concepts and ideas, as well as convey and receive constructive criticism. Strong relationships also speed up the creation of a prototype and facilitate cross-leveling of knowledge throughout a company.

Given that all of this is true—and that so many corporate mission statements at least nod to the pursuit of good relationships with customers, suppliers, and employees—why do so many management systems operate as if the whole world is against them? The answer to such a large question is not simple, but it does lie in perceptions of reality and corporate attitudes, much of which are tacit themselves. Most organizations reflect the environment they are operating in, both in the ways they are structured and in how they innovate. This is the well-known argument of "contingency" theorists in the field of management and organizational studies (Burns and Stalker, 1961). But other authors studying cognitive processes in business organizations have noted that the environment essentially becomes an internal, self-perpetuating feature of such places. The organization, so to speak, mirrors itself: it not only reflects the actual environment but the one it "thinks" it is operating in (Morgan, 1996).[1]

Therefore, when companies find that they are exposed to hypercompetitive environments, they mirror some of this competitiveness internally as well. Systems, strategies, structures, and perhaps even the organizational culture are influenced accordingly. Top management repeatedly conveys the message that the company is under fire and makes clear that the organization also needs to be internally competitive in order to adapt to changing environmental conditions. In effect, salespeople face more competitive incentive systems; engineers confront flatter and leaner organizational structures in which their prospect for building a career are not good; researchers find themselves in a competitive race to crank out novel ideas and to file the highest number of patents; and middle managers do their best to hold on to their ever more shaky positions.

The problem of mirroring hypercompetition is a grave one. It can effectively remove the key lubricant in any knowledge-creation process: care among organizational members. In other words, a hypercompetitive context is about as far away as you can move from an enabling context. It can lead individual members to act in an untrustworthy fashion, avoid helping out, engage in gaming, unduly criticize new and potentially valuable ideas, and refuse to offer their valuable feedback during the learning process. What is more, such an internal belief in hypercompetition may lead a company's strategists in the wrong direction, undercutting the very advantages that could bring success. A hypercompetitive context makes the organization rigid rather than adaptive, reactionary rather than pro-active, and very unpleasant as a place to work.

An enabling context, on the other hand, makes an organization appro-priately flexible, future-oriented, and a fulfilling place to spend time. We argue that the emphasis on cooperation and personal relationships that are the hallmark of an enabling context can also make a company more profitable. Chapter 8 delves into the specifics of organizational structure and the ways this structure can reinforce an overall enabling context. In this chapter, we present more general ideas about care in organizations and the role it plays in knowledge creation. We describe two contexts— hypercompetitive and enabling—and distinguish four different actions: seizing, transacting, bestowing, and indwelling. The last action, in par-ticular, can profoundly affect social knowledge creation. Indwelling involves all participants living with a new concept, seeing it from the inside out, and expanding on this vision together; that is, it relies on tacit knowledge as a source of innovation. We look at Unilever, Narvesen, and Shiseido as all three companies, in different business settings and national locations, exemplify how listening to customers with care can pay off. The chapter concludes with a list of practical initiatives, all of which can encourage care-based relationships in business organizations.

THE NEED FOR CARE: FROM WESTERN PHILOSOPHERS TO BA

Most people understand care intuitively because of their personal histo-ries. It describes the way a mother behaves toward her child, a teacher toward his student, a manager toward her employees, or a doctor toward his patient. As the opening quote from philosopher Milton Mayeroff acknowledges,[2] to care for others is to help them learn; to increase their awareness of important events and consequences; to nurture their per-sonal knowledge while sharing their insights. This can happen on an indi-vidual level, but the concept of care matters most in an organization when those in charge provide a context in which knowledge is created and shared freely. In our empirical studies and theoretical work, we have found that the concept of care quite satisfactorily describes relations that have a positive impact on knowledge creation.

A caring manager requires wisdom; he or she must understand the needs of the other as well as the needs of the group, the company, and society. He or she must integrate these needs in such a way that individu-als can contribute to the creation of social knowledge while also learning and experimenting on their own. This description of care, of course, has often been associated with women and "soft" management skills. More recently, many American researchers and commentators have studied the increasing number of female executives, along with the overall rise in the number of women in the workforce, and pointed to changes in the corporation. For these writers, women managers naturally have a more cooperative style, excelling at networking, team-building, mentoring—all hallmarks of a caring organization and an enabling context—and they are transforming their workplaces accordingly. Many take their cue from psychologist Carol Gilligan, whose ideas about women's "different voice" have influenced discussions of moral reasoning, alternative work styles, and the interconnectedness of social relationships.[3]

However, the concept of care is natural to all human beings, and an influx of women managers is not required to set corporations on the right track. In fact, the role of care in building a civilization was recognized long ago by Greek philosophers such as Plato, Plutarch, and Epictetus. Plato cared for the individual development of his students and recognized the important role he played as a tutor of the coming generation of philosophers. Plato believed that only through care could the philosopher ensure that ideas about morality, ethics, and the state would last over generations. The philosopher-tutor assumed a very wide responsibility for his students, creating an enabling context in which ideas would flourish. According to Foucault (1972), one of the key themes of Roman and Greek philosophy was also caring for the self as a part of a broader attitude of caring. Among the ancient followers of Pythagorean philosophy, care for the self and one's personal experiences meant focusing on reflection in solitude rather than dialogue. The typical Pythagorean was supposed to allocate time in the morning for planning the day, and time in the evening to reflect on the accomplishments of that day, including whether the plan had been sufficiently carried out. In addition, physical exercises that ensured a fit body were considered a prerequisite for a healthy working brain.

If we fast-forward to today's knowledge-creating companies, self-care of this sort, in which individual members allocate sufficient time for planning and reflection, still makes sense. However, in another important respect, the demands of the current postindustrial world take us beyond the ancient Greeks. In traditional Western philosophy, knowledge is believed to be unchanging and true regardless of social circumstances. The Platonic Forms—for absolutes like Beauty, Goodness, Truth—represent this view, as does Cartesian rationalism, and it is still strongly held by the cognitivists discussed in the last chapter. This view, however, fails to address the relative, dynamic, and human dimensions of knowledge. In this century, Alfred North Whitehead has stated, "there are no whole truths; all truths are half-truths."[4] As fellow constructionists, we also believe that knowledge is context-specific and relational. It is dynamically created in social interactions and has a subjective nature deeply rooted in individual value systems.

Knowledge is essentially related to human action, and the knowledge-creation process depends on who participates and how they do so.

This brings us to the Japanese idea of *ba*, which roughly translates as "place." Originally proposed by the philosopher Kitaro Nishida (1921, 1970), the concept of *ba* has been further developed by chemical scientist Hiroshi Shimizu (1995). Although we draw extensively from their works, our use of the enabling context or *ba* has been adapted to elaborate the conditions required for knowledge creation. Think of an enabling context as a place in which knowledge is shared, created, and used. In this sense, an enabling context does not necessarily mean a physical space. Rather, it combines aspects of physical space (such as the design of an office or dispersed business operations), virtual space (e-mail, intranets, teleconferences), and mental space (shared experiences, ideas, emotions). More than anything, it is a network of interactions, determined by the care and trust of participants.

THE DIMENSIONS OF CARE

Being nice to other people is generally a good idea; creating an enabling context that encourages cooperation, sharing, loyalty, and creativity sounds appealing. But you may still be wondering how care translates in a business setting. Even as a general term, *care* has been conceptualized in many ways by various authors. Some suggest it cannot be broken down into finer detail (Heidegger, 1962); others believe it does have behavioral dimensions. In our view, formulating such dimensions can help managers and others observe the extent to which organizational members show care for one another. Identifying these dimensions also makes it easier for management to systematically communicate the value of care throughout a company. To better convey what we mean by care in organizational knowledge creation, we delineate five dimensions here: mutual trust, active empathy, access to help, lenience in judgment, and courage. The implications of these dimensions are discussed in the following sections.

Mutual Trust

In every encounter with another person, you establish some degree of trust in him or her. If you think about it, your trust in some ways compensates for the knowledge you lack. You do not know all his or her motives, preferences, interests, personal background, opinion of you, reactions to your conversations, backing in the organization, ability to follow up agreements the two of you have made, and so forth. People often present themselves through stories that emphasize certain characteristics and downplay others, as we noted in Chapter 2, and in any case it takes time to understand another person's experiences. But you cannot help people grow and actualize themselves unless you trust them to use your teaching and recommendations in the best way possible. You have to trust them to add personal value to your lessons.

Trust is also reciprocal. In order to accept your help, the other person has to believe in your good intentions. For example, he needs to trust that you will not make him look incompetent in the eyes of a third person like a manager by "helping" him too much. In game-theory terms, your reputation and trust will be closely connected. If you play a number of chess games, your reputation will be based on the consistency of your moves over time. And to enhance the other person's trust and your reputation, you should behave consistently toward him, with a minimum of surprise, so that you help him grow over time.

Active Empathy

While trust creates the basis for caring, active empathy makes it possible to assess and understand what the other truly needs. Empathy is the attempt to put yourself in the shoes of the other, understanding her particular situation, interests, skill level, success, failures, opportunities, and problems. By active empathy, we mean that you proactively seek to understand the other. You care for the other through active questioning and alert observations. As we detail in Chapter 6, you practice conversational dialogue rather than advocacy, taking a listening and questioning attitude. This is often referred to as active listening by psychotherapists and counselors. On the most general level, active empathy is essential for gaining emotional knowledge—the stock in trade, so to speak, of psychologists. Although it is not necessary for managers to be confidantes or personal confessors to their employees, most companies, especially those in hypercompetitive mode, have a lot to learn from the helping professions.

Unfortunately, because there are numerous barriers to dealing with emotional issues in an organization, expressing needs, especially emotional needs, can be difficult for people. According to studies by Humphrey and Ashford (1994), many organizations suppress individual emotions through a set of "feeling rules" or procedures for how to tackle emotional issues. For example, a personal success should not be expressed too exuberantly; long-time frustrations should not be mentioned to colleagues; conflicts are best treated by carefully taking them out of the office or hiding them completely; a difficult customer pestering a salesperson should still be treated with a friendly smile. On the one hand, feeling rules serve an important function in creating an effective workplace. On the other, such rules can inhibit personal growth and development, since any learning process is associated with positive and negative emotions. Consider the relationship between the novice and a tutor in learning a new computer language. Sometimes it helps students to know that their teachers have felt the same frustration in learning the syntax and functioning of the new language, or that difficulty in learning the language's logic is not an indication of the novice's lack of intellectual capacity but an inherent characteristic of a long learning process.

Moving beyond strict feeling rules, therefore, you take on a questioning attitude in order to understand the needs of the other in a deeper sense. You pursue the deeper meanings behind what she may say, become sensitive to needs that may not be articulated and are quite tacit, and then help the other to articulate them. Offering a personal interpretation of the other's needs might be a useful way of going about this articulation process—"You've been working really hard this week to get out that marketing report. Maybe you need a day off." Alternatively, you can help others to find words that express their feelings and needs more effectively—"You seem frustrated" or "Whenever I struggle with a deadline, I start to feel like a failure."

This kind of tacit knowledge can be the hardest to make explicit in a business organization, because individual workers do not want to appear incompetent. Yet it is natural for employees, especially those who work hard and care about their efforts, to feel a whole range of emotions about their jobs. We believe a broad acceptance of the emotional lives of others is crucial for establishing good working relationships—and good relations, in turn, lead to effective knowledge creation. Sometimes the power of tacit knowledge can be found in airing feelings or thoughts that may seem negative. The key for caring managers is to acknowledge such feelings. At the very least, the feelings themselves will lose their power to distract or overwhelm employees. At most, an emotional struggle, once validated and understood, may lead to an innovative solution.

Access to Help

Active empathy prepares the ground for helping behavior, but care in the company has to extend to real and tangible help. In the relationship between a master carpenter and his apprentice, for instance, the master will teach the design of a tool, how to use the tool, how to maintain the tool, where to acquire new tools, and so forth. He not only shows by example how to do good carpentry through listening to the apprentice's concerns and questions; he also extends a helping hand. But the will to help has to be accompanied by easy access to the helper. What good is a master carpenter who is never available to his apprentices? And what about a master who protects himself from apprentices because he is scared to give away his preciously acquired skills and thus lose out in later competition? Under such circumstances, organizational members may commit to the idea of care and helping, but in practice they do not make themselves available. In companies with an overall enabling context, help is accessible to those who need it.

A possible remedy to this issue is to establish two responsibilities for individual professionals that should grow proportionally: the knowledge they acquire; and how accessible they are to those who need help. In other words, the more expertise you have, the greater your responsibility to help others. This goes beyond what Dreyfus and Dreyfus (1986) call "competent behavior," in which the organizational member starts to "assume responsibility for the outcome of his actions"(p. 26). Expertise should be equated with social responsibility beyond the outcome of actions. From our standpoint, a "caring expert" is an organizational member who reaches her level of personal mastery in tacit and explicit knowledge, *and* understands that she is responsible for sharing the process. She demonstrates to novices the link between action and outcome, and helps them get the practical training necessary for carrying out the same actions. Some organizational members will naturally assume the responsibility for helping as their expertise grows; others may need to be gently pushed in this direction.

In a microcommunity, where the level of knowledge differs among participants, accessible help is essential for knowledge creation. Caring experts in such communities need to assume responsibility for helping other participants so that further knowledge creation becomes possible. For example, in applying group software to create new knowledge, the caring IT-expert helps other participants to learn the basics. When applying mathematical formulas to the creation of a concept, the caring industrial mathematician explains the nature of the formula and its areas of application. In building a prototype and establishing a plan for manufacturing the product, the caring production expert explains the essentials of manufacturing to other group members.

During the course of knowledge creation, participants with different backgrounds will have to step into the role of caring expert. In microcommunities, caretaking is an essential skill for everyone involved, not just for managers or team leaders. Therefore, all organizational members must increase their awareness of this role, becoming proficient teachers or tutors as their own skills grow. Teaching goes hand-in-hand with knowing. Indeed, the knowledge-creating company thrives on the pedagogical skills of its caring experts, a point we return to later.

Lenience in Judgment

For care to be a prevalent feature of organizational relationships, helping behavior has to be complemented with a lenient attitude among organizational members. Lenience in judgment, as we understand it, comes close to the way it is practiced in a court of law. Although the evidence in a case might under normal circumstances support a stronger judgment, the judge, based on the advice of jurors, can take a lenient attitude toward the accused. That means the judge considers the context of the offense, the background of the accused, his or her psychological state at the time the crime was committed, lack of awareness of the consequences of the crime, and so on.

The legal analogy provides some guidelines for what mitigating circumstances might constitute in a business setting. It almost goes without saying that in any company individual employees will act incompetently, at some point. How such incompetence is to be judged, however, is not a simple matter of preexisting rules and regulations. In fact, for knowledge creation there are few criteria for competent actions. Neither the participant in knowledge-creation processes nor the observer of the outcome in terms of concepts and prototypes can fully judge whether a microcommunity was working at its best. Nevertheless, judgment is an essential part of creating individual and social knowledge. As human beings, we judge our own experiences and actions as well as the experiences and actions of our fellow employees.

Knowledge creation involves a considerable amount of mental and linguistic experimentation throughout the five steps, from sharing tacit knowledge to cross-leveling of the knowledge gained. Harsh judgment can prevent explicit knowledge from being created through externalization; at worst, it can stifle the remaining phases of knowledge creation. Say an engineer proposes an analogy of the evolution of civilization to express his understanding of computer developments. His stumbling attempts are met with laughter and tough criticism from other community participants. Not only will this prevent the engineer from trying out other analogies, it will also set the tone of knowledge creation in that community; it will effectively convey to the rest of the participants that far-fetched ideas are unwelcome, even to enhance creativity.

To help somebody grow, you need to let that person experiment. Just as the caring parent lets the child make mistakes, the master marketing manager lets the product manager experiment with a new package design. Through the eyes of the expert, the novice will always look like a fumbling beginner, and the expert may be tempted to break in and take charge. But in most cases, the caring expert follows 3M's excellent proverb: "Do like the captain of a ship: Bite your lip until it bleeds." That is, caring experts understand the value of experimentation for knowledge creation and will "bite their lips" in order to control their own judgmental impulses.

Courage

Last but definitely not least, care in organizational relationships is reflected in the courage that organizational members exhibit toward one another. Courage plays an important role in three ways. First, people must be courageous when allowing fellow group members or even themselves to experiment. For the marketing manager, courage is required in addition to lenience when allowing that creative product manager to experiment; biting one's lip or captaining a ship can be painful, after all. Second, participants in microcommunities of knowledge creation need to be brave when they allow their concepts to be exposed to a process of intense judgment.

Third, it takes courage to voice your opinion or give feedback as part of a process that helps others grow. Since feedback may be negative or disruptive for the individual, great courage is required by those who offer it, even if they are lenient judges. Those who participate in the justification process will need to give open and constructive feedback on the societal, economic, environmental, technical, organizational, and psychological aspects of the concept or prototype. If the critics are not brave during this screening and feasibility assessment, further knowledge creation can result in products and services that have negative social consequences, do not offer sufficient value to customers, or result in unsatisfactory business performance.

KNOWLEDGE CREATION AND CARE: TWO CONTEXTS

Based on our previous research, it is apparent that knowledge creation can take very different paths depending on the extent to which care is present. Organizational relationships range from a high level of care—in which there is considerable trust, active empathy, access to help, lenience in judgment, and courage among members—to a low level, in which the same behaviors are close to absent. Under conditions of low care, a process of *seizing* characterizes individual knowledge creation, and most social knowledge creation occurs through *transacting*. When care is high, however, knowledge-creation processes change to reflect stronger relationships. Individuals create knowledge through a process of *bestowing* their insights, and groups will create social knowledge through what we call *indwelling*. These processes are summarized in Table 3.1. As we

Table 3.1. Knowledge Creation When Care Is High or Low

	Individual Knowledge	Social Knowledge
Low Care	SEIZING Everyone out for himself	TRANSACTING Swapping documents or other explicit knowledge
High Care	BESTOWING Helping by sharing insights	INDWELLING Living with a concept together

make clear in our contrasting descriptions of a typical hypercompetitive and enabling context below, indwelling relies on good relationships that allow participants to share a vision, one that may largely derive from tacit ideas and feelings. When care is low, there is little acceptance of tacit knowledge as a source of innovation.

Low Care: Hypercompetition at Its Worst

With a hypercompetitive context, care runs low, and each worker will try to seize individual knowledge rather than share it on a voluntary basis. This seizing happens naturally; since the individual is left to his own devices, he expects little help from colleagues. If the individual is a novice, she will have to learn new skills by herself. In addition, any attempt to present new ideas, concepts, or prototypes will be met with harsh judgment by other participants in knowledge creation. In effect, individuals will end up building their own hegemonies of knowledge and then do their best to protect them.

They know that their future with the company depends on the expertise they exhibit about particular topics and disciplines; it is not based on the extent to which they help others. Listening to others and trying to understand their viewpoints will be seen as a waste of time. In this competitive context, sharing more knowledge than necessary will lead to reduced power and influence for the individual, with two important consequences. First, she will not be motivated to make her knowledge explicit or to share it except through clear transactions that benefit her. Second, in participating in creating social knowledge in a group, she will transact knowledge—"this document for that document" or "this explanation of how a machine works for that explanation"—with other participants rather than give it freely. Explicit knowledge will be shared based on expected returns.

It may be possible to swap explicit forms of knowledge like documents or mechanical schematics, but when care is this low, tacit knowledge is difficult to exchange. It would first have to be made explicit before the transaction partner could assess its value and decide what it was worth—unrealistic for most of the gut feelings, personal skills, and social history that constitute tacit knowledge in an organization. The whole notion of "transacting" something that is hard to articulate means that anything that cannot be specified has little perceived value. Since the organizational members would have to demonstrate their expertise to prove their worth, explicit knowledge would be expressed in a linear fashion. Concepts would have to be clearly defined, arguments "bullet proof," the data supporting a claim valid and reliable. Old findings rejected at an earlier stage of knowledge creation would be buried forever, and the presentation of a prototype would have to promise a significant impact on company performance. With little room for experimentation, the first and essential phase of knowledge creation—sharing of tacit knowledge—becomes virtually impossible.

Charles Darrah (1995), an ethnographer of the workplace, offers a case in point. His study describes the unproductive context of a computer-components supplier. The company faced severe productivity and quality problems. Management's response was to punish ignorance and lack of expertise among factory-floor workers; at the same time, whenever they ran into manufacturing problems, it explicitly discouraged them from seeking help from the engineers who designed the components and organized the production line. These workers gained individual knowledge through seizing: They worked on sequentially defined manufacturing tasks and tried to come to terms with the task at hand, without thinking through the consequences for the performance of other tasks at other stages of the manufacturing process. When a new worker was employed, he received little training. Yet for productivity and cost reasons, the novice would be put to work as soon as possible. Knowledge transactions between workers and engineers were very rare, and most of the knowledge on the factory floor remained tacit and individual. The tacit quality of individual knowledge was pushed even farther because the foremen would not allow personal notes or drawings to help solve tasks.

Concerned with the severe productivity and quality problems, a new production director suggested a training program for factory workers that would help to remedy the situation. The program was designed in a traditional teaching manner: The product and manufacturing engineers were supposed to explain the product design and give an overall view of the manufacturing process and the requirements for each step. At the end of the training session, the engineers would ask the workers for their opinions and constructive input—a knowledge transaction intended to improve quality and communication. The workers, however, knew the consequences of expressing ignorance and incompetence, and they did not discuss the problems they experienced, even if they knew those problems resulted from flaws in product design. Nor did they have a legitimate language in which to express their concerns and argue "on the same level" as the engineers. The workers mostly remained silent, the training program did not have the desired effects, and the director left the company shortly thereafter.

High Care: Indwelling and an Enabling Context

Compare this miserable situation with our second scenario. When care runs high in an organization, the individual member works in a context in which colleagues show genuine interest in her progress. She can trust her colleagues and will receive active help. She can access expertise whenever required and can afford to experiment. She knows her colleagues will welcome such courage and judge the outcome of open-ended knowledge creation leniently. When colleagues are supportive, individual participants are more likely to articulate their knowledge spontaneously, using new metaphors and analogies. And because a high-care organization allows for the expression of emotions, "fuzzy" logic, and ideas that are not rigidly specified, individuals will also share their tacit knowledge at the same time that they refine it. They will create knowledge while bestowing it on others, and their colleagues will do the same. Rather than trying to get a maximum grip on a task, the individual will aim for maximum leverage of other people's knowledge. This process of mutual bestowing leads to the kind of social knowledge creation that is the source of radical innovations: indwelling.

Indwelling is of particular importance to the sharing of tacit knowledge and concept creation. An authoritative source for the term is Polanyi and Prosch (1975). These writers suggest that dwelling in a concept can be understood as a dramatic shift of perspectives: you shift from looking *at* the concept to looking *with* the concept. For example, a management team discusses a future concept for the business, one that has been formulated in a vision statement. Initially, their discussions recognize major trends in the industry and the need for a dramatic change. Then they formulate a new concept of the ideal competitive organization. Here they are looking *at* the new concept. In order to achieve indwelling, they might assign positions in the future company among the participants and then describe the path the company will take in order to achieve the desired result. At this point, managers have begun to "live" with the new concept.

Suppose you want to develop a new recipe and an excellent cook has agreed to be your mentor. You start by observing him at work on your proposed dish. You view his movements, the way he organizes the kitchen, the ingredients he purchases, how he handles them, how he stores them, the sequence with which he blends the ingredients, and the temperature of the oven. You organize your observations in notes and perhaps a video-tape (all forms of explicit knowledge). But it is at the next stage that you shift from looking *at* the cook to working *with* him. From a caring per-spective, you offer to help out where you can, buying groceries, suggest-ing different storage containers, washing dishes. Help immediately provides you with shared experiences; you enter the domain of the cook's competence and become part of his world. Through a continuing dia-logue, both of you express some of the subtle aspects of cooking the dish, such as how it should taste, look, or smell. As you take on more of the cooking tasks, you develop the tacit judgment necessary for creating it yourself. And in caring for the cook, you have helped him to gradually uncover new practices and ideas that he can bring into his own work.

Indwelling is about commitment to an idea, to an experience, to a con-cept, or to a fellow human being. In developing shared tacit knowledge, the challenge for individuals in a microcommunity is to dwell in the experiences, perspectives, and concepts of other participants—to shift from a commitment to one's own interest to that of the group. In chang-ing such deep commitments, community members literally make changes in their lives. They begin to see the world through a new lens and to "passionately reason"[5] by using that lens. If we commit to the prin-ciples of chaos theory, for example, we start to recognize the world in terms of ordered structures that apparently result in chaotic events. If we commit to the principles of game theory, we see life as an eternal sequence of games that have to be fought and won. The trick here is to dwell in several perspectives at once, not just a single narrow view, in order to create a better understanding of the local circumstances for tacit knowledge and competence.

The prerequisite for indwelling is high care in organizational relation-ships. Experiences are shared through active empathy. Trust among par-ticipants makes it easier to articulate emotional aspects of an experience. Participants extend help to each other in finding new means to convey and share experiences; they practice lenience in judgment; courageously defend their ideas and offer constructive criticism of others. There are few filters that force knowledge into an explicit form, and therefore the shar-ing of tacit knowledge within an organization is enabled by care.

INDWELLING IN THE WORKPLACE: A PRACTICAL GUIDE

To be sure, creating the kind of care-based organization described earlier may seem daunting to many managers, who are often overwhelmed with deadlines and time pressures. Indwelling does require time and space in an organization, and a top-level commitment to the process. Yet there are certain steps managers can take to make indwelling a reality in their organizations. We list some suggested approaches below. Also, Chapter 5 provides an extended discussion of knowledge visions and the role they play in knowledge enabling.

1. *Review the knowledge vision.*
2. *Identify sources of tacit knowledge.* Possible sources may be customers and suppliers; strategic partners; microcommunity members; other organizational units and members who are not part of the community.
3. *Identify the likely impact of this tacit knowledge on the vision and how accessible the sources are.* Accessibility is defined by the ease with which relations can be established to the source and the tacit knowledge shared.
4. *Establish caring relationships with each source of tacit knowledge.*
5. *Build up a common experience base with each source based on caring.* In time, you will move from looking at the source as an outsider to experiencing the source's worldview from within.
6. *Allow for numerous reiterations of steps 4 and 5.* Do not forget that caring has to be a continuous process, not a one-time event. Building a common experience base may require several visits, conversations, and observations. Be courageous in allowing time for indwelling to occur, even when the pressure to realize a knowledge vision might drive you to quick-fix concepts.
7. *Evaluate the results of indwelling.* Because you can only hint at the potential strategic value of tacit knowledge before starting to tap it, it is important that you also do some ex-post evaluation of the knowledge acquired before developing it further into concepts and prototypes. Table 3.2 represents a sample evaluation form; in this case, a manager has assessed cooking suggestions made by customers at a retail outlet.

Table 3.2. An Evaluation Form for Indwelling

Knowledge source	What knowledge?	Impact on knowledge vision?	Additional indwelling required?	Is additional indwelling practicable?	Need to maintain relations to source?
Customers	Cooking suggestions	High— possible new products	Yes— two weeks	Yes— within budget and time frame	Yes— weekly visits
Suppliers					
Strategic partners					
Community members					
Organization					
Others					

As the sample evaluation form suggests, indwelling actions can also tap tacit knowledge beyond an organization's boundaries. For instance, Narvesen ASA, a major Scandinavian player in wholesale, retail, and catering, introduced the concept of "care-based shopkeeping" in their retail outlets, restaurants, and fast-food chains in 1997. Narvesen focuses on three components: (1) care for the customer—under any circumstance, help him or her to feel good in the shop by providing active service; (2) care for your shop and your colleagues—make sure that the shop runs smoothly by helping co-workers to do their jobs in a clean, effective, comfortable shopping environment; (3) care for your own experiences—make sure that whatever you learn about colleagues, customers, and shop design you retain for later use.

The last idea helps the company continuously improve its shop layout. Narvesen trains employees about the concept of care-based shopkeeping and encourages them to look at the shop through this lens. Some retail outlets discovered that for many customers, the shop is not just a convenience store but a meeting place: If they hang around for long, they often bump into old friends. Some Narvesen employees then suggested furnishing the shop with chairs and tables in the space available; they also began serving coffee, chocolate, and small snacks.[6] American companies like Barnes and Noble, with its bookstore chains, have also recognized that converting part of the retail space into a café gives customers a place to meet and linger.

Or consider Unilever, the consumer-products company headquartered in London and Rotterdam whose portfolio covers foods like Lipton Tea and Magnum ice cream, as well as personal care products like Calvin Klein CK1 perfumes. Caring for a consumer's knowledge is more than a slogan at Unilever. Dwelling in the mind of the consumer—through visits to consumer homes and intensive studies of cooking procedures—has led to the development of highly innovative sauces. A striking example is the company's gratin sauces for potatoes. Based on thorough consumer understanding (potatoes and cheeses are traditional favorites in the Netherlands), experimentation, excellent marketing, and patented technology, the product broke standard market boundaries because it was both easy to prepare and tasted good. The gratin sauces have been successfully introduced in a number of other countries. In addition to receiving several retailer and consumer prizes, this product won a Unilever Foods Innovation Award.

Such projects fall under the company's Culinary Knowledge Initiative, coordinated by Wouter de Vries, who is by education an information scientist and current unit leader of knowledge management specialists at Unilever. Care as a foundational value for the organization has been instrumental to the success of the endeavor. In the culinary area, for instance, the company has quite successfully applied softer incentives. While traditionally the performance appraisal of an innovation process has been strongly attached to the final product as a deliverable, under the Culinary Knowledge Initiative, performance appraisals are being revised to also include knowledge as a "deliverable." In fact, contributing to the overall knowledge of Unilever is considered a collective responsibility of any project team. Through mutual caring for the unique skills and backgrounds of all members, the team can achieve maximum leverage of individual knowledge and thus fulfill its responsibility. Knowledge creation is even defined as a basis for winning one of Unilever's coveted team awards.

The Culinary Knowledge Initiative also includes "knowledge debriefs." At regular intervals, as well as at project completion, the whole team engages in a debriefing about what they have learned and how they have made new knowledge explicit. In this way, the project teams start to see knowledge as an additional project output, and members care for the quality and potential of knowledge in the company. Although the major focus of these knowledge debriefs is social knowledge, experience has shown that project work also enhances individual learning. In any case, social events play a key role in stimulating care in organizational relationships and care for knowledge itself. The knowledge debriefs, project startup, and knowledge-sharing sessions are usually performed off site, thereby creating time for people to chat and get to know each other better. Such an approach ultimately results in deeper and more trusting relationships.

CARE AND KNOWLEDGE ENABLING:
HOW TO BUILD A GOOD FOUNDATION

As the successes of companies like Unilever and Narvesen imply, care should underpin all knowledge-enabling activities in a company. Put in another way, knowledge enabling cannot happen without it. In view of the importance of strong, positive relationships for knowledge creation, each of the practical initiatives we outline in the next sections should be seen as part of a stream of actions. It might be necessary to coordinate them centrally, perhaps through a knowledge activist. Later chapters on the five knowledge enablers will extend some of these ideas. But in all cases, managers need a good foundation of care-based relationships to make such efforts a success.

Creating Trust

Here we suggest three actions: create a sense of mutual dependence; make trustworthy behavior a part of performance reviews; and increase individual reliability by formulating a "map" of expectations. First, according to Smith and Berg (1987), "It is clear that a group can function only if members are able to depend on each other. It is ultimately the mutual dependency that makes the group a group. To deny this dependency or to try to make it into something other than what it is retards the group's capacity to come together as a whole" (p.140). Imperative to building trust among group members, these authors note, is this sense of dependency. Mutual dependency allows for successful task accomplishment, the reason that a group is formed in the first place.[7]

Alternatively, when a group member behaves in an untrustworthy fashion, other members will probably feel this sense of dependency even more strongly, as they do when the group is exposed to extreme situations. The management of a knowledge-creating company needs to make trust and mutual dependency a theme in their policy statements and strategy making. They can reinforce the role of trust in public speeches, policy documents, and other written materials. They should also come down hard on untrustworthy behavior in the company due to office politics (Harvey and Brown, 1992).

In convening a microcommunity for knowledge creation, you might start by sharing information on the personal backgrounds of each individual, and the kind of experience and knowledge each individual brings to the effort. This will make clear to community members that they are dependent on a variety in expertise; the manufacturing manager, the marketing manager, the computer whiz kid, the old industry fox all have their roles to play. At the outset, dependency is even more strongly forged when an ambitious knowledge vision and set of expectations drive the microcommunity, whether it is the development of a new drug or a new insurance service.

Furthermore, symbols can be used to reinforce group dependency and mutual trust. At Sharp, wearing a golden badge signifies that you are part of a Golden Badge project, one involving new product and technology development, and that this project reports directly to top management. The visible symbol shows the importance of your expertise; it indicates that you and your fellow project members carry a great responsibility for the company's future. Such trust is reinforced through a sense of dependency. Golden Badge members know that others who wear the badge also believe crafting future technologies will ensure the long-term survival of Sharp.

Second, managers should focus on trust in performance appraisals. In many companies, such appraisals emphasize the accomplishment of a set of predefined tasks and neglect other areas of organizational behavior (Hyman, 1992). In supplementing performance appraisals with a concern for trust, you can look at factors like reliability; the extent to which the person in question has kept her promises to other people, internally (co-workers) and externally (customers); the extent to which the person has acted consistently to build trust; and her reputation. This last factor indicates the quality of the person's organizational relationships over time and can be compared with previous performance appraisals. All the factors are based on a third person's observation of the way the person in question relates to other organizational members. Such an appraisal is obviously highly qualitative; the managerial point is not to pin down and strike out bad behavior, but to discuss performance in terms of how well the person works with others, as well as to suggest actions that might improve her relationships.

Third, create a map of expectations at the outset of knowledge creation. This is a tool that can allow participants in a microcommunity to structure their actions individually and collectively. As indicated earlier, trust can compensate for a lack of knowledge of other organizational members. After a short introduction of each participant's background, you might ask community members to share their expectations for themselves in the knowledge-creation process as well as the expectations they have for the community. They might start out by individually drawing maps of expectations, and then share these maps at a group meeting. Where the expectations are in concert, the group should have a solid basis for further work. Where they conflict or are incomplete, more discussion will be required to clarify what people really expect, which expectations will ultimately benefit the microcommunity, and how expectations can inform and inspire working relationships among community members.

A map like this has two dimensions: expectations for your own activities and performance, and expectations for how the microcommunity as a whole will perform. Expectations should be specified according to the following items: (1) time allocated for knowledge creation; (2) the physical and financial resources brought to bear; (3) the expertise involved, with special attention paid to each of the five knowledge-creation steps; (4) contact with other individuals or groups external to the microcommunity; (5) what you and the community will learn. Table 3.3, as a sample map of expectations, represents a hypothetical community developing a full-text retrieval system for heterogeneous, networked knowledge repositories.

As the knowledge-creation process proceeds, participants can keep going back to the map and discuss how their expectations have been fulfilled or have changed. The map, as such, should provide participants with greater knowledge of one another. It can also help bring some structure to behavior during a highly chaotic and unstructured process.

Table 3.3. A Sample Map of Expectations

Time Requirements	Resources Available	Expertise Available	Contact Network	Expected Learning
Own Performance				
One month	Lab space and Web access	C programming	Colleagues of a hardware manufacturer for keeping an eye on new hardware solutions, the Research Center of a software developer for radically new technologies	The architecture of full-text retrieval systems, and the range of application
Community Performance				
Three months	Three labs, marketing information	Marketing, Systems Engineering, Knowledge Engineering Applications	Top management for financial and moral support, marketing department for early involvement in decisions to launch the new product, various experts for access to benchmarking with Excalibur Technologies Corp.'s RetrievalWare, and Fulcrum's Knowledge Network	The business potential/business case for the new technology

Increasing Active Empathy

To reinforce active empathy, consider two actions. First, you might emphasize and even invest in training in listening behavior for organizational members. Listening behavior includes taking a listening posture, focusing the eyes, holding back the urge to exclaim your own opinions, picking up cues about what the other says that can serve for further probing questions, mirroring the questions of the other by providing your own interpretations, and so forth. The aim of training employees to be better listeners is to get them to see the world through the eyes of the other via probing and questioning— that is, to turn them into indwellers rather than distant observers.

Second, organizational members should learn to value attempts at active empathy when they experience it. Active empathy has to become an ingrained part of the value system of the knowledge-creating company; it is an essential component of an enabling context. In this sense, active empathy, like trust, has to be put on the management agenda as a dimension of caring for fellow organizational members. Repeating, enacting, and explicitly encouraging the message of active empathy will positively enable the work of microcommunities.

Fostering Helping Behavior

We have found at least four initiatives that can foster more accessible help in the organization: training in pedagogical skills, training in intervention techniques, making accessible help an element of performance appraisals, and sharing stories of helping behavior. First, teaching and training are often an intrinsic part of helping, such as when the master conveys her knowledge to a novice. The master teaches her explicit knowledge to the novice, then helps to build the tacit knowledge of that novice by training him in various practices. In general, you will create the much-needed "caring and sharing" mentality of a knowledge-creating company through developing such pedagogical skills. To some people, teaching and training come naturally; others have to build their pedagogical skills. The following issues should be addressed in training programs: how to assess the level of the other's expertise; what to teach and train; how to design good programs for training and teaching individuals (curricula); how to package explicit knowledge in ways that are understandable to others; and how to convey tacit knowledge through experiential learning.

Second, not all helping behavior takes place in the context of novice and expert. Especially in knowledge creation that involves radical experimentation—such as exploring a new technology, a new customer group, a new idea for a manufacturing method, or a new idea for a service—most participants in the microcommunity can be regarded as beginners. In this case, helping behavior is not based on expertise but on the idea that help in general will allow for mutual growth. In addition to providing training in appropriate listening behavior, you might emphasize other intervention techniques: clarification of standpoints, summarizing of arguments, synthesizing of standpoints and concepts, generalizing concepts from arguments and standpoints (Harvey and Brown, 1992), or creating new metaphors and analogies that will help unleash participants' ideas and express their tacit knowledge. Training for intervention techniques may also involve the use of visualization tools, ranging from complex flow charts to bulletin boards.

Third, help may not be accessible in the organization for numerous reasons. Therefore, you might want to include helping behavior along with trust as key factors in employee performance appraisals. Here are some good indicators of accessible help: the extent to which the person in question follows up requests for help; the time he or she spends on listening to the needs of the other and finding solutions; the time spent on conveying lessons to others; and the time he or she spends on intervening and providing help in articulating the knowledge of others. You might use performance appraisals of this sort on a project basis; after a completed knowledge-creation process or when separate phases of knowledge creation have been finalized, you (or the group) can conduct evaluations of trustworthy behavior and accessible help.

Fourth, compelling stories of helping illustrate caring behavior at the level of the microcommunity and thereby create a positive, softer incentive. You can tell success stories of support being given and received among microcommunities of knowledge, research groups, departments, divisions, and so on. These stories should be specific enough to include the point in the process at which the support was given, the nature of the support, and its positive result. The purpose of focusing stories at the group level is to avoid making it seem like something that depends merely on the goodness of particular individuals; those kinds of stories often result in responses like "That's great for him, but it's not my problem" and other defenses against offering help. Furthermore, open communication about caring behavior and the important role it plays for a group may counter possible "over-helping" strategies at the individual level. Keep in mind that receiving help should also be commended in the company. Receiving help with respect and care can be as difficult a task as giving it.

Lenience, Courage, and Mentorship

Lenience in judgment and courage are intrinsic values of a corporate culture, and the suggestions for increasing active empathy also apply here. Top management must communicate these values, by example and through oral and written statements. Caring means that you respect individual differences in observations and viewpoints, and that you allow individuals to develop their own distinctive skills and ways of operating spontaneously. Lenience and courage are essential for allowing employees their own individuality within an organizational context.

In general, a mentoring system in the organization will support all the dimensions of care. Mentors should exhibit high care in dealing with their protégés, building trust, listening patiently, taking the perspective of the other, teaching and training, judging their actions leniently, and being brave enough to offer useful criticism and to redirect their actions onto a successful path. The mentor works at developing what Boam and Sparrow (1992) termed *transitional competencies*. The need for transitional competencies arises when people are given tasks that are new, unfamiliar, and fraught with conflict, stress, or uncertainty. Under the guidance of a mentor, who has some experience with the task at hand, the novice can go through a learning process in which he or she creates the explicit and tacit knowledge required to accomplish the task.

Rather than letting new employees or team members sink or swim, then, mentorship allows people to develop more facility with transitions or "grace under fire." In fact, mentoring for transitional competencies can be focused on the knowledge-creation process itself. For example, a seasoned knowledge activist might help microcommunity members develop their general skills at identifying and sharing tacit knowledge, creating concepts, setting up justification panels, conducting justification workshops, creating prototypes, and assuming responsibility for cross-leveling of organizational knowledge.

As a part of mentorship, we would suggest that the processes of seizing, transacting, bestowing, and indwelling be explained to organizational members. This will allow them to understand the possible negative impact of low care on knowledge creation. It will also empower them to recognize and categorize knowledge-creation processes. For instance, a process might be inhibited by low care. One participant could bring the obvious seizing and transacting behavior to the attention of other group members. Together they might consider alternative actions, such as trying to practice more care, bringing in an outside consultant, changing team membership, changing the task, doing a new map of expectations, or changing the accepted conversational style.

THE BUSINESS ARGUMENT FOR CARE:
SHISEIDO AND BEYOND

For some managers in contemporary corporations, the ideas we have presented in this chapter may seem too "touchy-feely" to be applicable in a business setting. Although corporate cultures have changed over the past three decades, the language of the war room or a sporting event is still more familiar than that of caring or enabling. The worst critics may believe that with our emphasis on empathy, mutual dependence, and a process called indwelling, we have proposed nothing more than wishful thinking. Yet as the many company examples included in *Enabling Knowledge Creation* indicate, a new approach to organizational relationships and knowledge management can yield real business gains.

When Shiseido set out to introduce its Ayura cosmetics brand, for instance, the company created "communication studios" in three Japanese department stores for a trial period of one year. Shiseido wanted to learn more about what customers expected of such products and to differentiate Ayura cosmetics from other brands. Rather than setting up the usual situation in which salespeople supposedly "advised" customers about their beauty needs but often ended up forcing sales, the Ayura counters were designed to encourage conversation and knowledge sharing. Salespeople consulted with interested customers, but the products were not sold at that time. Instead, a beauty program was devised to match each individual's skin, accompanied by a week's worth of free samples.

At these innovative counters, customers were free to gather information and test Ayura products at their own pace. Shiseido created a world whereby customers were able to experience the Ayura brand freely and individually through a variety of information tools without pressure from shop assistants. The tools included a touch monitor for information about products, leaflets concerning beauty routines, a toll-free telephone number, personal computer correspondence, postcards that consumers could mail in, and a quarterly journal called the *Ayura Press*. In particular, the company wanted to create a consumer network that encouraged oral communication and allowed customers to play an active role in the development of products and services by offering their opinions.

Such a marketing approach also makes good business sense, of course, especially in the cosmetics industry, where consumers of high-end products often expect personal attention. Sharing information and ideas with customers is a good way to build brand loyalty; and Shiseido's marketers certainly hoped that the development of a consumer network, in which participants felt they had a voice, would heighten Ayura's popularity through word of mouth, drawing in the original participants' friends and acquaintances. It was this approach of understanding and taking care of customers' needs, of building relationships with them, and of renouncing an aggressive selling strategy that have made Ayura as popular and successful as it is of this writing. (The development of the Ayura brand is discussed in detail in Chapter 5.)

Still, we contend that such innovative strategies do not come out of a vacuum. Shiseido's management philosophy set the stage, as the wording for the company's "Criteria for Corporate Activity" indicates: "1. We seek to bring joy to our customers. 2. We are concerned with results, not procedures. 3. We share frankly with each other our real priorities. 4. We give free rein to our thoughts and boldly challenge conventional wisdom. 5. We act in a spirit of thankfulness." A company stricken by hypercompetitive *ba* would not express thanks to anyone.

At the deepest level, care matters for moral, ethical, and social reasons. We are not suggesting, however, that companies throw all business concerns to the wind. In a postindustrial economy in which customer loyalty, strong brands, and radical innovations often give firms the competitive edge, improving relationships among all participants, listening to new ideas, and having the courage to handle constructive criticism are absolutely necessary for effective business operations. Unilever, Narvesen, Barnes and Noble, Shiseido, and many other companies have good reason to create enabling contexts and to make care part of their business strategies. In the next chapter, we focus on how a company's strategy—often the bastion of hypercompetitive language and number-focused goals—can be connected to knowledge enabling.

·4·

STRATEGY
AND KNOWLEDGE CREATION

Ensuring Survival in the Present

and Advancement in the Future

To energize people, you need to cultivate their work place,
not manage it, because management implies control, and
the future is not about command and control.

—Leif Edvinsson, Vice President, Skandia

For managers, the importance of knowledge in organizations—and the whole knowledge-management movement—turns on what can be done with it practically in a business setting. Talking about the power of tacit knowledge or long-term competitive advantage does no good if knowledge creation is not part of a strategic framework. In the last chapter, we discussed an enabling context based on personal relationships and care as essential to knowledge creation; the business challenge is to take what may seem to be an anticompetitive approach and align it with good strategy. In the next chapter, we detail the first knowledge enabler—instill a knowledge vision—and, again, the challenge is to hook creative goals for a company to a practical plan of attack. Business strategy provides a necessary link between dreaming and doing, caring and following through; it can keep managers' feet on the ground during what may seem like a chaotic, unmanageable process—as long as a company's strategy recognizes that knowledge truly matters.

This last point is the issue, of course, since strategic discussions often focus on quantifiable results and objectives, as well as narrowly defined ideas before knowledge creation even gets under way. Such strategies may help companies control their operations in the short term, but they will not advance them into new markets or product areas; and considering the fast pace of multinational transactions and product development, they may not even allow a company to survive. As we noted in the Phonak story presented in Chapter 2, a company's strategy, as well as the management

69

required to carry it through, often involves achieving a balance between order and chaos. This picture may not appeal to the traditional strategist, but it is realistic. Knowledge, new or otherwise, always adds an element of uncertainty. Yet creating new knowledge—and, perhaps more important, effectively using the knowledge that already exists in an organization— has now become a core element of business strategy.

In a knowledge-creating company, the responsibility of management is twofold. The first responsibility managers have is to unleash the potential represented by an organization's knowledge into value-creating actions. That is, they need to identify what the organization knows, in what form, and to make tacit knowledge accessible and useable. In fact, the business community has begun to accept the knowledge challenge. In a 1997 survey of executives in eleven countries, conducted by the International Center for Business Information (ICBI), 97 percent of all respondents said they considered knowledge an essential part of value creation (ICBI, 1997). Pioneering companies like Dow Chemical, Canadian Imperial Bank of Commerce, and Skandia are charting the progress and use of their intellectual assets, connecting a vision of what knowledge they will need in the future with specific actions and objectives.

The second managerial responsibility is related to a company's competitive situation. Some consultants and organizational researchers suggest that the value of management to a company, and hence executive compensation, should depend on the extent to which managers are able to generate and exploit assets like knowledge more effectively than can their counterparts at competing companies.[1] This means that managers either need to ensure the creation of unique knowledge that can be unleashed in value-creating activity, or establish better use of public knowledge that is generally available to the company and its competitors.

In this chapter, we begin demystifying these responsibilities by presenting a new strategic framework. This framework breaks down the potential of knowledge creation into two basic strategies: *survival strategies*, in which companies focus on knowledge to maintain their current level of success and performance; and *advancement strategies* that emphasize future success and improved performance. We then look at how executives can strike a balance between the two and examine the business conditions that might influence them to opt for one or the other. The main point here, however, is that advancement strategies are necessary for knowledge-creating companies. To illustrate why advancement is often worth the risk, we detail the five steps of knowledge creation—sharing tacit knowledge, creating concepts, justifying concepts, building a prototype, and cross-leveling of knowledge. The chapter closes with the story of the Swedish company Skandia's "Future Center" and a discussion of how strategy is connected with knowledge enabling.

A STRATEGIC FRAMEWORK

Although it has become a business truism that knowledge yields competitive advantage,[2] not all knowledge has strategic value. Therefore, it is imperative that managers use a practical framework to assess the role of knowledge in relation to strategy. In general, we suggest that the ultimate goal of all knowledge-related activity is to ensure above average industry profitability for a company, both in the short and long term. This is a bold proposition, however, since many advocates of the knowledge movement tend to take a fairly operational view. In practice, the "knowledge issue" tends to become the responsibility of human resources, information technology groups, or corporate R&D; sometimes it is only part of isolated knowledge-management initiatives located deep within various business units. In addition, most theorists, with a few notable exceptions, pay little attention to an overall strategic view.[3]

As a consequence, top management rarely focuses on the strategic role of knowledge or the importance of knowledge-creation initiatives. One possible remedy is to reframe the way knowledge is viewed by senior executives and other company strategists. Rather than seeing it as an unknown quantity vaguely connected to creativity, absolutely necessary but impossible to objectify, they should consider it an asset tied to specific actions and business results. The framework shown in Table 4.1 highlights the strategic role of knowledge and corresponding knowledge processes. In the following sections, we examine each component separately.

Survival and Advancement Strategies

Von Krogh, Roos, and Slocum (1994) suggest that there are essentially two types of strategies: survival and advancement. Survival strategies secure current company profitability. This kind of strategy emphasizes current strengths and minimizes current weaknesses in the resources and knowledge base of the company; the aim is to take advantage of existing business opportunities and neutralize threats in the environment (Andrews, 1971). When conceiving of survival strategies, management counts on a fairly clear image of a known business environment.[4] Survival strategies attempt mastery of the company's current business environment. They allow for reducing the bargaining power of existing suppliers and customers; are based on successful product-market positioning compared with competitors; and meet the expectations held by a variety of stakeholders in the firm, such as society, the local community, employees, and the government. Survival strategies also make the entry of new potential

Table 4.1. A Strategic Framework for Knowledge

Strategy	Competitive Advantage	Sources of Competitive Advantage	Role of Knowledge	Important Knowledge Processes	Result
Survival	• current profitability • not implemented by competitors • those who try cannot replicate original advantages	• economies of scale • economies of scope • product/ service differentiation	• valuable, difficult to imitate, difficult to substitute • exclusively held or public • ability to transfer may matter more than content	• knowledge transfer • continuous improvement	• profitability higher than average of the industry
Advancement	• future profitability • not implemented by competitors • those who try cannot replicate original advantages	• potential economies of scale • potential economies of scope • potential product/ service differentiation	• new knowledge for process/ product innovation • transferable new knowledge	• knowledge creation • radical innovation	• future profitability higher than average of the industry

competitors unattractive, through experience effects and/or economies of scope, and prepare the company for possible substitutes for their products (Porter, 1990; Fajey and Narayanan, 1986).

Advancement strategies secure future profitability. Such strategies build on future strengths and attempt to minimize future weaknesses in the resources and knowledge base of the company; their aim is to take advantage of future business opportunities and neutralize future threats in the environment. When conceiving of advancement strategies, management's experience and understanding of the business environment is of limited use. Instead, the need is for creative approaches to strategizing, in which new images of the company and its business environment must be considered. Advancement strategies are typical of emerging industries like information technology, financial services, and telecommunications. The roles of various players and the corresponding bargaining power and product-market positioning are in continual transition (Levenhagen, Porac, and Thomas, 1993; Hamel and Prahalad, 1994).

In the development of advancement strategies, the experience of senior managers may count less than creative, intuitive, and insightful images drawn from the middle level or junior management ranks (Hamel, 1996). Advancement strategies should allow the company to see new aspects of the business environment in order to build up that company's mastery of its future environment. They outline how the company can gain influence in the evolution of the industry so as to increase future bargaining power over potential suppliers and customers. Such influence might, for example, be achieved by hiring scarce researchers, forming strategic alliances with research institutions, developing technological standards, or building strong links with future suppliers and customers. Advancement strategies indicate potential competitors and how they are likely to react to the company's initiatives; they emphasize new product concepts and services, as well as better market positioning of products compared with competitors. Advancement strategies also indicate how to meet the future expectations of the firm's various stakeholders.

Overall, a careful balance between advancement and survival strategies will allow a company to prepare for vanishing industry boundaries, rapid transition in the industry, the rapid devaluing of existing knowledge and competences, and the obsolescence of existing products and services. But because managers tend to prefer "actionable information" (Mintzberg, 1975), such as the kind that allows them to outmaneuver a difficult competitor in an existing market segment, survival strategies generally win the day in strategic conversations (von Krogh and Roos, 1996c). This imbalance may push management into a myopic and rigid view of industries and markets. Survival and advancement strategies both provide distinct competitive advantages, draw on particular sources of competitive advantage, put distinct demands on knowledge, and are associated with particular knowledge processes. Therefore, the proper balance between them is essential, and both require equal managerial attention, a point we return to later.

Competitive Advantage

A company that achieves superior business performance compared with its competitors is said to have a competitive advantage.[5] Under the commonly accepted definition, a firm implements a value-creating (survival) strategy that is not simultaneously being implemented by current or future competitors. For example, an aluminum producer might have lower factor costs because it owns power plants while its competitors have to buy electricity on the open market. This competitive advantage might be more or less durable, allowing the company to enjoy superior performance over a longer period of time.

A sustainable competitive advantage is one in which the company implements a value-creating strategy that remains unique despite attempts at imitation by current and future competitors (Barney, 1991). Competitors of the aluminum company might try to replicate its value-creating strategy by setting up their own power plants, but high initial investments prevent them from achieving the same cost level. Note, however, that few if any competitive advantages last forever. New knowledge, technologies, and products will at some point erode the competitive potential of existing knowledge, technologies, and products. Jorma Ollila, the CEO and president of the Finnish electronics group Nokia, has suggested that over the last few years the life span of Nokia's competitive advantages has been shortened by half.[6] Nokia and other companies continue to implement their current value-creating survival strategies, but their managers must think ahead to secure future performance through advancement strategies.

Sources of Competitive Advantage

Competitive advantages derive from low process cost—through economies of scale, scope, and factor costs—and/or product or service differentiation—the result of a unique product quality or product features that customers value; a unique geographical position; or unique skills and service offerings (Porter, 1990; Rummelt, 1980).[7] Survival strategies exploit current sources of competitive advantage: lower manufacturing costs than those of competitors due to more experience; lower quality costs because of a close collaboration with suppliers; shared R&D investments for a large set of products; shared services among various business units; ownership of patents, copyrights, trade secrets, or unique product designs. But advancement strategies explore future sources of competitive advantage: new low-cost manufacturing processes; new products and services with unique features; leveraging experiences gained from existing businesses to create new businesses.

Strategic Role of Knowledge

The role knowledge plays is different for survival and advancement strategies, and by making this distinction managers can begin to grasp the reasons that tacit knowledge has so much potential—often underdeveloped or actively ignored in traditional strategic models—for knowledge creation. In a business context, knowledge can be separated into two broad categories: unique knowledge held exclusively by the firm and public knowledge held by several competitors. For unique knowledge to be a source of sustainable competitive advantages, it has to satisfy three more criteria: it must be valuable, difficult for competitors to imitate, and difficult to substitute (Barney, 1991).

Unique firm knowledge is valuable if it can successfully be applied to value-creating tasks (competence) and if it can be used to capitalize on existing business opportunities. Since competitors, in developing their own survival strategies, are likely to benchmark themselves against the industry leader to level out performance, knowledge must also be difficult to imitate.

What first comes to mind in this regard is knowledge in the form of patents. Interestingly, the only processes or products that can be patented are based on explicit knowledge. Filing a patent is a time-consuming and costly process, but more important for the strategic role of knowledge, patent rights are difficult to enforce. An ever-increasing number of patent engineers in various industries complain that manufacturers at distant locations eagerly imitate their technologies. In some instances, patents can be circumvented by making incremental alterations in the basic technology, thereby even enhancing the value of a final product for the customer.

Tacit social or individual knowledge, however, is typically more difficult to imitate than explicit knowledge captured in documents and manuals. Either the knowledge is actually impossible to replicate, or the imitation process is so costly that it deprives the imitator of the cost parity it was to achieve. In 1980, a U.S. government study showed that Japanese manufacturers, on average, had a competitive cost advantage of $2,200 per car manufactured in the subcompact class, which was based primarily on better inventory control, personnel management, and quality control.[8] This realization then created a strong effort among American car manufacturers like Ford, General Motors, and Chrysler to tap the manufacturing knowledge of Japanese automotive companies. Numerous fact-finding missions were undertaken, several consulting assignments initiated, and numerous books written, but the source of the cost advantage proved tremendously difficult to imitate.

In fact, much of the knowledge in Japanese car manufacturing remains tacit; it is tied to personal relations, shared habits, and intuition, all of which are not easily documented. For example, quality problems in supplies are resolved by intense face-to-face interactions with supplier representatives, not just by exchanging manufacturing procedures, or transferring engineering documents and product specifications. This is possible because of the close physical proximity of suppliers and manufacturers. The average distance of suppliers from Toyota, for instance, is thirty miles; as a consequence, the company clocks 10,635 person days of face-to-face contact with its suppliers. This is difficult for Toyota's American counterparts to match. General Motors, for example, is located an average distance of 427 miles from its suppliers, and the resulting face-to-face contacts with them amount to 1,107 person days (Dyer, 1996). Moreover, better personnel management involves job-rotation programs and on-the-job training, which are either poorly documented at Japanese companies or difficult for an external observer to comprehend. Even in terms of inventory management, tacit knowledge plays an important role. Suppliers to Japanese car manufacturers are invited to share tacit manufacturing knowledge by working as guests during a company's manufacturing process, especially at the initial stages.

Tacit knowledge at such companies has another essential dimension: it is social, not just individual. Although such knowledge may be hard to document in a manual or computer program, it is shared by all relevant organizational members, as well as other stakeholders like suppliers. The competitive advantage of Japanese car companies, based as it is on tacit social knowledge, allows for a better understanding of how supplied parts affect final product quality, especially when the bottlenecks are located in the manufacturing process, the storage conditions for and usage of supplied parts, just-in-time manufacturing schedules, and so on. Suppliers are also integrated into the improvement of the car manufacturing process itself, continuously creating new knowledge that is difficult, if not impossible, for competitors to imitate.

Finally, for knowledge to be a source of sustainable competitive advantage, competitors must have difficulty achieving the same level of costs or differentiation by substituting other knowledge for the first company's knowledge. Efficiency in current operations, as well as innovation, can be enhanced by transferring and leveraging unique individual and social knowledge, and by sharing investments and costs across products, markets, and businesses. Some tacit knowledge can almost never be substituted because of what we call the "hegemonic effect": one or a group of companies (A) with the only source of tacit knowledge engages in knowledge sharing with another company (B) based on expected returns; but when those returns are satisfactory for A, future transactions with other companies (C) to achieve similar returns could be avoided. This typically happens when suppliers work closely with customers, tapping their tacit knowledge to provide future solutions to customers' problems. Once a company has successfully shared tacit knowledge with a given supplier, however, it is unlikely to continue such exchanges with other firms.

Consider Maekawa, a Japanese engineering company, and its customers. In the early 1980s, in response to increasing labor costs in the industry, food-processing companies knew they had to increase the effectiveness and efficiency of their processes through automation. One idea that arose in Maekawa was to develop an automatic chicken leg deboning machine (called *Toridas* in Japanese). But the process of chicken deboning is based on scarce tacit knowledge held by a small number of expert deboners. Maekawa promised to help the industry to increase automation, and selected companies involved in chicken deboning opened themselves to this supplier's engineers. These engineers focused for several months on chicken deboning, observing how the experts worked. After an eight-year development process, drawing heavily on the tacit knowledge they had gained of chicken deboning, as well as mechatronic and robotic technologies, Maekawa delivered a chicken deboning machine that truly fulfilled the expected returns. *Toridas* became one of the greatest commercial successes in its history. Yet now that Maekawa has satisfied their needs, its customers are reluctant to open themselves to other competitors, and this source of tacit knowledge is once again beyond the reach of those customers. In such a competitive situation, attempts at substitution become almost impossible.[9]

Given that a firm's unique knowledge often adds such value, can public knowledge ever allow a company to achieve a sustainable competitive advantage? Based on the above discussion, the answer would seem to be no. Typically, public knowledge is the technical sort shared in research reports, engineering drawings, conference publications, textbooks, consulting manuals, and classrooms; often it represents general technical solutions that are freely available on the market. It is predominantly social explicit knowledge, or individual tacit knowledge with the potential of becoming social in easily documented forms. Some public knowledge is of a narrative kind,[10] in which managers tell, hear, and retell stories about the industry, their competitors, the company, and themselves. Narrative knowledge often takes the form of "Did you hear that company A tested out the new XC 3400 machine with excellent results?" In this way, narratives give substance and life to technical knowledge and may catch the interest of the listener enough for him or her to investigate further.

While public knowledge may not be as obvious a source of competitive advantage as unique knowledge, we propose that the process matters more than the content; in other words, what the company eventually does with its knowledge in terms of applying it to value-creating tasks matters more than the public availability of that content. The ability to transfer generic knowledge to various areas of a business may play a key role in a company's success, and the process itself may be unique, valuable, difficult to imitate, and difficult to substitute. Shared public knowledge across organizational units in different products, markets, or businesses can improve innovation and ultimately secure the sources of competitive advantage. For example, Buckman Laboratories, a U.S.-based producer of specialty chemicals, built an electronic communications system to encourage relationships among its employees and to allow for the effective transfer of knowledge, both public and unique, throughout its worldwide network of companies. Buckman's success lies more in the commitment of employees to using the electronic means of communication than in the sophistication of the systems. In fact, the information technology itself can be imitated. But recreating Buckman's culture of communication, in which organizational members actively use the system to solve their local problems, is a very difficult task.[11]

Knowledge Processes

Survival and advancement strategies result in knowledge processes, and like the strategies themselves, they can be distinguished in two basic ways: those that create new knowledge (and generally contribute to advancement) and those that transfer knowledge (and generally enhance survival). Although there are elements of knowledge creation for survival strategies, the focus is one of rapid and effective knowledge transfer across the business. Knowledge is already at hand, and the effective utilization of this knowledge is what counts to sustain competitive advantages. While there are elements of knowledge transfer for advancement strategies, the predominant process is one of creating new knowledge for future sustainable competitive advantages.

BALANCING SURVIVAL AND ADVANCEMENT STRATEGIES

Despite the value of unique knowledge, current managerial practice is dominated by survival thinking and the formulation of survival strategies. Few managers seem to have the courage to think beyond existing knowledge, resources, customers, suppliers, and competitors. The knowledge executives use for strategizing is therefore limited to two scales—the company and the industry—and it is honed by identifying and utilizing current sources of competitive advantage. Perhaps this preoccupation with survival can be attributed to the difficulty of thinking in the future tense; admittedly, it is much harder to generate knowledge about something that *could* exist than about something that already does. And managerial horizons are predominantly influenced by the immediate needs of stakeholders: shareholders want their returns now, customers want excellent service now, employees want their salaries today, and so on.

There are many reasons that individual managers opt for business survival over advancement; few of the reasons are rational, but they are based on solid fears, anxieties, and threats to self-image. Some managers become focused on immediate needs and cannot see beyond the short term. Others just do not have time to develop advancement strategies. Some of these managers may well understand the importance of advancement strategies but hope that the negative effects of emphasizing survival will not surface until they have left the company. Yet others find that thinking about the future, developing advancement strategies, and creating new knowledge have high associated risks.

In a stable environment, of course, a firm can thrive with a survival strategy. If unique knowledge continues to be a source of competitive advantage, still difficult to imitate or substitute, such knowledge will allow a company to maintain its hold on unique products and services, geographical positioning, low manufacturing costs, high yield on marketing expenses, and so forth. But if the environment of the firm changes, or if the firm itself undergoes major changes—such as a major loss of executive or professional talent—a preoccupation with current survival will endanger its future (March, 1991). Changes demand the creation of new sources of competitive advantage; the firm's executives must conceive of and implement advancement strategies not simultaneously being implemented by current *and* future competitors, and the benefits of these strategies must resist attempts at imitation.

Strategic management concerns the formulation and implementation of strategies, and ultimately determines the areas in which a company will do business and to what extent it will be successful competing in those areas. Because strategy formulation is about resource allocation for maintaining current competitive advantages and developing new ones, this is the first place to restore the balance between advancement and survival. Some managers start with survival and advancement on a personal level. The senior vice president of strategic planning in an international telecommunications group, for instance, may spend one day a week in solitude to gain personal advancement that can be transferred to the firm. Some management teams spend a proportion of their time on team development, using "boundary-breaking" sessions in which team members must present unconventional ideas about how the industry or competitive environment could develop. Other management teams have structured their strategy formulation around survival and advancement, setting short- and long-term strategic horizons.

During such sessions, asking a number of questions can be helpful to achieve the right balance for a given company. You might consider the following:

Survival Strategies

1. How do we need to change our survival strategy to retain or improve our profit levels?
2. Who are the current and possible future competitors that are beginning to implement similar survival strategies?
3. What are our current sources of competitive advantage, and how do we need to improve these to sustain our competitive advantage over time?
4. How do we retain the value and uniqueness of the company's knowledge while securing it against possible imitation attempts and substitution by competitors? How do we transfer unique and public knowledge across our various products, markets, businesses, and organizational units more effectively than our competitors?

Advancement Strategies

1. What should our advancement strategy be if we are to secure future profit levels?
2. Who are the possible competitors that could implement similar advancement strategies?
3. What should be our future sources of competitive advantage, and how could these be made sustainable?
4. How do we create new knowledge that can become a source of sustainable competitive advantage? What should this knowledge encompass? How do we make this knowledge difficult to imitate and substitute at the outset of the creation process—in other words, *how can we use tacit knowledge to our advantage?* How do we transfer new knowledge across products, markets, businesses, and organizational units?

When you begin asking such questions, keep some ground rules in mind. First, in developing advancement strategies, a management team needs to go through a process of envisioning future knowledge, not just future business. We discuss the importance of developing a knowledge vision in the next chapter; for the moment, let us simply emphasize the link between vision and strategy, and point to how this may play out when balancing survival and advancement. Intel's reaction to the flaw in the Pentium processor at the end of 1995 indicates how business-based visions can outpace new knowledge creation.[12] For several years, Intel's management pursued a strategy of building consumer awareness of its processors. Seemingly, executives wanted to create differentiation advantages through marketing campaigns that told the consumer of the value of an Intel processor "inside" the computer. Ironically, Intel's marketing efforts in this regard were effective. The Pentium processor gained enough name recognition that when the flaw was detected, CNN broadcast the news (November 22), and customers immediately started complaining to the company. Intel first refused to deal with the problem explicitly. Only when IBM, a major Intel customer, halted shipments of Pentium-equipped PCs (December 12), did Intel's management understand the grave nature of the issue. By December 20, Intel announced a recall of the Pentium processor. Over the course of that month, its share prices declined from $66 to $57.

According to industry analysts, Intel got into trouble because it lacked the knowledge and skills necessary for building strong and positive consumer relations; the company embarked on a new marketing campaign but was not prepared to handle consumer complaints, especially in the wake of a major public relations problem. Intel's business-based vision — which, as it turns out, did help advance the company in the long run — could have been followed up by a strategy to create knowledge in consumer behavior, relationship marketing, and corporate communication, as well as a commitment to service, some of which would have included justified beliefs about how to deal with customer complaints.

A second ground rule for strategizing is to recognize that there are no natural authorities on the future. Senior managers attain their positions through experience, but this experience is firmly grounded in the history of the company, past knowledge, current competence and assets, the past competitive dynamics of the industry, and past stakeholder expectations. Because much of their wisdom may be based on past experience, top managers are not always the most in tune with future business needs. When formulating the future knowledge needs of a company, many voices should be heard. A broad perspective on potential changes will increase a management team's awareness of possible courses of action. Do not hesitate to broaden your management team with young participants who have unconventional ideas.

Third, the formulation of advancement strategies requires scaling. At the outset, the management team might talk about knowledge in broad categories in order to generate a more complete perspective on possible advancement strategies. These broad categories, in turn, can guide increasingly fine distinction making. For example, the management team of a computer manufacturer might start by identifying knowledge associated with four broad generations of computing: mainframe computing, personal computing, networked computing, and ubiquitous computing (MIT's Media Lab calls this last generation "things that think"). Then, for each generation, finer distinctions can be made. For ubiquitous computing, such distinctions might include "private computing" versus "public computing." Private computing could be broken down into "intelligent homes," "intelligent consumer products," or "intelligent communication devices."

Fourth, and perhaps most important, strategic conversations are an asset to the company. Strategic conversations represent the cradle of the future in the purest sense. Conversational records should be kept, and time should be allocated to reflect collectively on the conversations themselves. What insights did they generate? In which areas should the company seek more knowledge, and where is further fact finding necessary? Why were certain ideas abandoned for others? Did all participants have a say in the process? Was participation sufficiently broad in the first place? We revisit this subject in Chapter 6, when we take a broader view of conversations and knowledge enabling.

In general, escaping the trap of the past is essential for the formulation of successful advancement strategies. The challenge for managers is to strike a balance between survival and advancement thinking in daily practice—that is, to honor the past but keep one's eyes on the future. Some firms like 3M or Sencorp are aware that advancement must happen at several levels of the organization; they allow employees to spend between 15 percent and 20 percent of their time on new knowledge creation. But in most business organizations, even if new ideas are given lip service, advancement strategies are neglected. With this behavior, such organizations may undercut knowledge creation or are unable to grasp its competitive potential.

ADVANCEMENT AND KNOWLEDGE CREATION

Advancement strategies depend on the creation of new knowledge. As we have already noted, the knowledge-creation process comprises five steps—sharing tacit knowledge, creating concepts, justifying concepts, building a prototype, and cross-leveling knowledge—and we detail the different steps next. Managers cannot embark on an advancement strategy unless they understand how each of these knowledge-creation steps is related to the others and can be fostered. A failure to delineate the knowledge-creation process, not to mention ignoring it completely, will almost certainly lead to the barriers discussed in Chapter 2; at the very least, a lack of managerial attention will harden individual and organizational barriers that already exist. This is especially true for sharing tacit knowledge, the first and most essential step. As with so many of the other issues discussed in *Enabling Knowledge Creation*, a good advancement strategy must not only account for an organization's tacit knowledge but also channel it wisely.

Step 1: Sharing Tacit Knowledge

Tacit, explicit, individual, and social knowledge are all available to companies.[13] For example, when an individual experiments with new solutions for tasks, leading to better task definitions or results, she can share her explicit knowledge (through documentation, for example, or a new training program) with other organizational members. This knowledge becomes part of the company's explicit social knowledge in the form of organizational routines. These routines, in turn, can be shared and re-used over time and space. This much seems obvious. But the tacit knowledge related to highly complex tasks (for example, interpretation of economic trends) is harder to capture in formal organizational procedures. Rather, it relies on the sharing of experiences and expertise over time between senior employees and novices (mentoring and master-apprentice relationships), and among a fairly stable group of professionals (such as a community of financial analysts). Even when making individual tacit knowledge explicit and social is difficult, it is still central to strategizing in a knowledge-creating company.

Tacit knowledge is shared through the deep socialization of a project team, or what we call a microcommunity of knowledge. Socialization means that members of the community not only come to understand each other's definition of shared situations but also agree on a common definition and justified true belief about how to act in that situation. Such situations might, for example, involve the performance of a complex engineering task, the identification of a customer need, or the judgment of complex technical requirements. Socialization also means that each individual is motivated to extend his or her community membership into the future, there is mutual identification among members, and each member takes an active role in the welfare of other members.[14] When microcommunities share situations, they come to share the raw feelings evoked (Tolman, 1935), those emotions of community members that are observable but not expressible. The whole process of working together benefits largely from the mutual insight of community members into the reactions of others.

Because tacit knowledge is bound to the senses, personal experience, and bodily movement, it cannot be easily passed on to others. In fact, it requires close physical proximity while the work is being done. Here are some typical ways to share tacit knowledge:

- *Direct observation:* Microcommunity members observe the task at hand and the skills of others in solving this task, as in a master-apprentice relationship. Observers come to share beliefs about which actions work and which do not. They thereby increase their potential to act in similar situations.
- *Direct observation and narration:* Members observe the task at hand and get additional explanations from other members about the process of solving the task, often in the form of a narrative about similar incidents or a metaphor. The beliefs of observers are further shaped by these stories.
- *Imitation:* Members attempt to imitate a task based on direct observation of others.
- *Experimentation and comparison:* Members try out various solutions and then observe an expert at work, comparing their own performance to the expert's.
- *Joint execution:* Community members jointly try to solve the task, and the more experienced offer small hints and ideas about how to improve the performance of the less experienced.

Normally, tacit knowledge is shared through a combination of these mechanisms, but language is not the primary mechanism for this process. Take the simple case of bicycling. You can ride a bicycle and exclaim, "I ride a bicycle." This would describe to the observer what you are doing but goes no further than categorizing the tacit knowledge involved. If you want others to learn what you are doing, the intrinsic aspects matter much more (MacKenzie and Spinardi, 1995). Teaching someone to bicycle means sharing how to pedal and steer while keeping your balance and setting direction. A mixture of observation, imitation, narration, experimentation, and joint execution would be required for you and the observer to share such tacit knowledge in any practical way.

In addition, not all tacit knowledge has an extrinsic aspect. Studies of learning highly complex sequential tasks indicate how hard it is for humans to deconstruct, analyze, and verbalize even the steps of the complex process (Shanks and Johnstone, 1998). This is certainly the case for many business tasks. The transfer of tacit knowledge is likely to take substantial time and energy, and involves a good blend of reflection about group work and the mechanisms mentioned above. Routinized competence, which is based on some forms of tacit knowledge, is easy to observe and can be made extrinsic through reflections on how the task was solved and extensive conversations among community members. In fact, the first step in making tacit knowledge explicit will be to name or categorize it. Expertise, however, poses another kind of problem.

Experts have the ability to solve tasks that are not routine and to deal with the unexpected (Dreyfus and Dreyfus, 1986). While a master violin maker might share his tacit knowledge with an apprentice, the difference between the two lies not in the ability to select the right materials but to discard materials that might be flawed. Tacit knowledge represents judgment par excellence. If most violin materials are preselected by a supplier, discerning flaws will happen only sporadically. In such situations, the means for sharing tacit knowledge—observation, narration, and so on— will be difficult to apply. The casual observer might not even recognize that the expert has made a choice, and even the expert might not know that he has. Again, physical proximity and time are critical elements, as are caring relations among community members, whether violin makers or software engineers. Because sharing tacit knowledge may require new organizational structures, different kinds of project schedules, and new physical space to accommodate the work of microcommunities, this step has to be considered in a firm's advancement strategy—and is closely connected to establishing an overall enabling context.

Step 2: Creating Concepts

In this phase of knowledge creation, a microcommunity attempts to externalize its knowledge, making its tacit knowledge explicit. This is obviously another crucial step, one that may ultimately result in the advancement of a business through a new product, process, or service. Yet many business strategies do not account for the time it takes to express new ideas in a form others can understand, and many managers are not open to the playful use of language and metaphors necessary for sparking the creative process. Hence, the implementation of an advancement strategy through knowledge creation might be hampered as well.

To externalize knowledge means to express shared practices and judgments through language. A concept captures the blend of experience and imagination; it also comes about through throwing together already existing ideas (Husserl, 1931). Concepts like "intelligent cosmetics," "ubiquitous computing," or "adaptive clothing" all convey the thinking of communities that have engaged in knowledge creation in the most basic sense. Members who can mentally visualize a concept may be able to catalyze and coordinate knowledge creation at a company (some of these people will be knowledge activists). At Toshiba, for example, managers in the ADI division (Advanced Information, Intelligence, and Integration) are recruited based on their ability to mentally construct and "see" such concepts.

As Michael Dummet (1993) notes, "A language has two functions, as an instrument of communication and as a vehicle of thought" (p. 151). The central process in creating a new concept is coming up with a language for it that serves both to communicate new experiences and to guide new thoughts. The idea here is to look at language as a flexible stock of words and their combinations.[15] Playing language games can be an open-ended, intuitive exercise that serves the purpose of capturing tacit knowledge in flight; it feeds on creativity. A concept, as Wittgenstein suggested, derives its meaning in use. Therefore, community members must be allowed considerable time to experiment with different uses of a concept. Eventually concepts will begin to land; the community recognizes the power of a concept to externalize its tacit knowledge and will choose it. But if a company's strategy is too narrow to accommodate such a free-form process, it may end up strangling all chances for innovation and advancement.

According to Nonaka and Takeuchi (1995), a figurative language using metaphor and analogies is of particular importance for concept creation. The community talks about an experience as if it looks, sounds, or smells like something else. For example, members might suggest the "new wave of technology" or a "system for information digestion." George Lakoff and Mark Johnson (1983) put this quite strikingly:

> Because so many of the concepts that are important to us are either abstract or not clearly delineated in our experience (the emotions, ideas, time, etc.), we need to get a grasp on them by means of other concepts that we understand in clearer terms (p. 115).

A metaphor serves as a kind of intermediary concept, one that can be expediently used to shape thoughts and communication. Consider a microcommunity that intends to develop a new culinary product by watching how a sophisticated consumer bakes a cake. Perhaps the only way the community can conceptualize the cooking procedure is to understand this consumer as an artist, someone who blends ingredients until the result comes as close as possible to the experience of eating her grandmother's cakes on a hot summer day. From a strategic point of view, this may sound silly; why not focus on her shopping list, the cost of ingredients, a step-by-step process that can be easily documented? However, a literal approach may be fine for certain routines, but it cannot capture the tacit nuances of cooking or any other creative endeavor, from writing a screenplay to assembling a new computer language to formulating an effective marketing campaign.

Step 3: Justifying Concepts

After a concept has been created, evaluation of it needs to follow. It is here that a well-formulated advancement strategy—which should include certain business objectives, even if it allows for the open-ended nature of knowledge creation—can be directly applied to the group process. Concept justification can involve the community members themselves; department heads; business heads; top management; external stakeholders like suppliers, customers, and legal or government representatives; perhaps even performing artists and writers. Typically, the microcommunity is allowed to present its concept, then open dialogue about the concept, with constructive criticism, follows. If necessary, the community may be given a second chance to go back to the drawing board, repeating the first two steps of the knowledge-creation process to come up with a better concept.

Before engaging in concept justification, the community and other participants need to agree on a set of criteria. First, the concept should be reviewed for its impact on the company's advancement strategies. The key issue here is whether the participants in concept justification come to believe that the knowledge created is likely to generate a potential source of sustainable competitive advantage. The people involved might ask the following questions:

- Is the concept consistent with the company's advancement strategy?
- Is the concept consistent with the future values of the company?
- Will the concept be valuable for the future? Where does this value stem from?
- Could the concept remain unique in the future in spite of imitation or substitution attempts by competitors?
- Who are the customers that will benefit from the concept? How are they likely to react? Why are these reactions likely?
- Who should supply the necessary knowledge, raw materials, or technologies to make the concept into a service or product? What are their interests in the concept?

- What is the timing in creating a product or service resulting from the concept?
- What kinds of competences need to be established in order to further develop, manufacture, and sell the product or service resulting from the concept?

Few of the criteria mentioned here are quantitative, of course. If possible, this list of questions might be supplemented with other criteria, like pay-back time, return on investment, costs, profit margins, and so forth. The main point, however, is not to discard the concept too soon because of insufficient data. Justifying the concept against the advancement strategy should be more of a qualitative than quantitative exercise.

In addition, although new knowledge primarily contributes to advancement strategies, it might affect a company's survival as well. The new concept may improve existing product or service offerings, manufacturing technologies, routines, and processes; it could simplify logistics or enhance effectiveness of marketing. If participants consider it in terms of survival strategies, they might ask:

- What is the impact of the concept on existing competitive advantages of the company?
- How does the new concept contribute to the value, uniqueness of the company's existing knowledge, and/or the difficulty of imitating or substituting this knowledge?
- What is the impact of the concept on the company's current profitability?
- What are the likely reactions of competitors to the concept?
- How can the concept support existing markets, products, services, businesses, and processes?
- What will be existing customers' reactions to the concept?
- To what extent does the concept help achieve higher customer satisfaction for existing products and services?
- What kinds of new customers might be attracted through the concept?

Beyond specifying advancement and survival possibilities for a concept, participants need to be aware that a strategic focus can dominate concept justification too much, allowing an insider's view to prevail. This can happen all too easily, even though most successful product and service innovations are well adapted to new trends, developments, or events in society (Thomas, 1995). New concepts need to be accepted by stakeholders like suppliers, customers, educational institutions, governments, and society at large. For example, in the mid-1950s the British Government passed the Clean Air Act to reduce industrial pollution; a similar act was passed by the European Union in the late 1960s. European car manufacturers reacted positively to this, and pioneers like Volkswagen created socially beneficial knowledge in thermodynamics, air pollution, and engineering aimed at reducing emissions. One viable concept was that of catalytic converters, which reduce emission of carbon monoxide by more than 90 percent.

Participants in concept justification might ask these questions about stakeholders:

- Who are the stakeholders likely to be affected by and take active interest in the concept?
- What are their likely reactions to this concept?
- How should the company communicate the concept?
- How could the concept be changed to make it increasingly beneficial to society?

Finally, because knowledge is so intimately tied to people, it is emotional. Hence, concept justification should also be expanded to employ criteria that account for individual experiences and expressions. A concept is an expression of shared tacit knowledge, but it is not identical with tacit knowledge. Additional meaning will be given to the concept as the justification phase proceeds. All the participants in this process will bring their own views, thoughts, and emotions to the table, and the meaning of the concept itself will change through this group process. Although judgments about the goodness, truth, and beauty of a concept may seem very far away from business concerns, they play a role in creating something truly innovative.

Having an opinion presupposes the ability to express that opinion in language (Tomrey, 1971). In justifying the aesthetic value of a concept, a free and open language is necessary. The criteria employed can be romantic, adventurous, exciting, colorful, stylish, mystical, lively, graceful, or just plain entertaining. In some respects, this is an extension of the language games that help create a concept; it represents an open attitude toward what is considered relevant. Yet with their instrumental and rational stock of business words, few companies cultivate such rich and diverse language skills. They do not develop aesthetes, or people able to see the many meanings and aspects of a concept. They continue to rely on "aspect-blind"[16] managers trained in traditional business thinking, who may be excellent at judging the strategic or even social values of a concept but are blind to its aesthetic qualities. Therefore, few companies achieve aesthetic justification, even if aesthetic qualities may matter most to customers. A company may design an extremely functional suitcase, for instance, but customers will stay away in droves if they would feel embarrassed dragging the ugly thing around airports and train stations.

Skills in aesthetic judgment demand a certain kind of imagination that Harold Osborne (1986) calls "synthetic imagination." Regarding a concept, participants in the justification process must be able to review it in terms of the company's history: How does the concept relate to other knowledge, business, products, and markets for the company? They must also be able to project what the world would be like if the concept were introduced and developed into a product or service offering. This is what Sony tries to achieve when its project teams imagine the mind-set of the consumer and visualize how a new product could lead to a host of new opportunities. When participants compare and contrast the concept with others that are already out in the world, the new concept may come alive in the collective imagination. Last, those involved in concept justification must be able to imagine the process community members went through in creating it: What did they think they were up to? If the judges can answer this question, they will better appreciate the beauty of the concept and its reason to be.

Step 4: Building a Prototype

Once a concept has been justified, the next phase in knowledge creation entails prototype building. The prototype is a tangible form of the concept, and it is achieved by combining existing concepts, products, components, and procedures with the new concept. The people involved at this stage include not only the original microcommunity but also those from a wide variety of functions like marketing, manufacturing, maintenance, and strategic planning. This prototype team should have a charter at the outset that outlines what it is supposed accomplish.

Prototype construction is often considered a linear process in which design parameters are given. But in our view, building a prototype is a kind of self-regulating playful phase in which the participants assemble things at hand and make them into a new object without losing track of the original, justified concept. Controlled imagination plays a role in combining things; the participants should be creative in producing a physical object or an initial service offering, while the original concept gradually slips into the background. From time to time, participants can revisit the earlier steps in order to understand the various meanings attributed to the concept.

In order to speed up prototyping, a variety of things need to be at hand. Basically, it starts with pencils and paper, clay, or even Legos. At a more sophisticated level, three-dimensional CAD-CAM systems allow for visualization of a final product, and designers can experiment freely with different forms and functions. Some of these systems also include standardized design processes that help prototype creators think through the various aspects of the design. CAD-CAM systems can be equipped with programs that simulate movement and use of the prototype, and which allow designers to remove possible flaws at an early stage. Computer programs applying finite-element methods can calculate the deflection and strengths of mechanical solutions.

A database with standardized components is vital for identifying those components that fit with the concept; at the same time, it allows for economies of scope. A library of best practices in product design and manufacturing will help participants to identify previous lessons in product design—that is, what works and what does not. Videoconferencing or e-mail exchanges with key people off site can provide a short and effective feedback loop on the proposed prototype. Information about manufacturing and other procedures for similar products can help the team to conceive of the necessary tasks for eventually manufacturing the prototype. A list of competences and products of preferred suppliers will allow the team to assess what to develop internally or acquire externally. A overview of patents, such as the map developed by Dow Chemical that indicates the characteristics and potential value of about 25,000 patents (Petrash, 1996), can also be made electronically available to the team.

Prototypes can be shown to sample customers at an early stage to get their preliminary reactions to the design as well as to check out the market. The customer can be given some degree of freedom in operating the prototype while the designers watch his or her interaction. Service technicians are also natural participants in the prototype-creation phase, since their input will enhance serviceability of the end product.

Step 5: Cross-leveling Knowledge

The outcome of these four steps—sharing tacit knowledge, creating concepts, justifying concepts, and building a prototype—results in one of two things: a possible product/service innovation or raw knowledge. A company's advancement strategy can enhance cross-leveling of knowledge throughout an organization, even if a particular initiative does not yield a viable idea. The prototype itself displays knowledge in the physical form of drawings, specifications, or models, and it can be passed on to pilot manufacturing, full-scale manufacturing, distribution, and sales. At these later stages, the prototype will be further refined. The prototype, therefore, becomes a source of inspiration across organizational hierarchies and for other business areas, markets, or microcommunities developing their own products and service offerings.

Some of these alterations and knowledge exchanges may lead the original community to return to earlier steps of the process. Perhaps the lack of variety in members' experiences did not allow for the effective sharing of tacit knowledge, and the community must start anew. Or perhaps the concept created could not really meet the functional and aesthetic needs of consumers. In that case, community members will need to revisit concept creation. A new strategic direction or dramatic societal changes may mean the concept has been justified on false premises. Or the prototype may be impossible to manufacture or simply too expensive.

Although business strategists may plan otherwise, it would be too limited to view specific innovations as the only outcome of knowledge creation. The microcommunity involved has assembled experiences related not only to a concrete prototype but also to the very process of working together, the methods applied, and a variety of different concepts. In fact, such raw knowledge represents what Skandia calls organizational capital (Edvinsson and Sullivan, 1996). From this perspective, management has three responsibilities for organizational capital, all of which involve moving knowledge across many levels.

First, managers should shorten the time between knowledge created and knowledge received. The lessons from one knowledge-creation process should be applied by the same or a different community, and those who have created the knowledge can become teachers for other organizational members. For example, when one business unit has developed a new system for tracking the behavior of key accounts, this system needs to be disseminated as soon as possible throughout the organization.

Second, management should document the knowledge created. This can be done in the form of procedures or routines, job or competence requirements, or instructive videos stored on a CD-ROM. The new tracking system might be passed along in the form of a computer program, accompanied by an instructive CD-ROM that explains the benefits of the system and how to apply it. Each business is likely to have its own needs, but the information on common key accounts will be valuable, as will the inspiration from seeing such a system in use.

Third, management must ensure recirculation of created knowledge. That means encouraging and reinforcing future application of that knowledge. If the new tracking system helps workers understand how key accounts behave in various situations, they will be much more motivated to continue using the system. In another instance, business units might be asked to prepare short summaries of the recent insights they have acquired by looking more closely at targeted customers.

Leveraging knowledge organizationally does imply that transferred knowledge should be of value locally; otherwise, the organization will be overburdened with too much "knowledge push" (Sveiby, 1996). This, in turn, requires local justification processes that apply their own criteria for usefulness. One way of creating a "knowledge pull" is for various organizational units to post electronically the criteria for the kinds of knowledge they are looking for. Andersen Consulting does this through its issue mapping system. Various consultants or groups working on a project can post an issue, requesting help or answers from other consultants or groups.

However, a large amount of knowledge, particularly the tacit kind, is hard to transfer and disseminate organizationally. Whereas explicit knowledge can rely on groupware and networking tools, transfer of tacit knowledge requires sharing through socialization, physical proximity, and good relationships, although various collaborative computer tools can be extremely helpful to the process (Schrage, 1997). This makes cross-leveling of knowledge a tremendously challenging task—all the more reason for delineating each of the knowledge-creation steps when putting together an advancement strategy.

SKANDIA'S FUTURE CENTER: VISUALIZING AND CULTIVATING KNOWLEDGE

We now turn to a company that makes identifying its knowledge sources a strategic priority and has creatively addressed many of the challenges described earlier.[17] Skandia, a global corporation engaged in insurance and financial services, has a home base in the Nordic countries. Skandia Insurance Company Ltd. was established in 1855 in Sweden. Today Skandia has approximately 10,000 employees, and about 80 percent of its shareholders are non-Swedish investors. Our story begins with the Assurance and Financial Services business unit (AFS), where knowledge creation and strategizing have particularly blossomed. It was in AFS, now the leading business within Skandia, representing 80 percent of gross value, that the company's intellectual capital (IC) function first emerged in 1991.

Already in 1980, then-CEO Björn Wolrath and the head of Skandia AFS, Jan Carendi, realized that a knowledge-intensive service company's competitive strength would rely less on traditional accounting assets (real estate, equipment, inventories) than on intangible factors like individual talent, synergetic market relationships, and the ability to manage the flow of employee competences and skills. Wolrath and some other executives, together with Leif Edvinsson, then co-founded the Swedish Coalition of Service Industries, focusing on the problem of visualizing the untapped value potential of the service sector. By 1991, Skandia AFS had created its intellectual capital function and appointed Edvinsson as its director. His task was to develop new measurement tools and to visualize IC as a complement of the balance sheet. IC has since become a Skandia corporate function, and Leif Edvinsson is currently a vice president in that area.

Intellectual capital, as defined by Edvinsson, comes in two basic forms: human capital and structural capital. Human capital includes all individual capabilities—that is, the talents, knowledge, and experience of the company's employees and managers. Structural capital consists of everything that remains when the employees go home—that is, the infrastructure that supports the company's human capital, including the information technology and physical systems used to transmit intellectual capital. Based on these insights, Skandia constructed a measurement tool called the IC-Navigator (Figure 4.1) that offers a balanced picture of financial and intellectual capital.

One of the first steps in formulating an advancement strategy involves such identification of knowledge sources. The Navigator distinguishes among five major areas plus business contexts globally. The financial focus represents the results of the past, whereas the customer, human, and process focuses indicate the present situation of the company. Strategic use of knowledge—or what the company calls knowledge navigation for future earnings—is based mainly on renewal and development, which provides a predictive image of Skandia's future earnings capabilities.[18] IC indicators translate each focus into usable results with a key focus on strategic position, shift, and speed on shift, for example, navigation.

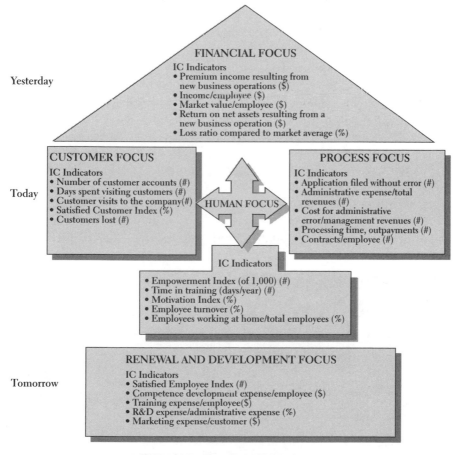

Figure 4.1. Skandia's IC-Navigator

Renewal and development is measured, for example, through the number of new launches per customer/year, time to market, or the percentage of business development expense in relation to administrative expense.

These quantitative indicators help to pin down the business results of a strategy based on knowledge creation. But Skandia's executives also recognize that to advance, they cannot just use numbers to predict the future or to determine how knowledge creation might best serve the company. Edvinsson talks about knowledge navigation in general and "futurizing" in particular. For him, futurizing is a proactive planning process in which managers do something now, not in the year 2020. He says,

> Since the future is unknown, you cannot draw a map of it, you can just use indicators showing where you are, the direction you are heading, and how fast you are on the way. If you see this over time, patterns of shifts start to emerge that might reinforce themselves like a wave. It is like sailing: not the straight line into the future, but more like tacking. This is what we call knowledge navigation, using the Skandia Navigator.

Skandia's executives believe that visualizing the company's hidden talents is a necessary prerequisite for futurizing. Whenever knowledge is visualized, it becomes explicit. To increase the visibility and transparency of its IC capabilities, Skandia has created many tools like the Navigator. But another means for visualizing knowledge is the Skandia Future Center, which serves as a unique laboratory for new organizational designs—that is, it provides an enabling context for knowledge creation.[19]

The Future Center was launched in May 1996 at the Villa Askudden in Vaxholm, on a Swedish archipelago 20 kilometers north of Stockholm (see Figure 4.2). During its first two years, a total of ten thousand visitors from within and outside Skandia have passed through its doors. The Future Center offers an arena for workshops and gives participants the opportunity to prototype, visualize, and "gestalt" their ideas. Initially, it

Figure 4.2. The Skandia Future Center

was run by Leif Edvinsson, management-developer Ingrid Tidhult (known as the "digital saloon cultivator"), other "futurizers," and networking specialists. Edvinsson and the futurizers meet "future teams" and organize programs to initiate what they call "mind-stretching," "gestalting," or "brainstilling."

At Skandia, stretching is considered an essential way to cultivate knowledge. The company encourages employees to stretch their talents from the known to an exploration of the unknown. During brainstilling exercises, participants focus on explicit sensory experiences, such as the smell of flowers or the feel of an old work desk, and are asked to consider what the tacit implications might be. To activate people, their physical and emotional responses must be addressed as well as their conscious thoughts; the whole idea is to achieve peace of mind. Brainstilling programs therefore use icons of the five senses to help participants internalize these experiences. Brainstilling can be achieved, for example, through hearing a rhythm such as a waltz.[20] Ingrid Tidhult says of her programs: "After 15 minutes, daily business stress decreases and people start to sense differently. The Villa Askudden serves as an energizing place for meeting the future."[21]

This enabling context encourages participants to experiment with the way a work space is designed or with how people work together. The Future Center's programs include a knowledge safari, knowledge games, and a knowledge café. Regarding the last, Edvinsson notes, "Talents used to meet in a café, as in Vienna. Historically, knowledge was often created in such cafés, as was the case in the development of continental stock exchanges." The implication is that traditional offices may not be the best way to spark new ideas, and most of these insights are already part of the office design at Skandia's headquarters in Stockholm. Like the Phonak House discussed in Chapter 2, the design of physical space is considered essential to knowledge creation, both as a representation of open-ended thinking and as a way to help employees form stronger relationships.

At the Future Center, visitors can play with a room's layout, the arrangement of chairs, the contribution of information technology, even the smells present. Because everybody senses differently, people need to experiment and try this out for themselves. In "future workshops," visitors are given whiffs of fresh bread or hundred-year-old sofas, and asked to consider how an office needs to smell to make it as comfortable as home or to nourish innovative rule-breaking. They may try working in the knowledge café, standing at tables instead of sitting at desks, or listening to their favorite music. Ideas can also be visualized by shooting video movies, or producing knowledge handicrafts made from all kinds of materials. Such works have been put on display in a special exhibition space. Ultimately, Skandia hopes participants will return to their own offices and change the work space, the titles on their business cards, even their positions. As

Edvinsson explains: "Things which don't happen at other places we will prototype here. Instead of running around and pushing for things to happen, we invite people to a space for testing how to start a wave. Then it usually is amplified when visitors bring it home."

Approaches like visualizing, brainstilling, and gestalting help unleash tacit knowledge, especially by appealing to the senses. By creating new gestalts of a company's structural capital—the supposedly fixed-in-stone aspects of a physical office space or organizational hierarchy—workshop participants can begin to see alternatives for creating their own enabling contexts. And the use of playful language, the emphasis on new perspectives and aesthetic angles, the need to share tacit experiences, all encourage more productive knowledge creation. Although creative workshops may seem very far away from a company's strategic calculations, they inspire exactly the kind of thinking required for advancement strategies.

Consider the five future teams, each consisting of five persons, that were assembled at Villa Askudden in May 1996 when the Future Center first opened. The members were not selected because they had any special insights into Skandia's future; rather, they were meant to represent a mix of nationalities, cultures, skills, generations, and functions from this competence-oriented global company. They began by focusing on five key issues: world economics, technology, demography, organization and leadership, and Europe's insurance market. They were supposed to recognize critical questions, identify a variety of trends, stretch minds by meeting different people, and read new signals.

But the work of these teams was not just a matter of group discussion and research; they were asked to turn in a manuscript by September, one that encapsulated their insights in the form of a "future drama" that could be performed by professional actors. Activating more senses, such a drama is a sophisticated way to share knowledge; it has a deeper impact on one's sensibilities than a mere report. More important, the future teams generated a kind of collective intelligence about strategic issues through their on-going dialogue.

For example, the ideas on Europe's insurance market were expressed in a family scene. The Brooks family, with father Anthony, mother Eva, and daughter Mirjam, were having dinner on a Friday evening, talking about their experiences of the day. Eva had returned to her car at 10:00 A.M. after shopping and found it damaged. She values the insurance company's service. She called the insurance company, identified herself, and was given advice as to where to take her car for repairs. Since there was no filling in of forms and the company took her car for repairs, organizing a loaner car right away, she could keep her schedule.

Anthony works as an engineer in a high tech company. He had attended a course at the university for the whole day to update his engineering skills. Feeling the need for continous learning five years after his graduation, he had subscribed for a competence insurance program. This program allows him to maintain his competencies by attending courses in his subject wherever available.

Mirjam is in her 20s and has already made plans for her retirement. She recalls that late in the twentieth century, young people were known stereotypically as latte-drinking, goateed slackers. The reason for this change in attitude was the rising awareness among young people that the financial advantages gained by investing in mutual fund accounts early are tremendous, and also that life insurance costs are far less when purchased early.

The future teams' insights was gestalt in a future cafe in London. After the drama was performed by professional actors, discussion took place. At each of the twenty-five tables a future team member was sitting together with five Skandia managers. They were expected to exchange, reflect, and discuss the five key issues with 125 Skandia managers. A software system called Ventana was used to capture the dialogue and new thoughts. Developed at the University of Arizona, this groupware program allows for question-and -answer sessions, visualizing and documenting the results in real time. The dialogues were sent over the Net and simultaneously revised by a group of editors who were sitting in another location. Via a collective screen, all dialogues were visible and audible to everyone. Observing the collective intelligence of the teams, the editors stretched to recognize strategic patterns. Based on the patterns, they formed a map that, together with innovative questions raised during the process, was passed on to various managers to be shared within the company. The next step was to initiate projects within the most interesting areas. The impact of this event was that people realized that questions are more important than answers to cultivate collective intelligence, turning Skandia into a prototyping question and answer organization. Since that event, mobile future cafés are held regularly.

As a result of the networking of the SFC among internal but mainly external visitors, UNIC (Universal Networking of Intellectual Capital) was created to cultivate these networks and to represent a larger virtual community. Communication is facilitated by KenNet, an information system that is Internet-based and can rapidly package, refine, and share ideas throughout Skandia and its partners. Internal and external experts' intelligence is therefore accessed and transferred. One outcome of such a knowledge community has been the IC-Index, which was cooperatively developed by American Skandia and Intellectual Capital Services of London. UNIC has also facilitated cooperation with another one of Skandia's strategic partners, Asea Brown Boveri, with the goal of creating an ABB Future Center.

From brainstilling workshops to a networked community—from sharing tacit knowledge to creating concepts based on new perspectives to distributing the resulting knowledge across many levels—the ideas behind Skandia's Future Center all indicate the link between advancement strategies and knowledge creation. This company's executives firmly believe that nourishing knowledge work will create future earnings capabilities. As Skandia's current CEO, Lars Eric Petersson, says, "The Skandia Future Center has helped turn Skandia into an Innovation Company."[22] This is also an illustration of continuosly moving between tacit and explicit knowledge, as well as internal and external knowledge.

MANAGING THE ENABLING PROCESSES

The Skandia story illustrates that knowledge creation is not just a matter of the right business strategy or caring organizational relationships or a concerted effort to dismantle barriers. Managers need to think of all of these elements as connected, since it is almost impossible to discuss one without reference to the others. That is why an overall enabling context must underpin other knowledge-creation initiatives. At Skandia, the Future Center as an arena prototypes and models what an enabling context looks like, helping participants to apply these techniques to their own business situations, or at least to carry home a new mind-set about knowledge.

The point here is that good strategy relies on more than traditional business models and approaches; it is based on knowledge enabling rather than only rigid management goals. For Skandia's Leif Edvinsson, "cultivating" is the key word, one that matches our definition of enabling and the new roles managers must play in knowledge-creating companies. "Cultivating energizes people, whereas management discourages them," Edvinsson says. "If the energy level of these people is just raised from 20 to 30 percent, that would be a 50-percent increase—and a huge potential could be unleashed."

To summarize how all this relates to the five knowledge enablers, the enablers do not follow a set sequence, but strategy certainly goes hand-in-hand with vision. When you are getting started with knowledge creation, it is important to create an advancement strategy that explains the rationale for this process in terms of establishing new sources of competitive advantage and by broadly outlining how knowledge creation should happen in the company. *Instilling a knowledge vision* is an integral part of creating an advancement strategy. A company's knowledge vision will more specifically outline the "what" of its advancement strategy.

Continual dialogue among organizational members can spark both vision and strategy—remember Skandia's on-line future teams; this is why *managing conversations* is also crucial. As soon as your advancement strategy indicates the need for knowledge creation, you should develop mentoring, incentive, and training systems that encourage care in the organization, as well as a good atmosphere for effective conversations. *Mobilizing knowledge activists* will trigger new knowledge-creation projects and motivate people to form or join microcommunities. In addition, some initiatives will already be running in the company, and the knowledge activist's job is to bring these to the attention of the organization, to coordinate various knowledge-creation projects, and to relate them all to the knowledge vision.

Creating the right context will ensure that knowledge-creation projects are successfully carried out through an organizational structure that reinforces enabling and is aligned with strategy. At the very least, this might require adding a project layer to a traditional hierarchy. Workers would then be able to split their time between knowledge projects and the more routinized tasks defined by the traditional structure. Finally, by *globalizing local knowledge*, you can dismantle barriers on a continuing basis throughout a multinational organization. Some barriers will initially endanger the formation of new communities: Managers may be reluctant to give up their best people, individual workers may have little motivation for embarking on new tasks, a new project may represent an uncertain future. Key processes for dismantling such barriers are the initial triggering of knowledge exchange, packaging/dispatching knowledge, and re-creating knowledge locally. Again, a supportive vision, a functional structure, free-flowing conversations, and knowledge activists that act as organizational glue will considerably ease the process.

In many respects, knowledge enabling consists of a feedback loop, in which the knowledge created must circle back to strategic efforts, continually altering or adapting a company's advancement strategy as well as its vision. Changes in a knowledge vision, in turn, may call for a new way of structuring the organization, point to new areas in the company that require the help of knowledge activists, identify new knowledge-creation projects, or suggest new barriers to dismantle in order to create future competitive advantages. In the following chapters, we describe the five knowledge enablers more precisely, starting with a look at how companies develop their knowledge visions.

·5·

ENABLER 1

Instill a Knowledge Vision

The absence of any measure of the total stock of knowl-
edge makes quantitative statements about it more akin to
poetry than to mathematics.

—Kenneth Boulding

One of the major challenges for managers in the knowledge economy will be figuring out what their companies ought to know for
the future. This is a tough question, because the future of a business can be very hard to predict. Yet executives cannot avoid thinking about
what is to come, or what might possibly happen, or even what will probably never happen (but if it does, watch out). The present ignorance of managers can end up being their company's worst enemy. Consider the
problems IBM confronted in the 1980s with the arrival of personal computers (PCs). In the 1970s, IBM executives sensed that a new technology
was about to replace the mainframe computer; the company even established a separate research facility that produced the first PC. However,
blinded by fear that the company's mainframe business might be threatened by personal computers, IBM failed to respond to market and customer demands—that is, it did not develop sufficient knowledge about
what customers wanted in a PC. As a consequence, for years IBM lagged
behind an "upstart" like Apple Computer (see Hamel and Prahalad, 1994).

The typewriter company Facit made the same mistake. Along with
other competitors at the beginning of the 1980s, they focused on reducing
manufacturing costs to stay competitive in a declining industry rather than
on acquiring knowledge of a radically different kind that would have
helped them to meet the new challenges. Investing in manufacturing
assets specific to the typewriter industry bound up their capital and
heightened the exit barriers for many companies. While typewriters were

gradually replaced by personal computers, typewriter companies contin-ued to cannibalize each other. If we consider knowledge to be justified true belief, such a resistance to exploring new knowledge comes from holding on to old patterns of justification and existing beliefs. Companies like Facit insisted for far too long that typewriters would always have a func-tional advantage over computers: portability. The current popularity of notebook computers indicates just how detrimental holding on to old beliefs can be.

Fortunately, history is also full of stories about companies looking ahead. Take IBM again. Despite initial missteps as the personal computer market developed, the company did manage to turn the business around, especially by letting Microsoft keep the rights to the DOS operating system and allowing other firms to clone the PC. Although many would argue that these strategies were not necessarily based on brilliant foresight—up until the mid-1990s, various commentators believed IBM had "sold the farm" when it allowed competitors to produce cheaper clones—today DOS/Windows-based PCs represent over 90 percent of the installed base of personal computers. Ironically, Apple, which refused to allow clones of its computers, has now become only a niche player.

In the seeds and agriculture industry, Monsanto was one of the first to follow an aggressive investment plan in building biotechnology knowl-edge. In the 1970s, Monsanto began converting existing natural drugs into synthetic drugs based on fermentation, as well as developing new drugs through biotechnology. This knowledge was profitably transferred later to other businesses, including pharmaceuticals. But in many pharmaceutical companies two decades ago, employees who even thought about biotech-nology were labeled "oddballs" or "heretics." These individuals may have been visionary in their own right, but they were unable to accomplish any-thing under the existing regime.

There are many reasons for the difficulty in predicting the evolution of knowledge. The first is its accelerating growth. The change in Apple's for-tunes offers just one example. Economist and philosopher Kenneth Boulding (1995) strikingly points out that "we can perceive . . . certain accelerations in the growth of knowledge; that is, the rate of growth increases all the time. Thus knowledge is like a sum of capital that accu-mulates at continually rising interest rates" (p. 13). However, even capital accumulation cannot be predicted accurately on this basis, only the rate of change. Instead of trying to predict the evolution of knowledge, Boulding suggests that organizational planners train themselves to expect the unex-pected. To deal with the unexpected development of knowledge in their industries, managers therefore need a structured approach for thinking through what their company ought to know—not what it *must* know.

A structured approach should help managers to change preemptively their justified beliefs about customers, technologies, competition, suppliers, the workforce, and so on. It involves *instilling a knowledge vision*, one of the key enabling conditions for knowledge creation. When managers instill an effective knowledge vision, they help encourage the formation of microcommunities, concept justification, and cross-leveling of knowledge throughout their organizations. Knowledge visions can also enable concept creation and prototype building. They have less impact on the sharing of tacit knowledge within a microcommunity, but the process of instilling a knowledge vision does rely, ultimately, on unleashing tacit knowledge to drive innovation. At the very least, the vision must acknowledge that not all organizational knowledge comes in explicit forms.

In strategic terms, a company's knowledge vision gives its business plans a heart and soul; it is the raison d'être for an advancement strategy. Looking at this formulation from another angle, an advancement strategy establishes the need for knowledge creation in competitive terms. It lays out the basis for future competitive advantages and performance. However, the advancement strategy needs to be tightly coupled with a knowledge vision that gives more substance to the strategy. The vision encompasses the types and contents of knowledge to be created, and thereby provides clear direction to members of the microcommunities within an organization. A good knowledge vision will inspire the company to search out knowledge in certain areas and to build up a stock of knowledge that can be of use for meeting future business challenges.

More important, it will emphasize knowledge creation as an activity, putting it on top management's agenda. Indeed, such a vision has to express a commitment from the very top of the company. In this chapter, we discuss the criteria for a good knowledge vision, using Shiseido's creation of its Ayura brand as an illustration of a real company's approach. We then lay out five specific management actions for instilling a knowledge vision, as well as indicate some possible pitfalls that may be encountered during the process.

WHAT IS A KNOWLEDGE VISION?

Any company vision has both a present and future component. By vision, we do not mean only foresight about a future state; we also believe vision of one's present situation is necessary. We want to emphasize this point, because it counters other definitions in the strategic management literature. A knowledge vision is firmly connected to an advancement strategy, one that emphasizes a company's future performance and success. But just as companies must balance advancement and survival strategies, they need to envision a future based on current conditions and even some sense of the past.

In fact, foresight depends heavily on the current vision of the world held by a company. We believe knowledge is socially constructed rather than a concrete representation of reality. Based on this constructionist perspective, managers continually have to investigate and reinvestigate their current beliefs and justifications. A knowledge vision therefore gives corporate planners a mental map of three related domains: (1) the world they live in, (2) the world they ought to live in, and (3) the knowledge they should seek and create. We consider each of these domains below.

1. *The knowledge vision should provide a mental map of the world organizational members live in.* This part of the vision is the easiest to understand and develop. It can specify various disciplines (organic and inorganic chemistry, nutritional or medical science), technologies (biotechnology, genomics), and areas of expertise (fermentation, process control, genetic engineering). The purpose of including all three of these scales is to motivate organizational members to think of their activities as part of a larger picture. An engineer in a knowledge-creating company, for example, needs to think about more than the knowledge that affects her daily activities and job position; she should also look for sources of knowledge that can help the company as a whole.

2. *The knowledge vision must include a mental map of the world organizational members ought to live in.* One of the main responsibilities of management is to communicate positive ideas and values, stimulating workers to feel good about their jobs. This second part of the vision should motivate organizational members to trust in the future of the company. A map of the world members ought to live in could include the merging of current disciplines, technologies, and areas of expertise, as well as the emergence of new disciplines, technologies, and areas of expertise. Again, the purpose of including all three scales is to indicate the connections among the world the individual will live in, the technological opportunities available to the organization, and the evolution of society and its possible impact on disciplines like medicine or science.

3. *The knowledge vision should specify what knowledge organizational members need to seek and create.* While the first two parts of the knowledge vision provide images of the present and future, this third domain actually indicates how to move from the present to the future — it offers a road map, so to speak. It might identify streams of knowledge that have to be developed in order to reach the future state. These can cut across disciplines, technologies, organizations, functions, and areas of expertise.

Labeling the streams of knowledge in language easily understood by everyone in the organization is important. For example, Sharp's knowledge vision involves promoting Optoelectronics as a field. Some of this company's knowledge streams are labeled "processing of electronic signals," "accumulation and storage of data," "transmission of electronic signals," and "input/output of electronic signals." At this level, Sharp's knowledge vision makes sense to an engineer working in the area of CD-ROM storage devices (accumulation), a researcher working on optical computers (processing), and a sales representative promoting and selling telecommunications equipment (transmission). The knowledge vision enables them all to see the stream of knowledge to which they contribute, how their stream relates to other streams, and how it may affect the current and future landscape of knowledge at Sharp. Note that in this example the streams are all parallel and do not involve any sequencing or development steps. However, streams of knowledge can also be broken down into finer detail by identifying, for instance, various stocks of knowledge that have to emerge sequentially.

In practice, a company's knowledge vision may take the form of a mission statement, a set of corporate values, a document about management philosophy, or a plan that looks more like a strategic outline. A company's mission statement might include lines about knowledge and thereby act as a knowledge vision. The point is that managers can either articulate a knowledge vision and call it this by name, or they can integrate ideas about knowledge into other corporate statements. Sharp has a written statement it calls a "knowledge vision"; Unilever has incorporated statements about knowledge into its guiding principles, which are repeatedly communicated from the top of the organization. Skandia's Future Center, which we detailed in the last chapter, involves participants in a variety of processes designed not only to spark its advancement strategy but to encourage visionary thinking on a continual basis. Although financial services firms are not known for innovation—a pharmaceutical company, for instance, is more likely to focus specifically on advancement formulations like "invest 18.5 percent of turnover in R&D"—Skandia shows that executives can design advancement strategies even in a conservative business. In such cases, the knowledge vision is almost more of an ongoing process than a written document; it is lived by everyone in the organization rather than formally codified.

THE CRITERIA FOR A GOOD KNOWLEDGE VISION

The next question is what characterizes a good knowledge vision. A vision can be communicated in a number of forms, and there are plenty of corporate mission statements or official philosophies that amount to no more than empty rhetoric. We believe there are at least seven criteria for assessing the quality of a knowledge vision: commitment to a direction, generativity, a specific style, a focus on restructuring the current knowledge system, a focus on restructuring the current task system, external communication of values, and a commitment to shaping competition.

Commitment to a Direction

The knowledge vision requires a strong commitment from top management. Executives should identify themselves with the current landscape of knowledge that the company is operating in, as well as the future landscape they hope for. In broad terms, they should construct the road map, or the way to achieve the knowledge vision, quite carefully. The vision also relies on the commitment of middle-level managers and front-line personnel, which requires a certain stability. If the knowledge vision dramatically changes every two months, organizational members will have a hard time figuring out what knowledge to seek and create.

To achieve a high level of commitment, a knowledge vision must be effectively communicated, a process that may benefit from the use of new technologies. After the merger between Sandoz and Ciba-Geigy in 1997, for instance, the resulting pharmaceutical company Novartis was perhaps the first company in the world to develop a knowledge vision of the life sciences. For this company, "life sciences" means all scientific activity, including creation of biotechnological, toxicological, and manufacturing knowledge, aimed at creating and sustaining life. Its vision basically covered the areas of pharmaceuticals and consumer health. Novartis developed a CD-ROM called "The Science of Life," which depicts its knowledge vision through images, text, and music, and is used to communicate these ideas internally.

Generativity

A knowledge vision should spur new thinking, ideas, phrasing, and actions (von Krogh and Roos, 1997); in short, it should generate new organizational imagination. Jean Paul Sartre suggested that imagination is a departure from the real: "For consciousness to be able to imagine it must be able to escape from the world by its very nature, it must be able by its own efforts to withdraw from the world. In a word, it must be free" (Sartre, 1987, p. 267). The knowledge vision of a company should enable individual members to escape from their current perception of the organization and allow them to think imaginatively about what the organization should and could become. It should help create what Sartre calls "imaginative knowledge" in the organization.

Against this rather fuzzy backdrop, we suggest that the phrases in any written version of the knowledge vision need to be open-ended instead of immediately and directly measurable. Perhaps the knowledge vision could be formulated as a set of broad questions or hypotheses. Keep in mind that the vision should inspire new knowledge creation, which by its very nature is explorative rather than exploitative. It should foster a kind of "directed improvisation" in which members start thinking in new ways about creating their future; again, consider the Skandia Future Center and its brain-stilling exercises.

But it should also generate new ideas about how existing knowledge can be effectively exploited in order to reach the future painted by the knowledge vision. From high commitment comes the wish to apply, utilize, and improve. For example, the knowledge vision should inspire the formulation of concrete learning goals for individuals, groups, and departments.[1] When looking at the vision—where the company is, where it should go, and how it might get there—one may discuss these broad domains operationally, at least for the short to medium term. Individuals, groups, and departments might be encouraged to develop sequential learning goals for their own knowledge creation. In addition, by communicating these learning goals, they can increase the mutual awareness of other colleagues, groups, and departments about what their activities are likely to be over the next few years, as well as how they hope to contribute to the overall knowledge creation of the company.

Specific Style

We find that just as organizations tend to develop their own style for vision statements, they will do the same for knowledge visions. Some select an almost haphazard, bold, creative phrasing—such as "We want to be the world leader in the knowledge area of genomics to create and sustain future and present life"—while others go for more down-to-earth, systematic, concise phrasing—"enabling ubiquitous computing." The choice of style matters, however, and is too often neglected by management. The discussion and group negotiating that goes into designing a knowledge vision can take a substantial amount of time, but the actual phrasing is often left to the very end. A junior assistant may be chosen almost at random to turn all that work into a couple of readable phrases, and the result is the empty rhetoric mentioned above or, even worse, a stylistic clash with the values and practices of the organization.

It is possible to buy standardized vision or value statements—plenty are available via mail order—but we would never recommend doing so. Such posters or banners may have great slogans, but they will have little to do with the identity of a particular company. We believe managers would do well to pay attention to the distinct style of their organizations and make sure the documented vision reflects that style.

Any text designed for public consumption, whether it is a marketing slogan, instruction manual, or novel, will create a response. The trick is to come up with text that elicits the response you want. Vision statements need to maintain a balance between generativity and clear direction. The phrases in a knowledge vision should be in tune with other messages from the organization in order to fulfill the expectations of everyone involved. Last, the means of communication should match the style. Perhaps an innovative knowledge vision, rather than being presented in traditional text, will be better served by a video showing possible technological developments, a CD-ROM, or a series of workshops in which the vision is repeatedly discussed and reinforced.

Focus on Restructuring the Current Knowledge System

When it comes to using organizational knowledge effectively, members need a push in the right direction. By this, we mean that the knowledge vision should extend beyond the experience gained through past successes. It might, for example, provide a new interpretation of the strategic history of the company. In looking at a pattern of divestitures, mergers, acquisitions, and alliances over time, the vision might focus particularly on what knowledge was gained through these strategic actions. Take biotechnology knowledge acquired through strategic alliances with universities and entrepreneurial companies. A good knowledge vision might put this into context by suggesting that this knowledge will contribute to the overall development of foods that have healing effects—a new product area for the company.

Focus on Restructuring the Current Task System

While the knowledge vision may help the company to rearrange knowledge in new ways, or to interpret its history of knowledge seeking and creation differently, it should also indicate where the company needs to change how such work gets done.[2] To apply new and existing knowledge to a new business, the knowledge vision should indicate the consequences of value-creating tasks. At some point, it needs to incorporate answers to a number of questions: Should the organization discard some of its current key tasks? What new tasks in manufacturing, marketing and sales, R&D, logistics, and administration should be designed for the future? In particular, restructuring the existing knowledge system has to be related to innovative tasks. It requires a new approach to innovation, one in which participants from various functional areas in the organization participate (Souder, 1987). For instance, an insurance company might provide better "lifestyles" consulting to private clients. Marketers could combine their knowledge of promoting these initiatives with insurance mathematicians' knowledge of the risks associated with an unhealthy lifestyle.

External Communication of Values

A knowledge vision should communicate to all stakeholders what kind of knowledge (and hence value) the company will be seeking. This kind of signaling behavior will open new opportunities. The company may attract talent from many countries and disciplines, alliance partners from various industries and locations, new technologies, or new and innovative sources of finance. The vision can also signal to suppliers and customers what they should expect from the company over a longer time frame, and how they might contribute. They should come to view the company as a knowledgeable partner for the future, or as a knowledge source that contributes to their own survival.

External communication with stakeholders is likely to reach competitors, instigating a different reaction. Some will reposition themselves, developing alternative visions, or even no knowledge vision at all. But others will imitate a good knowledge vision and figure out their own ways to use it for knowledge creation. While Novartis may have been the first to embark on a life-sciences vision, others like Hoechst and Monsanto have followed. But such imitation should not be a cause for alarm. It should be clear by now that knowledge is much more than the explicit ideas captured in a few phrases. A major portion of knowledge creation will be tacit, as is the road (as well as parts of the road map) to realizing future knowledge. Perhaps the winner's vision will most speedily and effectively generate new knowledge creation by inspiring organizational members to pursue their learning goals consistently.

Commitment to Shaping Competitiveness

The acid test for any knowledge vision is whether it helps the company keep its competitive edge. Not only must the vision help a firm to allocate resources for the creation of knowledge in important areas of future business; it should also inspire current knowledge creation so that the process is faster and more productive than competitors' efforts. Moreover, if the phrasing of a knowledge vision is open-ended enough, it will be better able to shift with and adapt to competitive dynamics. If competitors make too much progress in one discipline or technology, the company may need to do more intensive knowledge creation in similar areas, with more effective knowledge transfer, and to allocate resources accordingly. Alternatively, executives may need to reallocate resources for knowledge creation in different areas.

THE AYURA STORY:
NEW BUSINESS CHALLENGES CALL FOR NEW IDEAS

Shifting competitive dynamics certainly influenced knowledge creation at the Japanese cosmetics company Shiseido, leading to an entirely new brand. In the messy real world, a firm may not spell out all three domains in its knowledge vision, or adhere to every one of the criteria for a good vision. But a successful approach to the future almost always balances a firm's present business situation with future goals. To illustrate, we have analyzed Shiseido's development of the Ayura brand. The company's history, present business conditions, and its vision of how cosmetic concepts should evolve all played a part in this story.[3]

The Shiseido Company was founded in 1872 by Yushin Fukuhara, who had been a head pharmacist in the Japanese navy. He opened the first Western-style pharmacy in Japan, which was located in the bustling Ginza district of Tokyo. From the first, Yushin Fukuhara wanted to introduce the latest Western medical practices to Japan. While the country underwent the transition from samurai feudalism to civilized modern state, his vision of a modern pharmaceutical concern became an instant success. The Shiseido pharmacy introduced Japan's first toothpaste as well as its first soda fountain. Shortly before 1900, it began introducing its own brand of cosmetics, just as Western pharmacies did; Shiseido's first skin lotion, Eudermine, is still on sale today.

This Western influence on Shiseido intensified under Shinzo Fukuhara, Yushin's son. He earned a degree in pharmacology at Columbia University and worked as an industrial chemist in New York. When Shinzo returned to Japan, he recognized the potential of developing Shiseido's cosmetics business. By 1915, cosmetics had replaced pharmaceuticals as the core product of the company. Shinzo's technical skills—and the aesthetic sensibility that made him one of the best photographers of his day—were a better match for the cosmetics business than running a pharmacy. In addition to the technology required to manufacture a variety of skin care, makeup, and fragrance products, Shiseido introduced American marketing and promotional concepts to Japan just after World War I. Shinzo implemented artistic advertising for Shiseido products, through which many Japanese of the time first encountered Art Nouveau and Art Deco designs. Because he believed corporations should take an active role in collecting art, he even opened a gallery in the Shiscido headquarters building in Tokyo.

In 1927, Shiseido was incorporated as a joint-stock company, with Shinzo Fukuhara appointed its first president. Under his leadership, Shiseido introduced many aspects of Western culture to Japan, but the fusion of complementary cultures — Eastern spirit and Western sophistication — always lay at the core of its corporate values. From its founding to today, Shiseido has tried to meet the highest standards not only of technology and quality but also of aesthetics and creativity. In the Japanese market, Shiseido offers an array of makeup and skin-care products, toiletries, professional beauty salon products, pharmaceuticals, foodstuffs, high-quality chemicals, and fashion goods. In the global market, Shiseido currently has operations in more than fifty countries and manufactures exclusive fragrances and skin- and hair-care products. In fiscal year 1998, consolidated net sales advanced to $5.1 billion, and the net income was $87.5 million.[4]

Shiseido's research facilities are equally impressive. Since its first facility was established in 1939, the company's research centers have grown until there are now laboratories in seven fields: basic research, life sciences, pharmacological science, innovative products, pharmaceuticals, advanced skin research, and safety and analysis. In both scale and quality, these facilities are unrivaled within the cosmetics industry. In addition, Shiseido's Institute of Beauty Science opened in 1953 to foster a more holistic approach to R&D, one that encompasses the mind, body, and skin. Its role, in effect, has been to research cosmetics from the standpoint of the end user. Shiseido's R&D activities expanded globally with the opening of a European Techno-Center in Paris in 1988 and another in Connecticut in 1989. During the same period, the company jointly helped to create the Massachusetts General Hospital/Harvard Cutaneous Biology Research Center, the world's first comprehensive facility dedicated to basic dermatological research.

Yet despite continuing profitability and state-of-the-art R&D, Shiseido confronted serious business challenges in the late 1980s. After the sudden death of the preceding president, Yoshiharu Fukuhara, grandson of the company's founder, assumed office in July 1987. At that time, Shiseido proudly maintained its number-one position in Japan, with a 30 percent share of the domestic market. However, that share fell over the next few years as the company grappled with an increasingly harsh external environment. For one thing, none of the major cosmetic makers, including Shiseido, were adequately responding to contemporary women's skin concerns. The number of brands and products available from each company rose steadily as cosmetics became more complicated and specialized. The different functions of products were often unclear, and many kept changing or were discontinued. In addition, customers were flooded with makeup information through magazines and television, leaving them confused.

An increasing number of consumers turned to cosmetic manufacturers that developed and offered alternative products, such as the Body Shop. Companies that advertised "all-natural" makeup with no synthetic additives began gradually eroding Shiseido's market share. Because the growth in new cosmetic products countered Shiseido's basic conception and vision—that is, sophisticated products created through Western technologies and a scientific approach to beauty—the company found itself out of step with the business times. Shiseido's cosmetic philosophy had become outdated; at the very least, it did not have as much support as in the past, which prompted top executives to use the technical research base at their disposal to develop a new brand.

The Formation of a Cabinet

In 1993, development of the new Shiseido brand, called Labo (short for "laboratory"), commenced, and a "cabinet" was organized to smooth the way. The cabinet was a cross-divisional project team that had a "prime minister" (Yoshiharu Fukuhara) and eight other members who were the heads of various departments (marketing, design, product planning, management, production, R&D, and beauty-science R&D). In addition to the participation of Shiseido's top executives, the cabinet was supported by a total working staff of forty-five people, including many young members. The development of the new Labo brand advanced with the collaboration of the cabinet and the working staff. The results of staff discussions (particularly disagreements or unresolved issues) were raised with the cabinet and reconsidered there.

This kind of participatory system for new product development had not been seen before at Shiseido and was adopted to ensure that the product concept was clearly reflected in the final product. This in itself reflected a new strategic approach and a shift in vision. In the past, product development had followed a sequential process of planning, research and development, package design, factory activities, and trial manufacture. The drawback of the old system was that lack of communication regarding technological complexities and interdepartment activities led to an improper reflection of the initial concept in the final product. Structural boundaries between departments impeded effective communication across them and thus negatively influenced organizational knowledge creation.

Setbacks and the Search for a New Concept

The first proposed concept for the Labo brand was "from chaos to cosmos: a peaceful alternative for the skin and mind." According to this concept, the mission of the Labo brand was to release "customers' skin and minds from the chaotic situation characterized by dissatisfaction with confusing cosmetics and the lack of confidence in manufacturers, thereby allowing customers to realize a true sense of peace in their cosmetic routine." High-flown as this description may sound, it encapsulates the idea that a radical reconsideration of past knowledge about skin care was necessary. The researchers' first ideas centered around transforming skin through purification and strengthening rather than the old emphasis on basic care and beautification of normal skin. In accordance with this concept, ideas for purifying and strengthening products (cleansers and lotions) were offered to the cabinet. The image and positioning of these products inclined more toward that of medical goods than cosmetics; hence, these proposed cosmetic treatments were referred to as "cosmeceuticals."

However, there was nothing innovative about this concept. Our quick summary of Shiseido's history indicates that the company had envisioned cosmeceuticals from the very beginning. The cabinet and staff workers went back to the drawing board in search of another idea. The fact that other companies were emphasizing the natural element suggested to Shiseido executives that they should strengthen the company's position in this area. Accordingly, the cabinet decided to merge the cosmeceutical idea with that of "natural therapy." Although this was not an original concept for cosmetics per se, it constituted a new approach for Shiseido.

Note that opinions regarding this concept varied significantly among cabinet members. Those involved in beauty-science R&D were used to incorporating Eastern ideas into their work, and they understood the natural therapy concept quite easily; but general researchers, who were more technical and used to a rational scientific approach, were initially resistant. In this case, previous knowledge and the mind-sets closely related to that knowledge influenced the interpretation and acceptance of a new concept. The cabinet's challenge was to make sure that such resistance did not undermine the very real need for Shiseido to create an innovative brand.

From Modern Times to Postmodernism

Since the 1970s, discussions of postmodernism have become popular in many circles. Yet in the cosmetics world, past values continue to dominate. Shiseido's original vision of modern science and Western beauty practices was closely linked to Japan's own history of modernization. Shiseido actively looked to Western Europe, particularly France, to integrate European methods with its Japanese elements, and Shiseido products became a symbol of modernity. However, the current postindustrial world has exposed the limits of modern rationalization. Values constructed during the twentieth century are collapsing, and as we face the twenty-first, a new system of values has come into play.

In their effort to maintain Shiseido's dominant status, the cabinet and working staff members became conscious of the need to shift with the postmodern times. In January 1994, at the fifth meeting of the cabinet, a new concept was unveiled to counter the limitations of modern practice. This was phrased as "taking an Eastern holistic approach to life-force cosmetics." The Eastern ideas and culture that formed the basis of this new brand constituted a significant shift for Shiseido cosmetics, which had, until that time, looked to modern Europe.

The new brand image was based on the fundamental philosophy of Eastern medicine, in which the skin, body, and mind are all central. Rather than selling products as drugs or "hardware" for the skin, the new brand would promote a range of "life cosmetics." In other words, skin issues could not be isolated as such; they were the concern of the whole person and affected by one's overall nutrition and health, mental state, even spiritual concerns. Instead of applying remedial treatment for poor skin, attention was directed at improving the quality of skin through holistic care. The cabinet and working staff studied the quest for harmony and balance represented by Eastern sources, and after a number of philosophical discussions, they merged these ideas with ultramodern technology. The result: a new brand called Ayura.

Shiseido's Ultimate Success

In March 1995, Ayura was launched. The brand was named for *ayus*, the Hindu word for life. In addition, the "A" of Ayura represents a person in Chinese characters, while "Y" symbolizes a developing bud. For Shiseido's marketers, Ayura's logo represents an unexpected encounter between two people and the success that may be achieved through mutual cooperation. The brand symbol shows the germination of one seed, a growing branch, and an expanding root, which in due time will become the tree of life (see Figure 5.1). In accordance with the life-cosmetics concept, yellow was selected for the Ayura logo because it is the color of the sun—the source of all things.

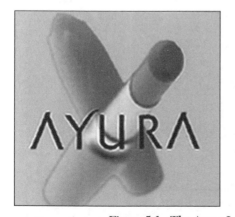

Figure 5.1. The Ayura Logo and Brand Symbol

The Ayura branding campaign included a unique "beauty routine." This encompasses practices previously not considered for skin care, such as breathing methods, meditation, circulatory massage, and acupressure. It is also worth noting that the Shiseido name did not appear anywhere on Ayura's product packaging. Shiseido's traditional product image contradicted the postmodern positioning intended for the Ayura brand. The cabinet and working staff members recognized the limits of brand diversification within Shiseido's modern (that is, old-fashioned) culture, and they envisioned a different future for Ayura products.

For the most part, they have succeeded. As we discussed in Chapter 3, the number of shops stocking Ayura products was initially restricted to three department stores for a trial period of one year. Through an alternative consultation approach at sales counters—one that does not force sales of cosmetics on customers—Ayura became increasingly popular at the trial stores and gained name recognition. For this brand, three important marketing strategies were employed: interaction (customer consultation and information exchange); retention (continuous development of good customer relations); and evolution (reflection on customer comments and continued attention to the evolution of products and services). In the vision represented by Ayura, activity regarding new cosmetics knowledge is not one-sided; it involves the mutual cooperation of producers and consumers, and entails two-way education to help improve the products.

In addition, the kind of individual beauty consultations advocated at Ayura counters provide an opportunity for the company to obtain tacit knowledge about what customers want as well as the condition of their skin. In fact, you could say that individual tacit knowledge about skin can come only through direct interaction and intuitive insight. More to the business point, although the company implemented an innovative alternative to forced sales and "scientific" skin analysis, there were practical reasons that Shiseido wanted to maintain the consultation system that already existed at many cosmetics counters. A 1996 *Nikkei Business* article argued that Shiseido's refusal to forgo the counseling system, along with its own consultation sales method, are both tied to the stability of value and high profit potential derived from such practices.[5]

Even though Ayura products proved extremely popular, Shiseido avoided a sudden increase in the number of stores stocking the products. It opted to take its time in expanding in order to nurture the brand's position and relationships with customers. In September 1996, twenty stores were selling Ayura products in Japan; that number had increased to 135 stores by March 1999. Of course, the fact that Shiseido has promoted the Ayura brand does not mean the company's knowledge vision has become entirely postmodern. The Ayura brand development has been Shiseido's only attempt at incorporating such alternative product ideas into its strategies. But while the results are not complete—knowledge visions at any forward-looking company are always evolving—there are some indications that the life-cosmetics vision has begun to filter into other R&D proposals at Shiseido.[6]

When a new system of values emerges, or when the way knowledge ought to be is questioned, a shift in vision becomes essential for those who pursue knowledge. Without continually questioning your own impression of how things ought to be, it is impossible to exceed the bounds of current knowledge. For those who become complacent in their triumph over the modern knowledge realms of science and technology, painful self-denial may first occur when confronted with the "irrational" challenges of today's global marketplace. This was evident when the Ayura cabinet and working staff grappled with Eastern concepts to arrive at new knowledge, a process they described as "the decoding of a code." Whether deciphering the Ayura code will cause changes at Shiseido or provoke a response among those not involved, this brand became a success because participants managed to break through organizational and individual barriers. Ironically, they ended up blending Western and Eastern values—a combination that was based as much on the original vision of the company as its postmodern future.

MANAGEMENT APPROACHES: THE 360° PROCESS

While our definition of a knowledge vision and the criteria for a good vision are generic, the process of instilling such a vision can vary substantially from company to company. The Ayura story makes clear how much the particular identity and business conditions of a firm determine the style of any resulting knowledge vision, as well as whether that vision will be applied to specific projects or become more pervasive. The key distinguishing factor is where the knowledge vision resides in a company.

At least four different management approaches can be identified: top-down visionaries, expert visionaries, distributed visionaries, and 360° visionaries. In the first company category, *top-down visionaries*, the knowledge vision is instilled by top managers; alternatively, a knowledge officer acting on their behalf formulates the areas of knowledge the company should seek out in the future. The advantage here is speed and efficiency; a knowledge vision will be ready for implementation quickly. The disadvantage is the limited view of the future often held by top management, which may result in the omission of key knowledge areas. Moreover, since the vision is imposed from above, understanding and commitment among middle-level managers and lower organizational ranks can be weak or very mixed. Some people will embrace the vision, while others may starkly reject any proposed effort in which they had no say.

The second group of companies, *expert visionaries*, assign a corporate technology department, R&D department or committee, or any similar body the task of formulating their own knowledge vision and then communicating it throughout the company. Shiseido essentially took this approach for the development of Ayura, although the new brand received a definite push from top management. The advantage is that the knowledge vision will be closely allied with the research expertise, research activities, and core technologies of the company. It will be solidly grounded in the appropriate research disciplines, perhaps with some cross-functional elements related to manufacturing, marketing, and distribution. The disadvantage is that the vision will probably contain a narrower view of the company's knowledge in areas that are not technical or research-oriented. Such a knowledge vision may function well for an R&D department—or for the marketers involved in a branding campaign like Ayura—but it will not push for the full utilization of knowledge potential in the rest of the organization. Again, the current uncertainty at Shiseido about whether the new product-development process for Ayura will extend to other areas of the company indicates the limitations of this approach.

A third group of companies, *distributed visionaries*, allow various groups, departments, and even individuals to develop their own knowledge visions. The advantage to this approach is that the visions will be closely connected to current knowledge and employee activities; they are more likely to inspire a high level of commitment and understanding among organizational members—as far as they go. The disadvantage is obviously a clear lack of coordination among the many visions that may exist at a company, which can result in an overall lack of direction for knowledge-creation efforts.

Finally, there are the companies we have chosen to call 360° *visionaries*, the ones we believe might have the best chance of creating a knowledge vision that will satisfy all the criteria outlined above. Skandia and Phonak come close to a 360° approach in their strategic and visionary efforts. Such companies recognize knowledge creation as an overall organizational activity, not just something that resides in research and development. Visionaries represent the full circle, or 360 degrees, of knowledge at a company; they include every organizational level when creating a knowledge vision, moving laterally, horizontally, and all the way around. Since the process concerns the cognition of individual organizational members, instilling a knowledge vision will inevitably elicit emotional responses. Negative emotions can pose a serious threat if people are not involved in the process, yet tapping positive feelings can get members to commit themselves more wholeheartedly. Good knowledge visions require coordination to have a significant impact on future business. Therefore, people from various layers, functions, and departments need to involve themselves in the vision process.

ACHIEVING A 360° VISION: FIVE MANAGEMENT ACTIONS

Now that we have identified the 360° approach, how does a company begin instilling a good knowledge vision? Including every bit of a firm's knowledge potential sounds good, but this is obviously the most difficult of management approaches. A 360° knowledge vision may evolve over time, and for practical reasons it may begin with one of the other approaches — such as an expert or distributed visionary effort — sometimes a necessary stop before a company can come full circle. Shiseido, in time, may indeed arrive at a full knowledge vision or enabling context. Still, there are some definite steps managers can take to help their companies become 360° visionaries. We describe five useful management actions next.

Management Action 1: Identify and gather participants, and organize the process. Peter Senge (1990) suggests that leaders need to ask for support from organizational members in developing any vision of the future. Start by selecting people from various microcommunities, departments, and levels of the organization. Allow these groups to have strategic conversations in which they explore issues with unlimited scope and impact, just as Skandia's future teams did. These conversations often become the primary source for a knowledge vision. Then gather these preliminary proposals and discuss them in a "vision committee" composed of select top executives and other company representatives, something like Shiseido's cabinet. The vision committee acts as the main coordinating body, the one that ensures convergence of what may be very divergent proposals. As with Shiseido's cabinet, provide feedback from the committee to the larger group of participants and allow them to reflect on it.

Be sensitive to differences in opinion that will surface among various microcommunities, departments, or other groups during this process. They all represent a history of knowing, which has been shaped by their history of competent task performance; Shiseido's "hard" research scientists, for example, had backgrounds that emphasized technical expertise and rationality, which made them resist more holistic ideas. In any case, all participants will bring various expectations for the future to the table. Understanding where different microcommunities are coming from, what factors shape their beliefs about the future, and what types of knowledge may be important for future business is an essential part of the vision process.

To a large extent, beliefs about the future will be tacit, often in the form of hunches or intuition. Therefore, all participants in the vision process, including top executives, must make a commitment to dwelling in the tacit assumptions of others. As we emphasized in Chapter 3, indwelling relies on a high level of care in the organization, as do strategic conversations and the relationships formed in microcommunities. Indwelling helps unleash the sort of tacit knowledge— emotional, intuitive, creative—that underpins any effective knowledge vision.

Management Action 2: Build a common understanding among participants of what a knowledge vision is and the seven criteria for a good one. To reiterate, the seven criteria for a good knowledge vision are (1) commitment to a direction, (2) generativity, (3) a specific style, (4) a focus on restructuring the current knowledge system, (5) a focus on restructuring the current task system, (6) external communication of values, and (7) commitment to shaping competitveness. The key here is to create a common vocabulary. When Shiseido's cabinet and working staff started discussing new product concepts, they went through several phases of honing the language used to describe concepts—from "cosmeceutical" to "new super natural cosmetics dealt with by high-tech" to "Eastern life-force cosmetics." The Ayura participants called these phrases "key words," and the search for a common vocabulary to express the new product concept drove much of the process.

In knowledge-enabling terms, of course, this process requires management. An uncontrolled explosion of concepts, words, theories, and methods can stifle the vision process rather than expand it. A good place to begin is by developing a vision map with participants based on the three main domains of a knowledge vision. The map can identify generic areas such as "technology" and "society" that may affect a company's future business and provide answers to the following questions: What is the world we live in? What is the world we ought to live in? What knowledge should we seek and create? Table 5.1 provides an example of how a hypothetical management group at a computer company might proceed. As a starting point, the reader might try to fill out the following matrix for himself. Use

Table 5.1. A Sample Vision Map

Questions	Technology	Society	Culture	Political and Legal Norms	Economy
What is the World We Live in?					
What is the World We Ought to Live in?					
What Knowledge Should We Seek and Create?					

this map actively in the knowledge-vision process to identify areas in which the three questions should be asked. Organize discussions around the map, and let participants think freely about these elements.

Management Action 3: Write up and use narratives of the future as platforms for the vision process. While the vision concerns the total company specifically, narratives can become "mental maps of the future,"[7] covering several broad factors like technology, social and demographic structures, political systems, legislation, the economy, or the environment. Consider the future dramas that Skandia's future teams scripted for professional actors. Then there are the stories from Statoil, the Norwegian oil company, of what would happen if alternative energy sources became socially acceptable and economically feasible, stories that this company developed in the early 1990s. They require ample consideration of knowledge development: What sources of new knowledge for alternative energy sources are available? What developments are likely to occur in exploitation technologies that would make oil and gas production even cheaper? What are the technical hurdles likely to slow down the development of new technologies?

In general, a narrative of the future should have a fairly simple structure: (1) it begins with a description of the current situation concerning knowledge in society, the economy, or in a specific discipline; (2) it lays out the forces pushing for new knowledge development in various directions (societal, political, economic); (3) it indicates future events, developments, and trends that the story's main players can see; (4) it provides rationales for these forces and discusses the plausibility of various events, developments, or trends; (5) it concludes with what an audience might expect to experience in five or ten years. In the future drama in chapter 4 about Europe's insurance market, a family's future relationship with their insurance company was illustrated: The twenty-year-old daughter got assistance in making plans for her retirement, the father benefited from a competence insurance program, and the mother took advantage if the car insurance service.

Based on these stories, any vision process might unfold.[8] The main questions would be these: What if the future state happens? How should our company be positioned with respect to knowledge? How do we achieve that position? What knowledge do we need to seek and create? The narration is a way to break the vision process free from a narrow focus on past wisdom; strategic conversations that are open, coupled with creative writing, are essential for the process. Because discussions about the future can be hampered by current concerns, personal interests, and micropolitical games, some companies have chosen to rely on outside experts or consultants—supplier representatives, university researchers, customers, even philosophers or economists—to spark new narratives of the future. These experts can bring in a fresh view, one that is uninhibited by corporate mental traps and unquestioned wisdom.

Management Action 4: Allow ample time for instilling a vision. Allowing sufficient time is perhaps the most important point, but it is basically a passive action that involves waiting, holding back, letting the process take its course. Instilling a knowledge vision should not be a managerial "hobby" or simply another job that has to be carried out under the burden of tremendous operational stress. Allow the necessary time and resources for open conversations and broad active participation. Do not push for closure, but keep conversation about the future going at several levels throughout the year. We believe it would be a mistake to set a deadline for a knowledge vision. If participants push to reach that deadline, the company may end up with a static vision that will soon become obsolete. In addition, the underlying narrative behind the vision must be continually updated with respect to validity—does the narrative still hold?—and reliability—to what extent are these images of the future still plausible?

Management Action 5: Consider the knowledge-vision process a learning process. At the heart of instilling a knowledge vision is learning. This process can achieve mutual understanding about future expectations for the business environment and the company among a wide variety of microcommunities and departments. The process helps to put issues, concerns, and possibilities on the managerial agenda. It should become a vehicle for helping the company to learn more about itself. More precisely, through the process, managers can learn about the "horizon of expectations" the audience for the knowledge vision will have.[9] The communication of a vision statement will lead to various reactions, some overly positive, others skeptical, still others neutral or focused on the status quo. These reactions will tell management and the vision committee something about what the organization as a whole truly expects of the future. These reactions, in turn, can be incorporated into a gradual revision of the knowledge vision—hence, our use of "instilling a knowledge vision" as the description of this enabling process rather than just referring to a knowledge vision as the desired endpoint.[10]

In addition, the vision process will explore potential patterns of knowledge development that participants may believe in but cannot be sure of. As the discovery of the future proceeds, the knowledge vision and its underlying narratives will be put to the test. An organization cannot wait to compare its narratives with the emerging future, and it cannot wait to realize the knowledge vision under future conditions. The company must proceed, full steam ahead, using the vision as a road map or navigational chart.

Last, the vision process itself must be learned. Conversations about the future require careful mastery (von Krogh and Roos, 1996d), and the process of instilling a knowledge vision should incorporate learning along those lines. What behavior enables conversations about the future and what is detrimental? What rules should a conversation follow? Once again, strategic conversations play an important role in developing a vision, as well as in getting as many people as possible to accept it. In the next chapter, which focuses on managing conversations, we return to this point.

PITFALLS IN THE KNOWLEDGE-VISION PROCESS

As with any process that involves many participants and organizational levels, instilling a knowledge vision is prone to pitfalls. For one thing, the resulting vision may be only cursory and not representative. At the same time, too much generativity can lead to chaos. The knowledge vision needs to be finely tuned but broadly discussed during the 360° process and experimentally tested in the organization.

Another problem involves fluid styles and too many messages from top managers. Do not overburden your organization with eloquent messages about the future. Attention spans within any busy organization are limited, and the knowledge vision has to compete for this attention in the midst of all sorts of other corporate and public messages. Select messages that will satisfy the criteria outlined above, but also communicate the essentials of the knowledge-vision process, its organization, and timing.

The final pitfall of note is lack of openness to serendipity. Rigid knowledge visions can block perception of unexpected technological discoveries, unexpected events that may affect development of a particular stream of knowledge—especially a crisis that may blow up out of the blue—and unexpected exit or entry of expertise in the organization. To remedy this problem, keep the knowledge vision open and flexible, and make the process one of feedback and learning.

Consider the issue of search costs from this angle. As an organization grows in size, the cost of searching for knowledge to solve an ad hoc assignment or a repeated task becomes increasingly problematic. One of the main goals of a knowledge-management approach is to reduce these costs, of course. In doing so, managers may create a more responsive, agile, and effective organization; coupling tasks with knowledge at a minimal cost may even represent a source of competitive advantage in some industries, where incumbent competitors are large. But a strict approach to search costs also has the limitations inherent in knowledge management: an overly quantitative emphasis, a focus on present business conditions, a narrow view of the future.

From a knowledge-enabling perspective, search costs are the total costs incurred by an organization's efforts to get individual members or a group to act effectively. Thus, the total search costs (TSC) have the following components:

$$TSC = DSC + ISC + KSC$$

where

DSC = data search costs
ISC = information search costs
KSC = knowledge search costs

Lest number-crunchers get too excited, however, let us caution that this is not an exact mathematical formula. Rather, it is simply another method for thinking about the cost of digging into knowledge. In these terms, human cognition is a value-creating activity in which new data are selected (such as a price trend) and related to existing data (other trends), and new information is created by putting it in context ("the combined trends represent a danger to our profitability"). Information, in turn, is combined with experiences, motivations, emotions, aspirations, and hopes to create knowledge. Knowledge enables the person or a group to act ("we will increase our efforts to gain bargaining power over customers by acquiring a competitor"). Therefore, it would be wrong to calculate only the cost of locating data in the organization. The total search cost has to cover each step, from identifying the data source to enabling a person or group to act on a task. Not only do you have to calculate the cost of collating data, putting it in context, and identifying its significance, but you also have to account for how new information will be acted on in the local context of an organizational member or group.

Now, to reduce the total search cost, three requirements have to be fulfilled. First, existing data and information have to be made visible by establishing categories of expertise, documents, databases, procedures, routines, and lists of individual organizational members or groups that can fill them. Second, a knowledge infrastructure has to be established that is accessible to a high number of potential users. If search costs are to be kept low, this infrastructure has to be easy to use. Third, the TCS can only be recouped insofar as the knowledge is available to solve a value-creating task, such as conducting work on a technical installation for the customer. Hence, knowledge management generally involves some sort of inventory management for the information available. Such inventory management indicates the stock of information, where it exists, and the experts who know how to use it for relevant tasks. This implies a need for stable categories—data and expertise have to be categorized in ways that a user of knowledge can immediately understand—and it is precisely here that the danger lies.

In the worst-case scenario, the only knowledge that will matter is the knowledge that can be searched for within an existing infrastructure. In other words, only knowledge that can take an explicit form is recognized. This can make the organization a prisoner of orthodoxy and entirely closed to serendipity. Existing information that can be categorized will be favored over new information and knowledge that is difficult to pigeonhole. Unless the knowledge infrastructure is highly dynamic—which means its maintenance and search costs will inevitably go up—the new seeds of information, knowledge, and innovation will not become visible to the company.

Rather than just investing in information technology (IT) solutions that may potentially facilitate the reduction of search costs (the DSC and ISC of our formula), management should invest in building relational values among organizational members. Only through good relations can the sharing of tacit knowledge happen, making such knowledge available to a larger group of people and creating an overall enabling context. When relationships are strong and positive, organizational members will actively seek out areas in which their knowledge and expertise are needed, thereby contributing to the reduction of total search costs; but if care is low in the organization, no infrastructure or sophisticated computer network will make knowledge freely available.

The main problem with an overly controlled approach to search costs—or instilling a knowledge vision, for that matter—is not really the need to make information or knowledge visible, or to establish a knowledge infrastructure, or to use an inventory system, or the application of information technology; it has more to do with a lack of appreciation for the highly dynamic nature of knowledge creation. As part of the human condition, knowledge creation fosters constant, incremental changes. That means the categories that meaningfully capture a company's knowledge have to change, too.

EXPECTING THE UNEXPECTED

The main hurdle for any vision exercise is that the future is unpredictable. In particular, knowledge has qualities that make accurate prediction of how it will evolve highly unlikely. Nevertheless, instilling a knowledge vision is a process that can enable organizational members to expect the unexpected. Despite the dynamic nature of knowledge creation and the importance of serendipity, it does help to think through the future in a structured manner. It is better to envision possible threats and opportunities than to hide from what may happen.

Instilling a knowledge vision will also be related to the other enabling processes. For instance, managing conversations will encourage open-ended thinking and a higher level of care in the organization, both of which are necessary for becoming a 360° visionary. Mobilizing knowledge activists will provide some overall direction for knowledge-creation initiatives. And creating the right context by choosing an appropriate organizational structure will help dismantle organizational barriers, as will globalizing local knowledge.

To improve knowledge creation at your company, you might consider starting with instilling a knowledge vision. Yet keep in mind that the vision must be flexible enough to allow for the new insights that will inevitably flow from local initiatives. The general law of knowledge unpredictability is bound to hold for your own organization, and you should not neglect interesting developments by clinging to a tightly defined knowledge vision. In the next chapter, we focus on one of the most basic ways to encourage knowledge flow: Getting people to talk to one another.

.6.

ENABLER 2

Manage Conversations

*Nor do I converse only with those who pay; but any one,
whether he be rich or poor, may ask and answer me and
listen to my words.*

— Socrates in Plato's "Apology"

The most natural and commonplace of human activities—conversations—often end up in the background of managerial discussions about knowledge. It is quite ironic that while executives and knowledge officers persist in focusing on expensive information-technology systems, quantifiable databases, and measurement tools, one of the best means for sharing and creating knowledge already exists within their companies. We cannot emphasize enough the important part conversations play. Good conversations are the cradle of social knowledge in any organization. Through extended discussions, which can encompass personal flights of fancy as well as careful expositions of ideas, individual knowledge is turned into themes available for others. Each participant can explore new ideas and reflect on other people's viewpoints. And the mutual exchange of ideas, viewpoints, and beliefs that conversations entail allows for the first and most essential step of knowledge creation: sharing tacit knowledge within a microcommunity.

Consider, for just a moment, the power of conversations. You can connect your ideas to those of other participants, experiencing how some ideas take on a life of their own. One person's comment about the difficulty of using the Internet, for instance, may lead to an extended group discussion that results in a new concept for a user-friendly interface. Forget who originally "owned" the idea or where it came from; community members provide the energy for an evolutionary process in which loosely formulated ideas turn into concepts, concepts are justified and turned into prototypes, and these may ultimately turn into innovative products and services. In other words, to *manage conversations*, our second knowledge enabler, affects not only tacit-knowledge sharing but all the other phases of the knowledge-creation process.

In productive microcommunities, conversations can unleash the creative powers of individual participants and fuel knowledge creation beyond the capacities of a single mind (Galvin, 1996). Occasionally, as an interesting conversation unfolds, the distinction between the self and the group vanishes. You become absorbed in the themes discussed, and the good of the group drives your participation, not just your personal agenda, interests, or beliefs. This kind of conversation will take on a different rhythm: Each contribution will lose its personal aspect, as all participants start identifying with the themes discussed. Beyond the purpose of sharing individual knowledge, such lively conversations lead to new shared insights that everyone involved owns.

Indeed, the birth of Western philosophical thought occurred through ancient Greek conversations in the form of dialogues. Texts by Aristotle and Plato are often accounts of conversations among philosophers representing various viewpoints. Lengthy conversations about beauty, friendship, death, and other timeless topics, along with arguments and counterarguments, are presented to the reader. The whole process of knowledge creation is laid open and can be inspected by those who want to understand the evolution of such themes. Take, for example Plato's masterpiece, the "Gorgias" dialogue, in which he analyzes the roles and functions of rhetoric in politics and society. Rhetoric is the art of speech that has a convincing nature. Plato imagines a dialogue between the master of rhetoric, Gorgias, the philosopher Socrates, the young and ambitious aristocrat Callicles, Socrates' friend Chaerophon, and the young orator and writer Polus. Through the dialogue, in which Socrates poses several questions and raises issues from a philosophical perspective, it becomes clear that rhetoric has a strong ethical side. A convincing rhetorician must be good and just in order to do no harm. The tension between Gorgias, the defender of rhetoric, and Socrates produces insights into the main theme. For the reader, the Socratic method of questioning reveals the virtues and weaknesses of rhetoric as a discipline.

In contemporary business settings, conversations are still an arena (or modern-day agora) for creating social knowledge. For one thing, they help coordinate individual actions and insights. Outlining a new strategy, crafting a knowledge vision, and justifying beliefs about the business success of a new product all require talking to other people. For another, conversations function as a mirror for participants. When a group finds individual behavior unacceptable, they will mirror their reaction through body language, corrective comments, and so forth. Just as the ideas being discussed evolve, so do the rules for conducting conversations. Good conversation requires the right pacing and etiquette to achieve the kind of mutual insights discussed above. In his dialogues, Plato certainly represented Socrates as a skillful conversation manager. If his followers had all talked at once or been consistently rude, few ideas about the nature of society or morality would have been generated or would still be worth discussing today.

Yet conversational skills often seem like a lost art in current management circles. Even if conversations that inspire knowledge creation require a number of Socratic ingredients—openness, patience, the ability to listen, experimentation with new words and concepts, politeness, the formation of a persuasive argument, courage—conversations in business settings are often fraught with hidden agendas, issue-selling, unquestioned advocacy, domineering attitudes, and intimidation. Despite their importance for long-term business success, conversational skills are not part of management training in business education. Military metaphors and old-fashioned assumptions about competition still hold sway: To talk is to fight—period. Using brute force, the conventional wisdom goes, managers enter the battlefield to win, leaving colleagues in a bewildered, confused, and battered state, hoping they will never have to confront the winner again.

In scientific studies of management, the role of conversation has also received relatively little attention, with a few notable exceptions. Westley (1990) has looked at the participation of middle-level managers in conversations about strategy; von Krogh and Roos (1996c, 1996d) have studied the difference between content and style in conversations focusing on operational issues and strategic perspectives; Peter Senge (1990) has examined conversations as instruments to revisit, renew, and improve ineffective or flawed practices. As we noted in Chapter 3, a number of researchers emphasizing female management styles (Helgesen, 1990; Tannen, 1994; Rosener, 1995) have discussed alternatives to the hypercompetitive, battlefield talk so common in business organizations.

Still, no studies specifically examine conversations in business settings as part of an enabling context or *ba* for knowledge creation. Therefore, this chapter focuses on how conversations can be managed to produce the kind of knowledge—individual tacit knowledge that has been shared and expanded with others—necessary for innovation. We start by outlining two distinct conversational purposes: knowledge confirmation and knowledge creation. Although knowledge confirmation is the most prevalent mode in most companies, managers need to work on developing the second type of conversation. Next, we define four guiding principles for conversations that enable knowledge creation: actively encouraging participation, establishing conversational etiquette, editing conversations appropriately, and fostering innovative language. We conclude with examples of the varying approaches successful companies like Maekawa and General Electric have taken to conversations, and a discussion of the different ways conversations need to be managed during each step of the knowledge-creation process.

CONVERSATIONAL PURPOSE:
FROM KNOWLEDGE CONFIRMATION TO CREATION

Conversations that take place in business organizations usually have one of two basic purposes: They either confirm the existence and content of knowledge, or aim to create new knowledge. Let us start with the first conversational purpose, since in our experience it is most common for business activities today. Conversations for knowledge confirmation are relatively clear-cut. They focus on the present, on facts, on solid reality. The scope and impact of issues discussed is quite limited. The purpose is mainly to confirm explicit knowledge. Furthermore, the concepts used in the conversation already exist and have been justified. Any model or prototype evoked will already be at hand, and the knowledge used will be limited to the conversation's specific situation (von Krogh and Roos, 1996a).

Such conversations confirm and reconfirm established expertise, and they allow for effective problem solving. Imagine, for instance, a conversation in the back room of a production line, in which the operator comes to the foreman with a technical problem concerning one of the instruments. The foreman, with more work experience on the line and having seen this instrument fail before, can inform the operator about the cause of the problem, the supplier to contact, and the necessary procedure for replacing the part. This conversation confirms knowledge about the production line; it is effective and efficient. Neither the foreman nor the operator needs to reflect on the way either guides and manages the conversation; they just need to get the job done.

However, when creating new knowledge is the purpose of a conversational exchange, simply confirming existing knowledge does not work. There is no sound knowledge base on which expertise can be established if it has not yet been created. In this situation, no solid facts or explicit models are at hand to indicate whether the participant is right or wrong. The purpose is for participants to establish not only new knowledge but a new reality. The focus is on the future, or knowledge of what ought to be, such as a new product concept, service, or manufacturing process. These are the conversations most directly related to a company's knowledge vision, and the scope and impact of the issues to be discussed are essentially unlimited at the outset.

As we have already pointed out, conversations play a part in all five steps of knowledge creation. The 5 × 5 Grid first presented in Chapter 1 is repeated here (see Table 6.1) to emphasize how strongly managing conversations affects each of the knowledge-creation steps. We review the steps again, this time with an eye toward the key role conversations play.

First, the tacit knowledge held by individual participants has to become shared in an atmosphere of high trust. In microcommunities of knowledge, members need to share and synchronize their mental ideas, even their body language, to create a rich field of interaction. Redundancy in themes and communication characterizes this phase of knowledge creation. For example, at Mettler-Toledo Albstadt, a German producer of scales that range from sophisticated tools for chemical production to those used commercially in fish markets, people are encouraged by CEO Reinert Tickart to create a constructive atmosphere for conversations. Organizational members are allowed to make small talk, raise personal issues, and make jokes at work. Even when he is present, conversation among people on the shop floor often involves non-job related issues, with his blessing. For Tickart, what he calls "high communication density" allows for more effective conversations that do involve work.[1]

Second, such open-ended conversational interaction, in which members learn to trust each other and have established a caring atmosphere, generates new concepts. A creative conversation allows individuals to bring in their own ideas and insights through multiple reasoning methods like induction, deduction, and abduction. Abduction, which refers to the use of metaphors, analogies, and language games, is particularly important during this phase; it will provide the group with new terms, key words, descriptions, and meanings for the concepts they begin to define together.

In the third step of knowledge creation, new concepts must be justified according to organizational values, a knowledge vision, a business strategy, costs, return on investments, and so on. Through justification, unaccept-

Table 6.1. The 5 x 5 Grid: Conversations Affect All Five Knowledge-Creation Steps

| | | | KNOWLEDGE-CREATION STEPS | | |
KNOWLEDGE ENABLERS	Sharing Tacit Knowledge	Creating a Concept	Justifying a Concept	Building a Prototype	Cross-Leveling Knowledge
Instill a Vision		√	√√	√	√√
Manage Conversations	√√	√√	√√	√√	√√
Mobilize Activists		√	√	√	√√
Create the Right Context	√	√	√√	√	√√
Globalize Local Knowledge					√√

able and unattractive concepts will be screened out. Conversations about the worth of a new idea walk a fine line between constructive criticism and harsh judgment. In fact, conversations are often fraught with hidden assumptions and values. Participants may claim that a certain concept does not meet the ethical standards of the company, for example, without really revealing what those standards might be. In this way, a potentially interesting product might be discarded even before it reaches the prototype-building phase.

In many respects, concept justification is a process that, when undertaken in good faith, moves participants beyond hidden assumptions and hidebound vales. It can occur when the language of a new concept is gradually merged with that of ongoing organizational conversations—that is, by actually applying the concept in daily speech. In Chapter 3, we described how Narvesen, a leading retailer, has created the concept of "care-based shopkeeping." As Narvesen's top managers continued to bring up the concept in their conversations, repeatedly referring to key phrases like "care for your customer" and "care for your experiences," it gradually became related to the company's existing values, its corporate strategy, and a larger total quality management program.

In the fourth phase, knowledge-creating conversations spark the design and construction of a prototype. Technical solutions are brought up by participants and carefully discussed. At this point, knowledge-confirming conversations play an increasingly important role. Technical, production, marketing, or financial expertise is tapped, and the scope and impact of the issues discussed become more limited. Yet the transition from justification to prototype building is not easy. Sometimes it includes new conversational participants who have not gone through the original process of sharing tacit knowledge. And because the conversation is less open-ended—that is, too much brainstorming at this stage becomes counterproductive—it may require a deliberate change in style and behavior.

Finally, cross-leveling of knowledge involves sharing explicit knowledge and concepts throughout the company. Therefore, ongoing conversations need to extend beyond the immediate group who have built the prototype and to focus more on knowledge confirmation than creation. These conversations become more inclusive in order to benefit all possible departments, communities, teams, and individuals. The scope and impact of issues discussed become increasingly constrained, as the prototype and/or concept is presented throughout the company.

FOUR GUIDING PRINCIPLES FOR GOOD CONVERSATIONS

In his seminal book *The Nature of Managerial Work* (1973), well-known organizational researcher Henry Mintzberg reported that managers spend about 80 percent of their time on communication, including talk and conversation. Managers at companies like Phonak, which we described in Chapter 2, echo Mintzberg's research. In general, Phonak's belief in the importance of communication is boundless: According to company estimates, up to 80 percent of the information exchange within it takes place through personal dialogue. As CEO Andy Rihs says, "Knowledge written and stored in computers is effective only about 20 percent of the time: You can either read the operating instructions of your new video recorder for one hour, or talk to a colleague for five minutes to find out how it works."[2]

Visionary managers and researchers have been saying things like this for years, so why are conversational practices so rudimentary in most companies? Why do managers so often stifle the creation of social knowledge at the outset by messages or orders that interfere with the process? Assuming such interference is a matter of misunderstanding rather than bad intent, we believe it is imperative to identify some guiding principles for conversation management. From our perspective, the different steps of the knowledge-creation process each require their own form of such management. The four guiding principles we describe below also play greater or lesser parts in the different knowledge-creation steps. In essence, managers must adapt their styles along the way, an issue we revisit at the conclusion of this chapter.

In some ways, the conversation manager is like the director of a movie. The director wants each of her actors to be as creative and capable as possible, and she encourages everyone to play his or her role with maximum focus and energy. The first task of a director is to provide roles for the actors, just as the starting point for the manager is to encourage active participation in conversation, helping to form microcommunities where appropriate. Next, as she watches the acting unfold, the director occasionally makes cuts to ensure the quality of the movie. She makes cuts if the performance of a single actor is not working or when events interfere, such as incorrect lighting or a broken stage prop. The director also intervenes when the actors are not working well together, coordinating their behavior and offering hints about how they might mesh better. In a similar fashion, good managers will edit conversations when the quality of the concepts discussed is unacceptable or too many ideas are on the table. They will intervene in conversations where the participants apparently misunderstand each other or disagree to such an extent that further discussion is stalled.

Unfortunately, conversation managers, unlike directors, do not have a script to work from. Often there is no way to predefine how participants should relate. Therefore, the conversation manager must help establish constructive working relationships within the group, as well as the appropriate etiquette for group discussion, some of which will evolve as participants become more enthusiastic and their contributions increase. Of course, the process will go nowhere if people refuse to participate. That is why the first of our principles emphasizes recognition of the rituals required to enter a conversation.

Principle 1: Actively Encourage Participation

Conversations for knowledge creation need to include people with a wide variety of educational backgrounds, ages, professional skills, and functional responsibilities. By securing broad participation, managers can help trigger creativity throughout the company. But before all this potential is unleashed, they have to get people talking and give them good reasons to keep talking. The first task of the conversation manager, then, is to establish entry points for everyone who should be involved. Managers can set up at least two entry points, or "doors," into a conversation: (1) they can encourage participation by making the knowledge-creating purpose clear; and (2) they can make sure entry rituals are fair and relatively easy to understand.

First, *managers must create awareness for knowledge-creating conversations*. In some cases—department meetings, a development project, a strategy group, a customer focus team—awareness will be immediate. Participation in the conversation is secured through the group or activity. At other times, however, managers will have to invite discussions. Ongoing conversations about a product, process, or service innovation need to be announced broadly. Then, people will have the opportunity to voice their interest.

Setting up doors into the conversation at various points will help. For example, certain parts of the conversation can be opened to a larger audience. Many companies consider every conversation about strategy strictly a top management concern; but others—Skandia comes to mind, with its future workshops and cross-functional future teams—will open doors to broader conversations about strategic priorities, goals, and values. At certain moments, such conversations might even be open to the public. One German company offers occasional public forums attended by several hundred people. The purpose here is to have open discussions, allowing audience members a chance to provide feedback on the new management principles and techniques that have been discussed.

One way to determine who should be involved in certain conversations is to distinguish between a core group and a support group. While the conversations of the core group might require limited participation—say, only the experts on a chemical process—a support group that involves many more people throughout the organization or a department—perhaps anyone who is interested in the subject—could provide input on environmental and social issues connected to constructing a new chemical plant. Note that information technology can help to define and structure participation, through groupware or other formats that allow ongoing electronic conversations among a number of participants. Conversations, perhaps in a question-and-answer form in which the whole transcript is shown, can also be posted on a company intranet or local area network.

Second, *managers can help shape conversation rituals that encourage participation.* The sociologist Zali Gurevitch discusses the rituals for entering a conversation as if they were an elaborate dance or court ceremony:

> Upon entering a scene of participation, we send looks and utter words to be immediately responded to in the eyes, faces, and bodies of the other participants, acknowledging and signaling the opening of an encounter. Then come ... expected grunts and idiomatic phrases that serve as introductory bows. Rituals of entry are both the cause and occasion that structure behavior and the ways to minimize the abrupt breaking of silence by speech. They provoke and yet appease shyness, embarrassment, swallowing spit, stuttering, an inability to speak, or becoming highly conscious of the choice of words and gestures for the act.[3]

That is, entering a conversation can require a very complicated set of rules and procedures. In some instances, rituals change depending on the seniority of participants or their positions. In other cases, the rituals might involve a dress code for the conversations, who speaks first, what to do when one person is quiet, how to ask questions, and so forth. The purpose of the meeting might also affect the staging of entry—for example, a person has to give a little speech when he or she first joins the board of a professional society. Conversation rituals become even more complicated if we consider cultural differences between Japanese and Western participants, the bowing of heads, the exchange of cards, ritualized acts of politeness, and so on. These rituals develop because they provide a certain stability for the participants. When the staging of the conversation is set beforehand, such as through a written meeting agenda distributed to everybody at the table and a set of opening remarks by a team leader or top executive, the other participants can focus on the real task—to create knowledge. Because these rituals often allow people to work more effectively, they have value and may even be thought of as a form of organizational capital.

Sometimes, however, even if the doors of awareness are open, the doors of ritual are firmly closed. Not knowing the rituals, a new entrant may make blunders, such as telling a silly joke or personal story that falls flat. When this happens, the conversation will continue without any real participation from the new entrant. This person will be present in body, but not in voice. Even worse, other participants may disregard any ideas or comments from the new entrant, thinking him a fool or simply an unknown quantity who does not merit their attention. For the new person, this treatment will feel like a nightmare, and he will eagerly look forward to the time when he can be relieved of suffering.

Every conversation, at least if it is sustained over some period of time and participants meet repeatedly, will develop its own rituals. Even the most chaotic assembly of R&D managers discussing new project ideas will adopt rituals, although this may just come down to the seating order around a café table. Conversation managers, who essentially open and close the doors of participation, need to pay careful attention to these rituals. It will be their responsibility to explain them to new entrants. One method for doing so is a preparatory meeting between the manager/coach and a new entrant, in which previous conversations are recollected and some of the rituals spelled out.

Occasionally conversation rituals become permanently closed, and the key is lost. A product-development group, for example, might reject any new entrant because current members think they are working together just fine, and any newcomer would just slow down their discussions. But to establish the right enabling context throughout an organization, participation in the creation of social knowledge has to be broad. New people have to be introduced into product-development teams from time to time, and some of the participants have to leave. It is the responsibility of the conversation manager to revise the rituals for entry to encourage new participation.

Principle 2: Establish Conversational Etiquette

Knowledge-creating conversations require the right rules and etiquette to make them a pleasant and memorable experience. By etiquette, we do not mean politeness above any other form of behavior or old-fashioned good manners. Microcommunities of knowledge in any organization will be as varied as their projects, functions, and ideals, and sometimes members will need to confront one another or "make waves." That chaotic assembly of R&D managers, for instance, may be accustomed to interrupting each other or making wild jokes or criticizing ideas quite frankly at the same time that they productively create new knowledge together.

That said, too much chaos in group relations is not a good thing. At the very least, the aim of creating new knowledge should be shared by all participants, and the contributions of all participants should be connected. Most important for the work of microcommunities, a conversation should trigger other conversations at a later time. Therefore, knowledge-creating conversations depend not only on *what* is being said but on *how* it is said. Paul Grice (1975), a philosopher of language, suggests several maxims for conversational etiquette. Adapting his work, we believe the following rules will help almost all knowledge-creating conversations:

- *Avoid unnecessary ambiguity.* Do not deliberately confuse things to cover a lack of knowledge, but admit to ambiguous meanings when you are searching for the best possible expression.
- *Avoid intimidation.* Do not threaten other participants.
- *Avoid exercising authority.* Do not use your position or other sources of power to force a conversation in a certain direction
- *Avoid premature closure.* Do not push for conclusions when knowledge is being created.
- *Be brief.* Allow time for others to make their comments and statements.
- *Be orderly.* Try to link statements to other themes discussed at various points.
- *Help other participants to be brave.* Allow for free and courageous speech.
- *Do not knowingly make false statements.*

Such rules take many forms in companies, and their importance will vary depending on the composition of the group involved. In some cases, especially when executives are part of a team or community, the rules about exercising authority and intimidation will have particular relevance. The most essential thing is that the rules, whatever they may be, encapsulate the mutual respect and care required for knowledge-creating conversations.

At the start of a knowledge-creation process, the expected etiquette for participants should be made clear by managers. With practice, a conversational culture will evolve in which organizational members know when and how to distinguish the practical tasks of knowledge confirmation from the rules for knowledge creation. After all, learning table manners comes down to practicing, every day, acceptable conduct for eating.

Principle 3: Edit Conversations Appropriately

In knowledge-creating conversations, the clay that participants work with is tacit knowledge. This clay takes shape when those who are talking together give tacit knowledge new forms of expression or establish new themes for discussion, ultimately arriving at new concepts. But because the tacit knowledge of individual participants is embodied in their own physical experiences and emotions, selecting specific themes for discussion can be difficult. For example, in learning the skills of chicken deboning during the *Toridas* project at Maekawa, each of the engineers involved developed his or her own embodied knowledge of the basic operations for this procedure. They learned certain movements, such as how to hold the chicken, how to strip the meat from the bone, and so on. There are as many ways of expressing this experience as there are participants. Chicken deboning can also be described as "meat stripping," "meat cutting," "meat removal," or "chicken stripping." A knowledge-creating conversation about it, then, would have to allow for these personal forms of expression.

Yet the ultimate goal for this project was to come up with one concept in order to automate the process. We refer to this conversational editing process as making incisions or cuts (Gurevitch, 1995; Grice, 1975). When a knowledge-creating conversation has generated many concepts, with varying degrees of quality, these have to be edited down to the ones with the most potential. A conversation may begin with individuals discussing a variety of personal experiences, but as it proceeds, the expressions should converge into one or just a few concepts that become the group's focus. Such convergence usually happens in two ways: through *agreement* and/or *understanding* (von Krogh, Roos, and Slocum, 1994; von Krogh, Ichijo, and Nonaka, 1997).

In practice, understanding and agreement are often achieved at the same time. But agreement is a commodity that can be sold at too low a price. Frequently, when participants agree on an expression or a concept, the implicit assumption is that they also truly understand it. But group dynamics, the insecurity of participants, and the influence of dominant personalities can force agreement when some participants may lack a full understanding of the concept. In another instance, a group may simply get tired of trying to come up with themes together and will agree to an idea—any idea—too fast.

Understanding, in our terms, is not achieved until all participants in a group truly feel that the expression or concept corresponds with what they know tacitly, whether they wholeheartedly agree with the idea or hate it. The acid test for understanding is that participants feel comfortable or uncomfortable about a concept; in other words, when they internalize the concept, they can use it to revisit their own experiences. The concept may or may not work for them, but at least they understand how it expresses someone else's experiences. In internalizing the rules of chess, for example, you understand how the other players move their pieces, even if you do not agree with their moves.

Understanding does not presuppose agreement, but it provides the grounds for a constructive argument. Until the participants in a knowledge-creating conversation have achieved some form of shared understanding, they cannot agree or disagree. And in justifying a concept, the toil of achieving such shared understanding pays off in a constructive debate. When participants adhere to appropriate conversational rules, such as listening to what others say and not intimidating them, it will be much easier for the group to make the necessary incisions together. Participants will expect others to make genuine statements that serve the purpose of knowledge creation, reducing the number of descriptions and deciding on concepts that are broadly understood. However, conversation managers may have to intervene if no understanding of a concept can be achieved among participants, or if participants cannot agree.

The managerial issue here is making the right incisions at the right time. At the beginning of the knowledge-creation process, too much editing may close down a conversation; at other points, appropriate editing can keep things moving. Conversations can circle around a concept for too long, wearing it out. Yet once a tired management team embraces "core competences," for example, as a replacement for competitive strengths, their conversation may become reenergized and yield new insights. When Narvesen's management team decided to talk about *strategic intent* rather than a *vision statement*, replacing the old term with a new one had a tremendous impact on managerial discussions. Through the process of making sense out of strategic intent, these managers came up with a host of new ideas for catering services and different forms of sales and distribution.

Of course, like a product or service, any expression or concept has a life cycle. In knowledge-creating conversations, the life cycle of expressions, concepts, and prototypes has to be managed. Note that conversations can also be inhibited by the never-ending introduction of new terms. Participants can feel lost, and there are few points of linguistic reference. Sometimes new concepts are created that describe essentially the same old, useful, known concepts. Business organizations overflow with buzz words, although there are good reasons for why such terms proliferate. The old-wine-in-new-bottles phenomenon occurs often in knowledge-creating conversations, but one executive's buzz word is another's creative vehicle. At Narvesen, *strategic intent* really did generate something beyond the older term of *vision statement*, but at another company such a linguistic substitution might have sparked nothing at all. The impact of language, like tacit knowledge and any complex experience of events, depends on the people involved, the context, and a certain amount of serendipity.

A rapid growth of terms may also indicate that the right term has yet to be found. Observers of science like Paul Feyerabend (1975), suggest that a proliferation of terms that are not different semantically is a sign of possible "paradigm formation" (von Krogh and Roos, 1995b). That is, language accumulation has a threshold effect: Concepts cue up, until one finally makes it and becomes the lasting concept, directing further theory development. While "meat stripping" may seem very similar to "chicken deboning," the latter description became the one that Maekawa's engineers used to create a successful deboning machine. Therefore, although managers may be called on to edit conversations, they should not despair if the exponential growth of terms sometimes gets out of hand. This leads us to the last of our guiding principles.

Principle 4: Foster Innovative Language

According to organizational researcher Marlene Fiol (1991), a company's language represents one of its most important assets. Indeed, a knowledge-creating company lives on its language. There will be no new prototype, product, or service without a new concept, expressed in language that conveys its meaning. Many modern corporations recognize this and make clear statements to their stakeholders about the importance of language. Time Warner, for example, suggested in its 1996 Annual Report that it is in the business of creating a new language for the media industry.[4] Other companies like Novartis have created terms that inspire completely new perspectives on industries. Novartis's use of "neutraceuticals" describes the joint efforts of the pharmaceutical and nutrition industries to create foods with a healing effect.[5] Such neutraceuticals include a new generation of cereals that help prevent cardiac disease, or foods with soy additives that can help lower cholesterol levels.

Language is a medium for the expression of people's observations about the world, and their observations are required to create new knowledge. Hence, in order to generate innovative concepts, language needs to be extraordinarily dynamic during the knowledge-creation process. Participants should not only speak freely and honestly, they should also allow the words they use to be playful, vivid, silly, and not always "correct." In managerial terms, fostering innovative language during knowledge-creating conversations will help give new meaning to well-known concepts and terms; it will also inspire new terms that incorporate existing meanings, or new terms with entirely new meanings. Playing with language can stretch meanings and concepts, enabling participants to better formulate their ideas. By calling the management developer at Skandia's Future Center the "digital saloon cultivator," for example, this company's wordplay conveys the spirit expected of participants in its future workshops and programs.

Frequently, we say that those who have an ability for wordplay are articulate, charismatic, or witty; these are the people with the gift of gab, and they often energize everyone around them. In the course of doing the research that underlies this book, we conducted a number of interviews with executives. They were all highly articulate and linguistically innovative. For instance, Shun Murakami, president of one of Maekawa's independent corporations, says, "We do not put great importance on data as such when laying out our business plan every year. What is most important to us is keeping in close contact with various customers and reading their thoughts and desires. We come to understand what they want to do while talking with them about various things."[6]

To be sure, there are plenty of commentators who believe "proper" language should be guarded from the explosion of jargon so common today. The question is, do people have the right to play around with new words, expressions, and phrases? This question has puzzled philosophers of language since ancient times. Yet if language is instrumental in creating a person's perception of the world (Maturana and Varela, 1987), then human beings should have the freedom to experiment, the boldness to provoke, and the "geist" to furnish our concepts with a portion of meaning. Be aware of what George Lakoff (1987) calls "hypercorrection": draconian efforts to correct all mistaken words and phrases. This often undermines innovative language games and effective knowledge creation. As Lakoff points out, some people view any change in the way language works as a "corruption." The old form of a language is taken as the standard, and any difference from it is seen as problematic. But meaning is normally lost only in cases where it is gained somewhere else. Like any living thing, language evolves.

One visual technique for instigating knowledge-creating conversations involves drawing circles of meaning. This process evolves in four stages: (1) a new metaphor or analogy leads to a new concept; (2) the new concept sparks a conversation about what this might mean in practice, generating many interpretations; (3) the circle of meaning gradually tightens, and its boundary becomes increasingly visible; (4) the circle narrows even more, representing the group's shared understanding of and agreement about a new concept. Figure 6.1 offers an example of what circles of meaning might look like as the concept of neutraceuticals is discussed.

A second technique involves scaling, both spatially and temporally. From time to time during a conversation, it is useful to change the scale of discussion: Participants can be asked to look at a phenomenon, concept, or prototype from a bird's or ant's perspective. Scaling up a discussion on a prototype can be achieved by asking how a new product might influence the development of society. For example, a device like a Palm Pilot that incorporates a fax machine, electronic datebook, and access to the Internet may facilitate instant communication, relieving people from time and space constraints—but will it also simplify tracing a user's whereabouts, invading his or her privacy? Meanwhile, scaling down could focus the discussion of a possible product on how components known to the group can improve the functionality of the prototype. Time scaling might involve investigating the historical antecedents for the concept and prototype, and how one should understand the possible future development of a technology. Scaling is achieved through active inquiry and conversational editing, as well as a creative use of language. Indeed, what, where, how, and why should be asked from many different perspectives to enhance a microcommunity's knowledge-creation capabilities.

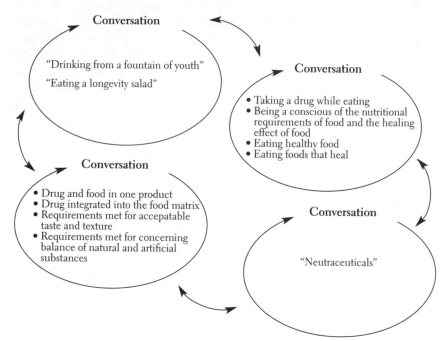

Figure 6.1. Circles of Meaning: An Example

HOW MAEKAWA AND GENERAL ELECTRIC GUIDE CONVERSATIONS

In practice, companies that emphasize effective group discussions and an open atmosphere for conversations combine these guiding principles in their approaches. Good conversation management is not only a key knowledge enabler in its own right but also a driving force behind the other enablers. It will help shape strategies and instill knowledge visions; it is part of an enabling context and will smooth the way for globalizing local knowledge. And the conversational abilities of knowledge activists can certainly help mobilize knowledge-creation efforts, the subject of the next chapter. Like care in the organization, good conversations inspire everything that knowledge-creating companies do. As such, they take on many different forms, depending on particular business settings and environmental conditions. Consider the following examples from Maekawa and General Electric, two very different but successful companies.

Maekawa Seisakujo (or the Maekawa Manufacturing Company) has developed and produced industrial freezers since its founding in 1924, and today it is unequaled globally in this field. At Maekawa, meetings are frequently held, and employees are encouraged to have face-to-face conversations. The company's executives believe, however, that conversations need to get at deeper issues than the superficial topics often discussed in a meeting format or informal gatherings; they believe it is critically important to understand what tacit ideas, beliefs, and feelings exist behind expressed words so that mutual understanding can be achieved among those involved in the conversation.[7]

For that purpose, all the company's many project task forces—or independent corporations, as they are called at Maekawa—are asked each year to summarize an annual business plan on a single, letter-sized sheet of paper. These business plans are distributed at a meeting where representatives of related independent corporations gather, and participants list the tacit ideas they believe exist behind the written words on additional sheets of paper. By continuing this practice, Maekawa has built a foundation for developing a common understanding or language of ideas in the company. This process is described as "approaching the whole by working together" (Maekawa, 1994). Indeed, comparison of plans does not happen just among independent corporations. The plans of all related "blocs" of corporations are examined and compared with each other at the top management group level in order to achieve consistency among them. In this way, business plans are created through discussions at three structural levels (corporation, bloc, and group) at Maekawa.

The annual business plans also help encourage conversation among organizational members on a deeper level. Each plan is supposed to present an image of the given independent corporation's business in the near future (three years ahead), a direction that corporation should take over the course of the coming year, and an implementation plan. When the business plan of each independent corporation is made open to other corporations in related areas, it is thoroughly "examined and criticized by them," according to Yoshio Iwasaki of Maekawa Research Institute. But because these plans are designed to fit on a single page, the quantity of information contained in them is limited. In this case, statistical data are not very important. What Maekawa people emphasize, according to Iwasaki, is "communication based on tacit knowledge":

> Our business plans come from our mind. Even if the plan's presentation is clumsy, it is evaluated highly if it contains a certain belief. While I am reading it, such a belief emerges in my mind. Something envisioned in the domain of their tacit knowledge must be accepted in the domain of our tacit knowledge. Otherwise, we would face a complete breakdown in communication.

Conversations with customers provide another source of knowledge at Maekawa, a subject we detail further in Chapter 8, along with the structural role the company's independent corporations play in creating the right enabling context or *ba*. At Maekawa, people do not ask for statistical data to read market trends. What they truly rely on are interactions with customers. It is not easy, however, to transform such interactions into a business plan. Maekawa executives must develop certain beliefs based on discussions with customers, then briefly summarize these on a piece of paper. Furthermore, such a belief must represent what the rest of their independent corporation believes, not just a particular manager's ideas. In short, all members of the independent corporation must share the same belief when laying out a business plan. They accumulate and talk about the same experiences with other members while committing themselves to a shared enabling context; that is, they constantly interact with customers, develop their own beliefs from these experiences, and then articulate and share them with other members.

In contrast, General Electric, whose businesses range from consumer electronics to a television network—and whose 1998 market value of $271.64 billion meant it ranked first in *Business Week*'s annual Global 1000 survey for the third year in a row[8]—might be said to have a more American style. The language of its strategies and improvement programs reflects this pragmatic culture, and its emphasis on rationality and militaristic metaphors could even be called old-fashioned. But for this company, the approach works. Take GE's Six Sigma quality program, currently its most important strategic initiative.[9] Sigma refers to a statistical standard against which figures can be multiplied: the greater the figure, the higher the precision or quality. By citing "six sigma" as its quality standard, the company aims for only 3.4 defects per million in whatever is produced. Six Sigma entails the formation of project teams, each of which is supposed to achieve such precision. The teams create products through a five-step process known as DMAIC—short for definition, measurement, analysis, improvement, and control.

Most Six Sigma projects last about four months. A project team is led by quality experts at GE known as "Black Belts," who are trained by "Master Black Belts." Both Black Belts and Master Black Belts work full-time on Six Sigma efforts. In addition, other "Green Belts" are involved in quality improvement efforts while holding down regular jobs in their organizations. "Champions" are senior management leaders in each division who are responsible for quality improvement, while coordinators or facilitators known as "Quality Leaders" roam the office like commandos. General Electric's Six Sigma initiatives began in the fall of 1995. In 1997, there were over 60,000 Green Belt project leaders who have received training and have completed at least one project.

In training programs for Six Sigma, GE people belonging to different small business units study together, and program participants are encouraged to share their experiences and learning. General Electric has developed over forty analytical tools for Six Sigma activities, and almost all are based on statistics. Therefore, statistical terms have become a normal part of conversations among GE employees. Six Sigma is really a study of statistical terminology, and this terminology is rapidly becoming part of the language GE employees use. Statistical terminology is hard to grasp at first, but it is an ideal tool for explicitly articulating knowledge that can be shared by different divisions. General Electric's small business units are very diverse in their business domains, but as this common language has evolved, all sales, production, and management people have developed a shared understanding of GE's quality efforts.

THE CONVERSATION MANAGER:
ADAPTING TO DIFFERENT PHASES OF KNOWLEDGE CREATION

Just as a particular company will develop its own approach to language and conversations, each phase of the knowledge-creation process is supported by its own style and type of conversation. For this reason, conversations can and should be managed, either by everyone involved, or a conversation manager who can moderate disputes, establish the right etiquette, and appropriately edit ideas. Management of conversations, however, is a subtle process. Rather than simply searching for levers to make a good discussion happen, the manager should attempt to understand the influence of any kind of intervention on the trajectory of a given conversation. Trying out a new concept and hearing someone say "that idea is just so stupid" will not only discourage the person who made the suggestion but also others who have witnessed such intimidation. Some participants may never raise their voices again. On the other hand, frank criticism is necessary during other steps in the process, and hearing generic encouragement like "great idea!" or "whatever anybody says is important" may actually hinder the discussion.

For another twist on an earlier analogy, conversations are like plays in which the manager directs the action. The audience—or larger organization—also affects the proceedings, adjusting its own role and participation depending on how the play unfolds. The conversation manager, then, carefully brings people together, drawing on their continuous efforts to give the creative work vigor and life. Rather than intimidating them, she inspires individual participants to be brave. Even more important, she creates a sense of belonging that allows conversations to take place. Conversation managers are by definition caring experts, because caring relationships are essential to talking freely, accepting constructive criticism with grace, and sharing one's personal beliefs with others.

Still, the guiding principles of managing a conversation depend on the purpose of the conversation. When the purpose leans strongly toward knowledge creation, the conversation plays out in a different fashion from the one it would follow if the purpose were to confirm or cross-level knowledge. As shown in Table 6.2, the guiding principles change for each phase of the knowledge-creation process, and conversation management should shift accordingly.

Conversations that help people share tacit knowledge, for instance, generally involve active participation, few incisions, and creative language games. The etiquette is welcoming and invites new participants into the process; it encourages open and unstructured contributions. In creating a concept, the doors to new participants start to close, but incisions are still few in number. Innovative language is also actively pursued, and the rules continue to encourage ambiguous statements and creative speech. During concept justification, broader participation is called for in order to thoroughly investigate the organizational consequences of further developing a concept into a prototype. The etiquette may shift to explaining and examining a given concept rather than encouraging a host of new ideas. Hence, authority and closure are more frequent features of such conver-

Table 6.2. Conversational Guiding Principles for Knowledge Creation Steps

	Sharing Tacit Knowledge	Creating a Concept
Active Participation	• Select participants • Create awareness for knowledge-creating conversations • Establish rituals and rules • Make sure everyone contributes	• Develop rituals further • Keep participation constant
Conversational Etiquette	• Allow for metaphors, analogies • Avoid pushing for closure • Allow for lengthy statements • Allow for chaos • "Check authority at the door"	• Give participants courage • Avoid pushing for closure • Allow for metaphors and a search for meaning • Avoid intimidation
Editorial Judgment	• Avoid incisions • Increase quantity of concepts • Start new concept life cycles	• Base incisions on quantity and quality • Reduce the number of concepts to two or three • Delete outdated concepts
Innovative Language	• Experiment with new concepts and meanings • Be playful • Practice temporal and spatial scaling	• Experiment with concepts and meaning • Practice temporal and spatial scaling

sations. Managers may need to do more editing with respect to the quality and the quantity of concepts presented. The language used becomes increasingly static.

In building a prototype based on the concept, the doors of participation close again, and the rules allow for increasing expertise and authority. Statements should be short and directed toward constructing, specifying, and improving the prototype. Incisions are numerous and basically refer to the quality of the solutions suggested for the prototype. Language is increasingly constrained, and the circle of meaning becomes more definite and closed. But in cross-leveling knowledge, the doors of participation open once more, and the conversational etiquette encourages friendly sharing and communication of the results of knowledge creation. By this point, a common language communicates the new concept across all levels of the organization.

Obviously, conversation managers have to be quite adept at adapting to the different phases of knowledge creation. Indeed, they are often the charismatic and articulate executives who become knowledge activists. As the next chapter indicates, knowledge activists can take many forms in an organization and may have quite individual styles. While CEO Jack Welch

Table 6.2. (continued)

Justifying a Concept	Building a Prototype	Cross-Leveling Knowledge
• Allow new participants into conversation • Identify groups with vested interest in the concept • Explain rituals of entry • Discuss usefulness of concept	• Review rituals of entry and make changes when needed • Disallow new participants	• Allow new participants into conversation • Make the rituals of entry democratic • Create high organizational awareness for the innovation • Review the progress of rituals and awareness in the whole process
• Consider an array of different viewpoints • Be brief and orderly • Take an examining attitude	• Allow authoritative statements from those with expertise • Do not allow ambiguous expression • Be orderly • Push for closure	• Make knowledge creation the basis for recognition of expertise • Communicate as clearly as possible • Explain the process of knowledge creation that the microcommunity went through
• Use justification to decide on the quality of a concept	• Use technical requirements to decide on a prototype's quality • Focus conversations through the deliberate use of language • Make cuts where needed to speed up prototype development	• Package the knowledge and describe the process in terms easily understood throughout the organization • Make incisions where knowledge developed does not apply to local environment
• Keep concept constant; change meaning depending on feedback of participants • Practice temporal and spatial scaling, depending on justification criteria	• Keep concept constant • Reach agreement about and shared understanding of concept • Use one scale only	• Keep prototype constant • Maintain agreement and shared understanding • Use one scale only

of General Electric emphasizes Six Sigma and statistical techniques throughout his corporation, Skandia's Leif Edvinsson talks about waves and knowledge navigation, and Helmut Volkmann of Siemens pursues "Xenia, the knowledge city." But all these visionary managers recognize the importance of inspiring and mobilizing their workers—through conversations, a sense of the many and varied sources of knowledge in any organization, and a firm focus on the future.

· 7 ·

ENABLER 3

Mobilize Knowledge Activists

Siemens people pass by my office and ask me about the future. They are interested in the things I do, and every day I get more supporters in the company.
—Helmut Volkmann, Senior Director, Siemens

Imagine you are part of a team that is developing a new service for your local customer group. Over the course of time, you start to feel that the project is doomed. Your boss tells you he has heard a rumor that another team tried something similar for a different customer group and had no luck. You call up a person from this earlier team, and she tells you that yes, they attempted the same thing two years ago and got nowhere. She adds sarcastically that she could tell you exactly why it failed, but why bother? It was a lousy idea. Discouraged, you go back to your team and break the news. Your teammates sigh, frown, express irritation for wasting so much time. One of them even mutters, "No more knowledge creation in this century!" No matter what you say, they have lost their sense of purpose. And all of you feel that no direction has been set for overall knowledge creation in the company, let alone your own project. You are discouraged that coordination of innovations happens so sporadically and ineffectively.

What this team desperately needs is a knowledge activist. If a manager is part of the team, he or she may be required to play this role. Alternatively, all the members may need to push for such activism in the company. Regardless, we believe that enabling new knowledge depends on the energy and sustained commitment an organization puts into knowledge creation. That is why our third enabler, *mobilize knowledge activists*, matters so much to the process. Knowledge activists are major players in at least four knowledge-creation steps. At the beginning of the process, they often form microcommunities of knowledge. They smooth the way for creating and justifying concepts, as well as for building a prototype. Most of all, activists are essential for cross-leveling of knowledge, since they are the people responsible for energizing and connecting knowledge-creation efforts throughout a company. Although they are seldom directly involved in the sharing of tacit knowledge within microcommunities and smaller groups, knowledge activists help establish the right enabling context—the essential space and relationships that allow tacit knowledge to be unleashed.

In other words, they are the knowledge proselytizers of the company, spreading the message to everyone. Knowledge activism can reside in a particular department or with a particular person; it can be situated in already existing departments and functions, or may be taken on as a special assignment by individuals or departments. It is not necessarily a job for one senior manager, although visionary executives like Helmut Volkmann of Siemens, Yoshinaru Fukuhara of Shiseido, Leif Edvinsson of Skandia, and Jack Welch of General Electric have certainly played this role.

Middle managers may also be knowledge activists. Indeed, they can be instrumental in forming the microcommunities that share tacit knowledge. While the whole notion of middle management and the hierarchical organization it implies is shifting in the current knowledge economy, managers at all levels of a company are still much better at motivating workers, getting people to talk to one another, and coordinating the often disparate efforts of creative professionals than are virtual networks or other forms of computerized communication. On the flip side, the increasing importance of innovation for competition indicates that knowledge activism is not just the responsibility of managers. In that sense, the team members in the example above needed to energize themselves as well as to long for a larger knowledge vision.

Such activism has six purposes: (1) initiating and focusing knowledge creation; (2) reducing the time and cost necessary for knowledge creation; (3) leveraging knowledge-creation initiatives throughout the corporation; (4) improving the conditions of those engaged in knowledge creation by relating their activities to the company's bigger picture; (5) preparing participants in knowledge creation for new tasks in which their knowledge is needed; and (6) including the perspective of microcommunities in the larger debate on organizational transformation. In this chapter, we cover all these purposes, discussing the three roles knowledge activists play—catalyst, coordinator, and merchant of foresight—the skills required to be an activist, and where knowledge activism may reside in the company. We also note a few of the pitfalls of knowledge activism and provide a closer look at the work of Helmut Volkmann—the "thought-maker" of Siemens.

WHAT A KNOWLEDGE ACTIVIST DOES: THREE ROLES

Once General Electric launched its Six Sigma quality program in September 1995, CEO Jack Welch encouraged the senior managers of the company's eleven businesses to spread the news throughout their organizations. Welch himself used every occasion—corporate events, e-mail, the annual report—to get out the message. In January 1996, Welch made an official announcement about Six Sigma at the annual operational managers' meeting held in Boca Raton, Florida. That spring, he distributed a brochure entitled "The Goal and the Journey." And he used e-mail to good effect.

Consider one message he sent to GE managers around the world on March 22, 1997. Welch made clear that managers needed to start Black Belt or Green Belt training (that is, to become Six Sigma quality experts) by January 1998 and complete it by July 1 of that year in order to be promoted to senior management positions. This message had a huge impact. Although Welch had frequently emphasized the importance of Six Sigma initiatives up to that point, it was not easy to convince as many as 240,000 GE people of the program's strategic importance, especially when the new efforts involved a steep learning curve and complicated statistical language. However, when managers were told involvement in Six Sigma was the minimum requirement for advancement, the number of applicants for Six Sigma training programs drastically increased.

At Skandia, Leif Edvinsson is another knowledge activist, connecting and activating internal and external intelligence experts from all over the world. He spends much of his time networking. During workshops at the Skandia Future Center, with local subsidiaries, or on a virtual basis via videoconferences or the Internet, Edvinsson challenges business ideas and daily routines. As a coach, he is at everybody's disposal. Contacts with him can be established through e-mail or a special newsgroup of Skandia's intranet. He connects people working on the same task within and outside Skandia, or people with corresponding tasks and approaches to problems. He attends conferences that may be only remotely related to Skandia's business future. As a global knowledge "nomad," Edvinsson's activities and geographical location change constantly.

As these two stories illustrate, knowledge activism comes in many shapes and sizes. An activist may be the head of a large transnational firm (Welch), or an executive who has the specific responsibility of emphasizing knowledge work within a company (Edvinsson). What such executives do will vary with particular business circumstances. In general, however, there are three possible roles for knowledge activists. They can be the *catalysts* of knowledge creation, *coordinators* of knowledge-creation initiatives, *merchants of foresight*—or all three.

Catalysts of Knowledge Creation

Conventional wisdom holds that social and organizational changes generally require a triggering event. Such events may be negative—an external shock to business because of changes in government tax policies, a breakdown of a power plant, the entry into a domestic market of a strong global competitor, a natural catastrophe. Others may be positive, such as the establishment of new government-funded research programs, reforms in medical-care services, or the advent of new information technologies. But change can also be triggered by the initiative of particular people, who may alert their fellow group members or managers to the impact of future events. For some chemical processes to occur, an active agent, or a catalyst, has to be present. In the same manner, some organizational changes will never happen without a catalyst in human form.

Since knowledge creation is a fragile process, often subject to strong barriers, it can require such a catalyst. In this respect, knowledge activists perform two functions. First, in traveling freely around the company, talking to organizational members across boundaries and levels, they are exposed to a variety of new data, ideas, insights, opportunities, questions, and problems. They can pick up on these signals and gradually formulate the necessary "process triggers." Process triggers might come in the form of questions: *Where* is the problem? *When* did you have that idea? *Why* is this happening now? *How* can it be changed? *What* would you do instead?

For example, a knowledge activist might come across a forgotten study conducted by visiting university students on customer retention for a certain product (that is, the percentage of customers who buy that product again). The data may show an alarmingly low retention rate, but nobody in the company has responded. An activist might then trigger changes that improve retention rates by getting the appropriate people at the company to consider these questions: Why is our customer retention for this product so low? Why does the customer prefer to buy our competitors' products after having tried ours? What changes do we need to make in the product, promotion, packaging, price, or distribution in order to better satisfy the customer? Note that deciding *who* should be involved in making these changes is a necessary part of the process, pointing the way to the correct site for knowledge creation. In answering this question, the knowledge activist can then try triggering changes with a sales representative, a marketing director, a product manager, or a product developer.

The second catalyzing function of an activist is to help create an enabling context for knowledge creation. As we have already pointed out, knowledge creation is strongly tied to participants' experiences as human beings, both spoken and unspoken. As such, knowledge cannot be separated from its context; it is part of the physical, mental, or virtual place in which it has been created. But knowledge creation within a company is not always easy. Conversations among group members, such as those of the team that opened this chapter, can inhibit people rather than spark them; microcommunities can fall apart, with all the knowledge gained through their personal interactions lost. Therefore, context can either encourage knowledge sharing and use or trap it within isolated individuals who may not be able to articulate what they know.

Establishing an enabling context will help participants in knowledge creation both use their personal experiences and relieve them of the heavy burden of what they know. While past experience is the source of many insights and observations, those who want to create new knowledge need to bridge the gap between what is already known and what has become obsolete. In the next chapter, we discuss the importance of an overall enabling context in more detail, relating it to various organizational structures that can enhance knowledge work. For now, we simply stress the key part knowledge activists play in developing the right enabling context, promoting the "knowledge spaces" or *ba* that encourage innovation.

Such spaces are often founded on a blend of physical architectural design; intervention and moderation techniques to inspire conversations; tools for visual communication; and a good mix of people from various cultural backgrounds and functional areas. An innovative architecture for knowledge creation, for example, might involve a building with different rooms for the different phases of knowledge creation, or one with an open plan that fosters intermingling and communication. The Phonak House described in Chapter 2 comes to mind. For other companies, good intervention techniques might matter more for the sharing of tacit knowledge and concept creation. Perhaps an external moderator sets the rules for knowledge-creation sessions and asks participants to adhere to them. Or she might apply creative techniques in which participants identify metaphors and analogies that make their insights and experiences more explicit, helping to "bundle" them into key words that finally form a concept. The Skandia Future Center detailed in Chapter 4, with its innovative management developers and workshops, creates a thriving enabling context in this way.

Tools for visualizing concepts and prototypes, including three-dimensional CAD-CAM systems and computer simulation techniques, also have their uses. But fascination with information technology often becomes an end in itself, and sophisticated tools have less to do with establishing an enabling context for knowledge creation than bringing together a productive mix of people. There is a positive relationship between heterogeneity and creativity in cross-functional teams, especially during concept creation, in which expertise is not such a factor. And in justifying a concept, a knowledge activist would be well advised to form a heterogeneous group that includes people from various organizational levels and with different cultural and functional expertise—even outsiders—in order to provide a broad range of perspectives.

The French sociologist Pierre Bordieu calls such an enabling context or space *habitus* (Bourdieu, 1980); it is a kind of socially constructed principle of regulated improvisation (Calhoun, 1991) in which tradition and creativity intersect to generate new knowledge. Note that creating the right enabling context is not just the work of a day or a few months; knowledge-creation initiatives require long-term attention, the kind that comes only with a substantial commitment from top management and a context that inspires continual knowledge creation rather than one-shot deals. Maekawa's efforts to create a new chicken deboning machine, for instance, took fourteen years.

In playing the role of catalysts, knowledge activists might recall sociologist Paul Ricoeur's advice that to speak of initiative is to speak of responsibility (Ricoeur, 1992). Ricoeur emphasizes the importance of an individual's will and intention to act in a social setting, as well as the stamina required to follow up on commitments, personal and group needs, and personal and group wishes. A knowledge-creation initiative sometimes depends on such mobilization to drive the process forward.

Coordinators of Knowledge-Creation Initiatives

Although a catalyst may not be necessary (experts somehow always find a way to introduce new innovations), coordinators of knowledge-creation initiatives are essential in almost any company. Large and midsize companies are bound to have many knowledge-creation activities going on simultaneously. On the department level, people come up with new product and service ideas, different ways of manufacturing, and new ways of thinking all the time. On the small-group level, new ideas are exchanged and developed, some of which may turn into a booming business for the company. Even individual organizational members often try to find ways to better utilize their personal creative potential.

Organizational researchers James March and Johan Olsen (1976) have described this as the "garbage can" model of organizations, where people, choices, problems, and solutions are loosely connected and come together at random. Say an engineer in raw aluminum production has some difficulty optimizing his manufacturing processes through the implementation of process-control tools. His first reaction is to search for solutions outside the company, and he contacts a number of technical consultants. What he does not know—and does not bother to find out—is that the manufacturing director at a different division producing ferroalloys had a similar problem a few years back. That director also bought external technical advice. The plant went through a series of trial-and-error runs before he and his engineers settled on one process-control system. Although the materials produced by these divisions are different, the engineers in the aluminum plant could have gained important insights from the ferroalloy plant manager, such as what consultants to work with, what factors to consider when choosing a new system, the experience of implementing a new control system, the time frame and budget for such a process, and so forth. Instead, repeating similar trial-and-error runs in the aluminum plant ends up costing the company a substantial amount.

For the knowledge-creating company, special emphasis has to be put on actively connecting local initiatives, an issue we address again in Chapter 9. The larger the company, the more effort has to be given to this task. Two departments working on similar concepts and prototypes can cross-fertilize one another by communicating more extensively rather than duplicating work. During knowledge-creation efforts in any company, a constant possibility is that a new concept developed in one department may be very similar to one developed previously in another department, even another country. The original department may possess a prototype product, or have accumulated negative experiences from trying to justify the concept and studying its implications for customers. The grounds for justifying the concept may have changed, but the work of the first department should, at the very least, be brought to the attention of the new effort.

Facilitating these connections is the knowledge activist's job. In delineating the role of coordinator, we believe it is useful to distinguish three conceptual issues that help shape what a knowledge activist does in this respect: the microcommunity perspective, imagined communities, and shared maps of cooperation.

The Microcommunity Perspective

Microcommunities of knowledge are not limited by group, department, and division boundaries, but may overlap within and across them. Note that we did not choose the word *community* by accident. All communities have their own rituals, languages, norms, and values. Our idea of a microcommunity is characterized by face-to-face interaction, and in creating knowledge, the participants also gradually get to know more about each other. The social knowledge they gain through this experience is the key to effective knowledge creation and to creating the right enabling context.

In large organizations, however, microcommunities also represent a coordination challenge, and it is here that knowledge activists play a crucial role. There are limits to the number of participants in knowledge creation, especially during the steps of sharing tacit knowledge, creating a concept, and building a prototype. Too many perspectives, too many sources of tacit knowledge, and too many cultural traditions can make knowledge creation difficult. Good activists will not only bring together the right people, forming creative communities and helping them to share tacit knowledge from within; they will also connect the disparate efforts of many small groups. Knowledge-creation initiatives depend on mutual awareness among microcommunities, yet such communities often evolve on their own rather than as part of a well-thought-out management plan. By maintaining the microcommunity perspective, activists recognize the value of knowledge creation that occurs in small groups, planned or unplanned, and ultimately link these "garbage can" efforts with a company's overall knowledge vision.

Imagined Communities

The term *imagined communities* is borrowed from the work of two sociologists, Benedict Anderson (1983) and James Calhoun (1991). Calhoun, for example, describes America as an imagined community: "I feel a oneness with other Americans I have never met, a sense of common membership with people I have never met or heard of as individuals, with people who in direct interaction might repel or anger me" (1991, p. 106). He goes on to say that this imagined sense of community may even lead people to fight wars for the common cause of protecting their traditions and ways of life.

From a knowledge-creation perspective, knowledge activists can also develop this sense of imagined community, one that is based on a common cause or value system. Identification with an imagined community (computer hackers, ad designers, scientists, artists, economists) rather than just people in one's immediate office space will help coordinate local knowledge-creation initiatives and is part of implementing a company's overall knowledge vision. While it is true that the successful knowledge-creation initiatives that spread throughout a company usually originate in microcommunities, these communities need to have an awareness of what other groups are doing in order to come up with ideas that are widely applicable. Each member has a mental image of their communion (Anderson 1983).

To create such imagined communities, a knowledge activist might share inspiring stories from different microcommunities, describing who is involved, how long they have been working together, their ideals and frustrations, the concepts created, their attempts at justifying concepts, and the great products that ultimately resulted. The activist must develop her narrative skills, in some sense becoming a poet—that is, someone who can make connections in a seemingly unconnected world.[1] She must monitor the progress of various microcommunities and distribute detailed accounts of their efforts, communicating a larger sense of community and vision that everyone should be working toward. She can create a sense of belonging to a movement by spreading the latest news through information technology, face-to-face contacts, and newsletters.

Shared Maps of Cooperation

When microcommunities throughout an organization share a larger sense of purpose, coordination of knowledge-creation initiatives is much easier. Yet the knowledge activist cannot stop at creating imagined communities. People know with whom they share a nationality, and they can also look at a geographic map to find out who is physically close or distant. But imagined communities can also be mapped, and activists can graphically illustrate how people relate throughout a company. A shared map of cooperation, for instance, will show how the knowledge-creation initiatives across a company are connected.

There are various types of shared maps. An organigram simply shows the location of different people working on knowledge creation; a project-management tool indicates the participation, budgets, milestones, goals, and time frame of knowledge-creation initiatives. A more sophisticated approach involves showing a knowledge-creation process graphically, from the sharing of tacit knowledge to cross-leveling of knowledge; for each step of the process, participation, budget, time frame, expected and achieved results, and responsibilities can be drawn in. Mapping competence configurations (von Krogh and Roos, 1992) is another powerful approach, one that depicts the tasks of various microcommunities and the knowledge they bring to the solution of these tasks. Here other microcommunities can openly discuss how their knowledge might contribute to performance at another site in the company; alternatively, they can see where to find knowledge that may be of use for their own task performance. See Figure 7.1 for a sample shared map.

Such maps of cooperation must be shared with all microcommunities. They need to be visually appealing, be easy to understand and use, supply coordinates for each participant, and show how each microcommunity contributes to knowledge creation in the company. Shared maps of cooperation will allow microcommunities to connect more easily at different points in time. Yet they must be expressed in a language and through a symbolic structure that is commonly understood by everyone.

Because knowledge creation is a journey into the unknown, these maps have to change with the terrain. Dynamic maps will depict how knowledge creation proceeds—what happens to the new concepts created, what issues are being considered during a justification process, the rise and fall of new prototypes, and so forth. In general, shared maps of cooperation will prepare microcommunities to engage in knowledge exchange, the kind that leads to cross-leveling of knowledge and true competitive advantage. But they also need to be thought of as tools for structuring an ongo-

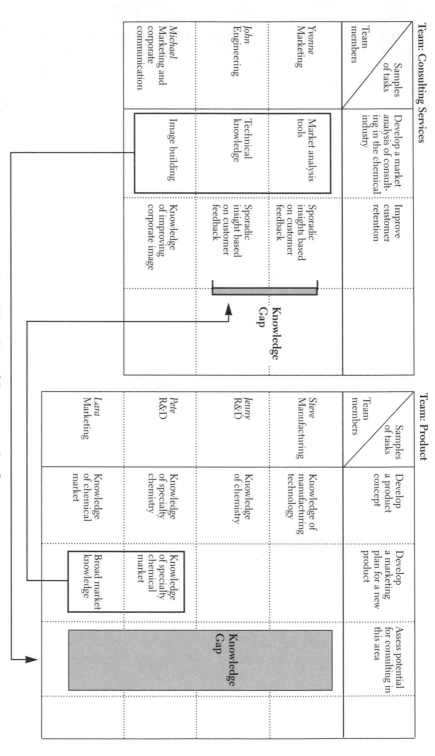

Figure 7.1. A Map of Competence Configuration

ing discussion of how diverse initiatives intersect, not as static entities that can never change. At regular intervals, a knowledge activist might produce "knowledge exhibitions" at which various microcommunities present their efforts to improve exchange of experiences.

Merchants of Foresight

Knowledge activists, then, must assume responsibility for getting shared maps of cooperation to fit with the terrain the company explores. They must connect knowledge-creation initiatives in which cross-fertilization leads to economies of scope and scale. Last, activists can assume a third role: They can be the merchants of foresight in their companies. By this, we mean that activists often provide the overall direction for knowledge creation in different microcommunities. As a merchant of foresight, a good activist will maintain the microcommunity perspective at the same time that he or she changes scale to encompass the larger vision. In other words, knowledge activists need to maintain a bird's-eye perspective as well, soaring beyond the many specific interactions in an organization to look at the company from above.

The key question here is how various microcommunities contribute to the knowledge vision of a company. As we discussed in Chapter 5, a knowledge vision should give organizational members a mental map of the world they live in and provide a general direction for the kind of knowledge they ought to seek and create. This mental map of the future is certainly connected with the imagined community of purpose an activist can promote and the shared maps of cooperation that may result. In essence, these are all tools for making the enabling context for knowledge creation more explicit and easy to grasp.

Business strategy is intimately linked with vision, of course, and merchants of foresight provide the right process triggers to get the two in synch. When playing this role, knowledge activists are responsible for understanding each microcommunity's contribution to the development of the company and detecting how initiatives throughout might change its strategic posture. An activist could ask important questions about advancement versus survival strategies, competitive advantage, sources of competitive advantage, and the role of knowledge, triggering changes that might make the company's strategy a better fit for its knowledge vision.

Selling the vision is also crucial, as Jack Welch has done so effectively with Six Sigma, connecting "the goal and the journey" with the need to create future sustainable competitive advantages for GE. Knowledge activists in this guise challenge participants to improve their contribution to the vision, suggesting how they might adjust their work to match the company's larger goals. Every microcommunity has to understand its work in a broader context, which is no easy task when bogged down in daily details. Knowledge activists have to fight against the myopia that often hinders the process of knowledge creation. (Recall that Welch had to send a clear message that managerial advancement depended on involvement in the new program.) Fighting myopia is particularly important during concept justification. A new concept, whether for a product or service, results from the tacit knowledge shared within a microcommunity; yet this concept will go nowhere if it cannot be justified in terms of the overall vision.

Selling a vision of the future is like selling oxygen—the customer cannot see what he is buying. The merchant of oxygen has sophisticated instruments that show the flow of gas in order to convince the customer that it exists. The working of these instruments and their calibration has to be understood by both the customer and the supplier. By the same token, shared maps of cooperation have to be linked with foresight. In effect, the activist needs a clearly calibrated map to indicate that knowledge-creation initiatives do indeed contribute to the knowledge vision. Like the oxygen merchant, she has to demonstrate that the vision really focuses knowledge creation in the company, and that the efforts of many microcommunities are of value throughout.

WHAT A KNOWLEDGE ACTIVIST IS NOT

In some ways, what we are calling a knowledge activist may resemble the position of knowledge officer now found in a number of companies. But an activist is not the same as an officer, and we want to address some possible misconceptions about knowledge activism before discussing who might play this part in an organization. First, knowledge activism is about enabling, not controlling. Even as a catalyst, connector, *and* merchant of foresight, activist efforts only influence the companywide processes of knowledge creation—they do not determine them. Because of the inherent indeterminacy of such activities,[2] anyone who wants to be a knowledge activist, or considers himself or herself one already, must give up, at the outset, the idea of controlling knowledge creation.

You can see why knowledge activists might conceive of themselves as knowledge controllers. They have direct and immediate contact with various microcommunities, as well as access to the explicit knowledge, concepts, and prototypes produced by these communities; they may adhere to the ideals laid out previously, yet even in our terms they are the ones who continuously edit the maps of cooperation. Indeed, if knowledge were an asset, stable over time and space, and something that could be adequately captured by standards, managers could apply technical procedures to control its development. True knowledge activists, however, have to remove themselves from the asset perspective of knowledge once and for all; they must take a constructionist stand, embrace *ba*, and revel in the context-specific and hard-to-define.

Unpleasant as this may seem to traditional managers, knowledge has an unpredictable character. It is fluid, dynamic, partly tacit, partly explicit, scalable, tied to individuals as well as groups, prone to serendipitous twists and setbacks. Any attempt to control knowledge creation will end up referring to the explicit historical knowledge that already exists, such as an engineering drawing, a market study, or a production manual. Yet this kind of knowledge rarely sparks the innovations and enabling context required to develop the future competitive advantages of a company. What matters is the process: People come together, strike the right tune for sharing private insights, dismantle barriers to fruitful cooperation, unleash the group's creative potential, stretch their minds to embrace new concepts, and carefully apply their technical wisdom to develop prototypes. With the mind-set of a controller, the knowledge activist would be just another frustrating barrier to knowledge creation.

In addition, knowledge activism is not only about connecting to others but about ensuring self-connections. As a merchant of foresight, the activist is in a vulnerable position. In trying to sell a knowledge vision, she will always confront the short-term considerations of different microcommunities, which have their own agendas, aspirations, and fears. She typically runs the risk of being dubbed a visionary without any solid basis in day-to-day business. The maps of cooperation might be seen as a fiction of her own rather than something that provides guidance for down-to-earth knowledge creation. To overcome this obstacle, knowledge activists must be very sensitive to the workings of each microcommunity. They will have to build up trust by demonstrating staying power and a desire for continuous collaboration. They will have to master the delicate art of attentive inquiry and dialogue, through which they can proceed to attach the intent of each community to the company's knowledge vision. It almost goes without saying that they have to act with integrity, at times proposing changes to the vision if it seems too ambitious, unclear, or in conflict with ongoing knowledge-creation initiatives.

Finally, assigning a manager to the position of "knowledge activist" should not be a cover-up for a lack of knowledge creation. It would be easy to say, "Look at us! We really take this knowledge stuff seriously—we even have this knowledge-activist guy who is responsible for knowledge in our whole company!" But if there is no substance behind the words, this is no more effective than calling someone a knowledge officer. Without a sustained commitment to creating knowledge throughout the company, a knowledge activist will just be an extra investment that does not pay off.

He can never compensate for a lack of knowledge creation at the business level, and even the most uninformed shareholder may start to question the absence of deeply rooted knowledge-creation practices. Do not forget that the activist only enables knowledge creation by catalyzing, coordinating, and trading in foresight. The activist cannot be looked at in isolation but as a part of a total package in which new sources of competitive advantage are being secured for the future. Only then will that knowledge activist guy or gal pay off.

WHO SHOULD BE A KNOWLEDGE ACTIVIST?

Since all organizational members from time to time activate knowledge creation in a company, you might well ask if it ever *does* pay off to consider knowledge activism a separate task. We believe it does. Even if knowledge creation can be triggered in microcommunities regardless of intervention, the concepts generated will not necessarily have a strong connection with a company's knowledge vision and overall advancement strategy. The project might lack foresight, and even well-intended initiatives—or the most terrific ideas for products—can end up being ignored by the rest of the company. When a specific person or group has the responsibility for knowledge activism, the coordination that gets good ideas out the door is much more likely to happen. Deciding who should take this responsibility, however, is not a simple hiring decision.

Knowledge activism flows from different sources in different companies. In many large diversified corporations, especially those with a lot of international research and development activity, we have observed that the role of the corporate R&D center is changing in this direction. Rather than conducting basic research, applied research, or even product development, these centers have increasingly taken on the role of coordinating R&D activity throughout the corporation. Applied R&D is essentially seen as a business-related activity linked to distinct industries, markets, customer groups, and products. Meanwhile, corporate R&D is now focused on connecting various research and development findings across businesses with the intention of creating economies of scope.

The corporate R&D center might also work as a catalyst for local knowledge creation by delivering basic research. They can trigger questions related to business activities, using basic research findings as a lever to get into innovation processes at the business level. At the same time, these corporate R&D centers are closely related to corporate strategy making and thus assume a particular responsibility in communicating a knowledge vision. This means that corporate R&D centers often coordinate knowledge-creation initiatives in such a way that they support the realization of the vision—GE's Six Sigma training programs, for example, are initiated

by the Business Initiatives Section at GE's corporate Headquarters unit—
or that they engage in intensive conversations with senior managers about
the need for a change in vision.

Still, this popular approach has pros and cons. These groups are good
representatives of corporate strategy and can therefore communicate and
influence the creation of a knowledge vision. But a center's interests might
conflict heavily with those of microcommunities at the business level,
especially if it has its own budget for R&D. The question of where knowledge creation should occur will be a recurrent theme, endangering the
success of knowledge activism. One possible solution is to restrict basic
research to corporate levels, and applied research and product development to the business level. But as many R&D managers probably have
experienced, the distinction between basic research and applied research
is inherently fuzzy. In a map of cooperation, the division of knowledge-creation labor would have to be solved on a case-by-case basis.

Consultant and researcher Gary Hamel (1996) has suggested that a
company's strategists need to be its activists, inducing change throughout
an organization and creating commitment to an ideal. Strategic planning
staffs and "foresight" centers like Skandia's Future Center can also play an
important role as knowledge activists. Since knowledge is a source of competitive advantage, strategists are bound to take knowledge and other intangible resources into consideration during strategic planning. This, in turn,
requires that they develop high sensitivity to the various knowledge-creation initiatives occurring throughout the company, communicating intensively with product developers, researchers, sales and marketing personnel,
corporate communication officers, and so forth. Strategists form the nexus
of information streams throughout a company, and they assume responsibility for scaling up and identifying patterns in an evolving strategy.

The good thing about using strategists as knowledge activists is that they
are close to the knowledge vision of the company and can communicate
and explain the direction to be pursued by this vision. They can work
actively as merchants of foresight, linking various knowledge-creation initiatives to external changes like the threat of new entrants, new technical
developments, intensifying competition, enhanced influence by suppliers,
and changing customer needs. The problem is that strategists are busy people, always in a hurry to keep up with environmental changes. Perhaps they
even lack the patience required for triggering knowledge creation. As coordinators of various initiatives they may do fine, but they often favor knowledge creation that is in line with a given strategy and vision, ignoring the
kinds of innovations that might change that vision. Strategists are often
identified with a well-defined strategic intent. They normally do not
acquire a reputation for picking up on local initiatives and amplifying them
throughout a company. For strategists to become excellent knowledge

activists, then, a mind set shift has to occur. They have to pay attention to emergent, bottom-up knowledge creation.

Some companies like Asea Brown Boveri (ABB) have established knowledge-and-technology-transfer (KTT) units that take responsibility for spreading technologies, best practices, and experience throughout the corporation. The purpose of these units is to disseminate local knowledge globally in a systematic and speedy fashion. The units normally work with engineering departments as sources and receivers of technology. They identify expertise on technology and the technology to be transferred, define documentation routines, develop training programs, and manage the transfer projects. KTT is becoming a discipline that has a considerable impact on the competitive advantages of the transnational corporation, and the ability to excel in this discipline will therefore have an impact on long-term industry performance.[3] In Chapter 9, we detail such a program at Adtranz, a former project of ABB's in India.

Once again, however, the pros and cons for knowledge activism are clear. As coordinators of knowledge-creation initiatives, KTTs are excellently positioned. Like strategists, these units function as a nexus of information, technology, and knowledge flows in the corporation. KTTs develop particular expertise in administering projects that connect knowledge-creation initiatives. They also take specific approaches to knowledge transfer, such as balancing the transfer of tacit knowledge through training with the transfer of explicit knowledge via engineering documents.

But because knowledge-and-technology-transfer units are quite contract- or project-oriented, connecting knowledge creation and cross-leveling knowledge beyond the project or contract is often unrealistic. The perspective of a KTT can therefore be quite short term. As merchants of foresight, KTTs would have to emphasize knowledge and technology transfer in the context of a knowledge vision. They would need to provide a sense of purpose and direction that can fall far beyond the purview of a given project. Another difficulty might be that, unlike a corporate R&D center, KTTs often lack the basic technical knowledge needed to catalyze knowledge creation. They might not be close enough to the market to pick up new signals from customers that could trigger new knowledge creation. Hence, these units would have to work closely with "listening posts" such as sales and marketing personnel, strategists, researchers, and alliance partners.

By this point, you may have decided that assigning one member of each microcommunity as a knowledge activist is the best idea. The pros of this approach would be local acceptance of this person in her own community and a profound understanding of the process of knowledge creation in general. The cons are also obvious, however, since each knowledge activist would pursue the interests of her own microcommunity and/or be suspected by other communities of doing so. It would also be difficult for her to instill foresight into the community's initiatives, because of her high commitment to the details of one particular knowledge-creation process.

So perhaps activists have to be some sort of manager, even if they are not senior executives. Much of the work on Japanese management has discussed the roles and responsibilities of middle managers (Hedlund and Nonaka, 1993). While some Western companies, in their exuberant efforts to downsize (or "rightsize"), have rid themselves of middle managers (Couldon and Coe, 1991), Japanese companies still retain them in order to achieve better connections between the overall strategic direction set by top management and operational efforts at the level of products and markets.[4] Many Japanese companies have also found that the presence of middle managers contributes to better motivation in lower-level employees (Nonaka and Takeuchi, 1995). In this respect, the middle manager has a good foundation from which to sell a knowledge vision to lower levels.

Electronic communication, of course, has the potential to replace much of the lateral and horizontal information brokering and dissemination previously done by middle managers, connecting employees in various departments and functions. Many commentators now believe an ever-decreasing number of managers will serve more people in the organization, and that electronic communication is the most powerful way to manage a new array of responsibilities. In such virtual companies, managers are like a "spider in the web" (Hedberg, Dahlgren, Hansson, and Olve, 1997), sitting in the middle of a vast network. As we describe in Chapter 8, computer networks and access to the World Wide Web can certainly encourage interactions among many players, creating a kind of "cyber *ba*" that contributes to an overall enabling context. Management consulting firms like Gemini Consulting, whose story we tell in Chapter 10, often rely on corporate databases, intranets, and e-mail to enable knowledge creation and sharing.

But even if this seems conceptually appealing, cyber hype also represents a major threat to the sharing of tacit knowledge in an organization. If a gathering of people is to develop into a microcommunity, they need to develop good relations, complement each other's skill sets, and have a genuine commitment to helping the group grow. Above all, intimate knowledge of people is required to form such communities. Emotional knowledge comprises tacit ideas and experiences of relationships, such as how people work together, their roles and functions on a team, their expectations, their strengths and weaknesses. This tacit knowledge does not lend itself to computer communication. In contrast with an executive who checks into a corporate database of people and skill sets to form a new community, activist middle managers have firsthand experience with who may work best together. This, coupled with their operational experience, often makes such managers excellent catalysts of knowledge creation.

In terms of coordinating initiatives, middle managers are in a position to know much of the covert, semi-overt, and overt knowledge creation occurring in their domains. Even here, however, there are some cons to making middle managers primarily responsible for knowledge activism. Free movement across levels, businesses, departments, and functions might be difficult for these managers. And because some companies like Canon make middle managers responsible for specific knowledge-creation initiatives, such activists may have a hard time obtaining a bird's-eye view of knowledge creation in the company. An overall commitment to a knowledge vision might conflict with the operational concerns and interests of middle managers, and they may be likely to favor those initiatives that are closest to achieving operational excellence within their own areas. Therefore, new knowledge creation may not depart sufficiently from knowledge already embedded in existing products, services, manufacturing procedures, or marketing practices, and will be driven by too much of an operational/improvement mind-set.

One way to overcome this problem is to create a "middle elite."[5] Such managers would get increasing freedom to move around the company, be informed by local knowledge-creation initiatives that broaden their perspectives, share their ideas with participants in these local initiatives, help to facilitate local knowledge-creation initiatives, and become a voice for the local initiatives in top-management discussions of strategy. Sencorp, a privately held, U.S.-based corporation involved in fastening tools, medical technologies, and fastening services, has empowered middle-level management in this way. The company encourages middle managers to initiate knowledge creation, drawing on human resources from all over the corporation (von Krogh and Roos, 1995a).

Yet another possibility is to create new job positions and assign responsibility for knowledge activism to an individual, a knowledge-activist team, or a separate department. The knowledge activist, in this case, would develop the three roles in a balanced way, seeking to catalyze new knowledge creation, to coordinate knowledge-creation initiatives, and to introduce some foresight into the local processes of knowledge creation. Although individuals can accomplish much, team work is probably more effective. A team of managers can define the role and function of knowledge activism in their company in a disciplined manner. It can also become a haven for tired activists, who may need to become reenergized by discussing issues and new opportunities with those who understand the work they do. In the case of a team, the number of members should be carefully adjusted to support the number of knowledge-creation initiatives throughout a company.

HELMUT VOLKMANN:
THOUGHT-MAKER AND MERCHANT OF FORESIGHT

The main lesson here is that knowledge activism can reside in many places and depends on a company's enabling context and business mix. Even that, however, may not be enough to explain why particular managers take on this role or are able to hop across organizational boundaries so well. On his business card, Helmut Volkmann does not list "Thought-Maker," his favorite job title. Instead the card prosaically says: "Dr. Volkmann; Senior Director, Corporate Research and Development." But based on what we have learned about his innovative programs at the Siemens corporation, we consider Volkmann a particularly striking merchant of foresight.[6] He can both scale up—taking a bird's-eye perspective of his company's future and that of society as a whole—and scale down—focusing on daily knowledge-creation activities at Siemens.

In 1847, Werner von Siemens, an electrical engineer, joined forces with craftsman Johann Georg Halske to build telegraph systems in Germany. In 1848, Siemens & Halske Telegraph Construction Company, the firm's original name, linked Berlin and Frankfurt with the first long-distance telegraph system in Europe. By 1867, Halske had left the company, but the name of the company remained Siemens & Halske for more that 100 years. Siemens's history of firsts includes Europe's first electric power transmission system (1876); the world's first electric railway (1879); one of the first elevators (1880); the world's first X-ray tube (1896); and the first European subway, located in Budapest (1896).

Today the Munich-based global electronics giant is involved in information and communication systems and services; semiconductor, passive, and electromechanical components; energy; health care; lighting; transportation; household appliances; and other industries. The company has offices in approximately 190 countries, and produces everything from power plants in Egypt to communications equipment in Thailand. Growth has been especially strong in Asian markets; as of 1996, the company had thirty-five joint ventures in China. In 1998, Siemens's worldwide workforce totaled 416,000, with 222,000 employees working outside Germany. The company had sales of about $66 billion and showed a net income of about $512 million.[7] For obvious reasons, Siemens has a vested interest in creating new knowledge, and this is the organizational environment that has molded and inspired Helmut Volkmann for more than forty years.

The Education of a Knowledge Activist

Volkmann entered Siemens in 1954 at the age of seventeen, starting as an apprentice who studied business administration and engineering part time. Later in 1969 and 1970, as a special representative of the board of managers, he was involved in developing the concept of group dynamics at Siemens. By 1977, he was head of software engineering, a department that increased to 300 people by 1986. During the intervening years, he completed a Ph.D. in political science and became obsessed with exploring the nature of the emerging information society; more to the point, he came to believe that "information" did not represent everything a society should become. According to him, "The knowledge society has to be more than just industry plus information technology." Volkmann did extensive research, wrote articles, and gave an increasing number of presentations on this topic. Yet this was too much "external" thinking for his immediate boss, who wanted Volkmann to pay closer attention to internal work.

Thus, in 1986, committed by the top managers of Siemens's huge R&D center in Munich, Volkmann at that time, was asked to choose one of two alternatives: to pay closer attention to the software development group he headed or to spend three years pursuing his philosophical interests, essentially as a resident thinker. Volkmann chose the latter: "This was a tough decision, because I thought I would be stuck on the side. But I was also sure that this would be the chance for me to think and probably to create something new." In fact, this was what happened, as Volkmann went on to spend far longer than three years thinking about the future of the company and taking a broader view of the society. As of this writing, he is still Siemens's thought-maker.

Volkmann is a strong believer in the butterfly effect of chaos theory. If a butterfly that flutters its wings in China can produce a tornado in the United States, perhaps Volkmann's efforts will trigger Siemens people all over the world to think in unexpected ways. When we asked him how one could apply for such a job at Siemens or elsewhere, he replied, "Without my previous thirty years at the company, I never would have gotten the job. And you should know that I am not just sitting here thinking. I attend conferences and exhibitions, give presentations to customers, and moderate workshops for interested people. Thus, the job is quite stressful as well."

Dr. Volkmann's "Virtual Team" and SATORI

Once Volkmann was free to think about the future of his company, he used a rather unconventional approach to focus on the emerging challenges of the information age. He created a "virtual team"—an imaginary group of people from the future who are able to visit the present and past. He created six members for the team, each with a special name and distinctive personal attributes. There was Tom Sawyer, based on an action-oriented hero whom Volkmann loved when he was young; there was Kai-Out-of-the-Box, a Berlin street-gang boy. Volkmann invented Medica-Twin because "twin means there are two souls in his body: that of a scientist and that of a reformer." Vips, the Little was like a naive child, always asking older people "why?" Eve Pragma focused on facts and everyday reality. The last member, Ingo, was an old engineer.

After he could imagine all six members clearly, Volkmann introduced a present-day entrepreneur into the mix. Under this scenario, the entrepreneur learned about the existence of the team from the future, contacted them, and said, "I would like to know more about the future and make my company the best for your society. Can you tell me how to do this?" Volkmann wrote more than a thousand pages about the adventures of this team, complete with in-depth dialogues. For over two years, he let the virtual team members converse in his head, telling stories and traveling to the future and past.

You may be wondering what kind of executive uses childlike stories to explore the future. Yet Volkmann was well aware of what he was doing. Even if he sounds like a creative writer rather than a manager, that is not his main job: "Most of the ideas people have are rebutted by others telling them why an idea cannot work. We come up with all sorts of creative ways to say something cannot be done, but we do not allow our minds to think differently. We have forgotten what children still can do—to wish."

It is from such "wishful" thinking that Volkmann began developing innovative approaches to the future for workshops at Siemens. Based on the dialogue between the virtual team and the entrepreneur, for instance, he generated the SATORI method of systems enhancement. The first letters of six key words—start, analysis, transcendence, occasions or opportunities, results, and innovations—form the acronym, which is also the Japanese word for enlightenment. As conceptualized by Volkmann, SATORI represents the different steps of knowledge creation. The method involves establishing open centers for information and problem solving, and in such centers, participants might explore questions related to each of the steps: What has happened? (start); Why has this happened? (analysis); What do we really want? (transcendence); What can we dare to do? (occasions and opportunities); What should happen? (results); What do we have to do concretely? (innovation). Volkmann used SATORI in many workshops. Based on an idea, a problem, or a requirement, participants have to go through each step of the method, answering the questions one by one. All thoughts and ideas resulting from answering the questions are retained (for example, they can be tacked up on bulletin boards) and are then restructured by the participants to get a solution or to develop an idea further.

But as early as 1973—long before Volkmann became the company's resident thinker and the SATORI method was developed—he and his colleagues wanted to change the traditional meeting approach, in which a series of different speeches is delivered to a passive audience. They did so for an information meeting of a thousand Siemens managers. The event, held in Munich's Olympic Hall, was very participatory. With twenty to thirty separate spaces on each of the hall's two levels, he and his team set up "information markets," each focused on a particular topic. At each market, managers came together and discussed or presented the issues they were interested in. This approach was so successful that Siemens held several information markets in later years.

Xenia: The Knowledge City

Another Volkmann thought experiment involves envisioning an entire knowledge city called Xenia.[8] For him, Xenia (which means "the hospitable one" in Greek) is a place where "learning, discovering, inventing, and finding can be done in a focused and concentrated manner. Visitors of this place know they can easily get access to existing knowledge. Thus, they can meet their objectives faster and also create new knowledge." Developing a list of things required for such an ideal place is a significant creative challenge for any workshop, and Volkmann intends Xenia as a vision that can spark innovative thinking. For example, a management team that wants to make its company more innovative might try envisioning Xenia in initial discussions.

In general, cities are places in which people go to shop, visit friends, work, be entertained; they are also complicated geographical and social spaces that require orientation on a number of levels. Most people are accustomed to cities, and even an imaginary one can awaken memories of the past that stimulate new discoveries. That is, cities reflect the sentiments of their inhabitants, require maps, and are a good metaphor for how an enabling context might be structured.

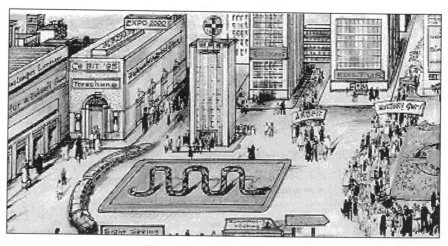

Figure 7.2. A Knowledge City

Think of a knowledge city as a meeting place for people in search of solutions. In Xenia, a new visitor might find experts who have the answer to his technical problem, or a group of thinkers might meet in a "knowledge garden" to arrive at a solution together. According to Volkmann,

> My vision is that there are cities where the knowledge of experts is not isolated and does not rest just in their heads. Knowledge is in the air, and everybody who is interested can use it. Someone who wants to solve problems and enters a knowledge city may end up finding something she did not expect or get advice just to try something different—like wading barefoot through a fountain. The main slogan for a knowledge city is "Meet people, communicate, think: gain knowledge through contemplation! Put knowledge into practice: act!"

Figure 7.2 provides an illustration of what Xenia might look like. Volkmann believes knowledge can be represented by the city metaphor in the following ways:

- the topology and layout
- the design of buildings (facades, floor plans, interior design of event and exhibition areas)
- a supply of intangible goods in multimedia form
- a display of meta-knowledge through signs all over the city

For instance, the names of streets and squares, as well as the types of buildings, signal different kinds of knowledge. A tower that can be seen from everywhere symbolizes a vision, and a big message on its front advertises that vision. To orient visitors, there are signs directing them to knowledge and topics of interest. Instead of billboard ads for products and services, you find ads for ideas, problems, knowledge, and solutions. The decorative and community-oriented facades of the buildings represent an enabling

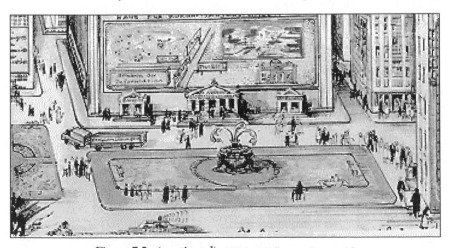

Figure 7.2. (continued) © Helmut Volkmann, Siemens AG

context for knowledge, just as Renaissance planners and thinkers conceived of a city-utopia.

We could keep describing Xenia in minute detail, but the idea here is just to introduce the approach. Overall, we urge readers to be open to the creative thinking such metaphors may inspire and not to reject out of hand innovative thought experiments like a knowledge city or the atelier for innovators described below.

In fact, Xenia is not pure fiction. Volkmann has built a physical model of the city with all its major features to visualize the idea. This was helpful in putting the concept across, as many people liked the idea but could not think of a concrete realization and therefore hesitated to utilize it. Based on the discussion of the physical model and after a presentation of the Xenia model by using very large outlines at the CEBIT (a major annual event for the European computer industry) in 1995, the idea of Xenia was transferred to a business division of Siemens for management consulting in 1997. This business division now also has the physical model for demonstration. Although Xenia is still at the conceptual stage, Volkmann can conceive of managers at other companies creating different knowledge cities—perhaps just as idealistic as Xenia, perhaps grounded in a harsher competitive reality—and also of a network of knowledge cities existing around the world someday. Each of these cities, whether represented virtually or through a physical model, could focus on a given topic, such as energy, health, education, ecology, or traffic.

Ateliers for Innovators

A related approach to thinking about the future involves what Volkmann calls ateliers for innovators, which are essentially knowledge cities in miniature. That is, they represent districts of a knowledge city. People meet to work on complex and innovative solutions in each district in a disciplined manner, using methods like SATORI. The ideas and results from several districts can be presented to others; in addition, participants of one district may go work for another, as districts form and evolve like microcommunities. Such ateliers—or carefully designed "homes" for knowledge workers—would be an ideal setting for sharing tacit knowledge, creating concepts, or prototype building. They are a metaphor for the kind of knowledge space that innovation requires, but Volkmann's atelier concept can also extend to an actual physical space that facilitates communication or to a virtual space or a mix of both. An atelier-inspired conference room, for instance, might include multimedia displays, colorful paintings and photographs, or anything else that encourages creativity. Meeting in such a room, group members might discover knowledge components they did not expect at first but that they can use for their assigned task.

Figure 7.3 depicts an idealized version of an atelier. In Volkmann's terms, the different working platforms shown in the drawing symbolize the division of labor for knowledge creation. Moderators, editors, model makers, multimedia designers, investigators, and logistical staff are there to help the primary group or microcommunity. Specialists provide the group with useful background information derived from research in databases and application programs. They support documentation of the process and give advice about presentation of the results. Primary participants also have access to various tools—from chalkboards to maps of cooperation to computer groupware that facilitates communication—to improve working relations and group dynamics. And if the process does not run smoothly, conversation managers, caring experts, and other moderators are on hand to give the group methodological advice and training. Technical support offers help with handling computer equipment and the infrastructure of the computer network by, for example, setting up dedicated phone lines or cables.

Again, all this may seem extremely utopian. But Volkmann has created an actual atelier for innovators at Siemens. Between 1991 and 1992, top management allowed him to use an old, 600-square-meter storeroom for this purpose. He put flowers, pictures, computers, charts, and other equipment in it, and Siemens participants were enthusiastic: "Here is really the place to think!" remarked one senior executive. For fifteen months, managers could brainstorm and discuss their ideas in this creative space, until the storeroom was converted back to its original purpose. With a gleam in his eyes, Volkmann told us recently, "Because people liked the place so much, I took a second chance." After Volkmann presented his ideas at the

Figure 7.3. An Atelier for Innovators
© Helmut Volkmann, Siemens AG

CEBIT in 1997, an atelier was set up in the same business division to which the Xenia idea has been transferred for management consulting reasons and which has the Xenia model for demonstration.

GROUND RULES FOR ACTIVISTS

Helmut Volkmann represents one end of the knowledge activism spectrum. He is a creative merchant of foresight, focused on alternatives for the future and communicating the possibilities accordingly. Not all activists will be so personally creative, but there are a number of general ways through which they can be the Volkmanns of their corporations. We believe that the ideas presented in this chapter, managed carefully, will have a positive impact on knowledge creation in a company, even if participants are not spinning tales about Xenia or a virtual team of the future. In order to begin mobilizing knowledge activists, try following these initial ground rules:

For Top Managers

- Reread the knowledge vision with respect to knowledge activism. Does it create room for activists to catalyze, coordinate, and trade in foresight?
- Establish knowledge activism as a concept in your company; include it in conversations about knowledge creation and innovation.
- Develop a history of knowledge-creation initiatives and use this as a platform to discuss the importance of knowledge activism.
- Start a broad discussion of how knowledge activism should work. Be open to discussing the possible reservations various people in the organization may have, and come up with ways to convert skeptics into enthusiastic supporters of knowledge activism.
- Discuss who in your organization has the characteristics of a knowledge activist. Do this with care, spending sufficient time and drawing on a number of people who have firsthand experience with the skills required of a good activist.
- Appoint a knowledge activist or group. Clarify and outline what you expect of activists and the roles they need to play.

For Activists

- Identify and name existing microcommunities of knowledge and decide where new microcommunities might emerge.
- Help to form new microcommunities of knowledge.
- Discuss the extent to which local knowledge-creation initiatives align with the knowledge vision.
- Connect microcommunities throughout the company by sharing stories and spreading the latest news.
- Develop shared and dynamic maps of cooperation—for example, graphically illustrating knowledge-creation activities, innovation projects, or centers of excellence.

- Distribute these shared maps to various microcommunities. Make sure to update the maps on a regular basis.
- Launch knowledge exhibitions—presentations of work by different microcommunities or companywide displays of knowledge-creation efforts.

As the above ground rules suggest, selecting the right knowledge activist is a major issue and will depend on the correct skill profile. In some of our research with companies, we have found it useful to create a skill profile at the outset. The profile should be matched with the three different roles knowledge activists can play. In considering a team or knowledge-activist group, you might look for complementary skill sets to fulfill all three roles. A possible skill profile is shown in Table 7.1. Note that the ideal listing of skills presented there is meant only as a tool for getting started. It is highly unlikely that any single person will be so talented. Nevertheless, the process of identifying skills will probably indicate what you really want from an activist, in practical terms, as well what kind of additional training you might provide for activists.

When the team solution seems most appropriate, knowledge activism will ultimately depend on the smooth work and cooperative spirit of team members. Such a team will have to develop and share the roles of knowledge activism, and the process they will go through is quite similar to that of other knowledge-creation efforts. They will have to share their tacit beliefs about what knowledge activists do, then create a concept for knowl-

Table 7.1. The Ideal Knowledge Activist: A Skill Profile

Catalyst	Coordinator	Merchant
Motivational skills	Historic understanding of the company's development	Ambassador for the company's knowledge vision
Interpersonal skills: Respected	Narrative skills: Detect, formulate, and tell stories of knowledge creation	Skills in strategic tools and analysis
Intervention skills: Improve group dynamics and relationships	Cartographical and visual skills: Develop and maintain shared maps of cooperation	Broad understanding of the company's strategy process
Analytical skills: Help the group to develop a charter of their tasks and responsibilities	Analytical skills: Draw connections between knowledge-creation initiatives	Motivational skills and to sell ideas
Broad social network inside and outside the company	Broad social network within and outside the company	Unconventional thinking and visionary skills
Operational understanding of the business, key products, and markets		

edge activism that will eventually be justified by top management, middle management, and other organizational members. This knowledge-activist team will need to create a prototype of the service it will provide. Once the knowledge gained through this process has been cross-leveled, allowing various communities, departments, and divisions to weigh in on the team's initial ideas, the importance of knowledge activism will not only be communicated throughout the organization but the team's service will also evolve to match what its various constituents want. If such an activist group of people consciously undertakes knowledge creation about their own roles, they will gain a firm foundation for their subsequent work. What you recommend to others, after all, you should first test on yourself.

THE IMPACT OF KNOWLEDGE ACTIVISM: DREAMING *AND* DOING

Which brings us back to Helmut Volkmann. Why does a company like Siemens pay an executive to think freely and produce boundary-breaking ideas? For knowledge officers and controllers, this may sound like a nightmare—or at least a waste of time and resources—because the company cannot really measure the performance of Volkmann in financial terms. But as we have emphasized throughout *Enabling Knowledge Creation*, a narrow definition of performance and value can end up undermining a company's competitive advantages rather than maintaining them. In the postindustrial knowledge economy, innovation is the name of the game, and true innovations sometimes depend on highly paid dreamers like Volkmann. At the very least, knowledge activists of this caliber—Leif Edvinsson of Skandia is another—create the kind of enabling context or *ba* that allows creative thinking to thrive.

Volkmann's work may be positive to Siemens's image. He says, "At different events where I have presented my ideas, such as at the CEBIT, the spectrum of opinions offered about what I do range from 'It's great that somebody looks over the mountain' to 'I did not expect this from a traditional company like Siemens' to 'Yes, I would like to be actively involved in further developing these ideas.'" He acts not only as a merchant of foresight outside his company but also within it. Volkmann connects external and internal knowledge initiatives. He has organized an increasing number of workshops for new projects at Siemens; he moderates sessions with the company's sales force and its customers; most of all, he is available when anybody is curious about his ideas.

Of the five enablers, mobilizing knowledge activists may seem to be the most practical first step. Managerial expectations can be spelled out when developing this position, and the concept of knowledge activism can be made to dovetail with knowledge-creation initiatives throughout an organization. Yet keep in mind that effective activism also relies on a carefully crafted knowledge vision and ongoing conversations. Without these, activists will find their task difficult to accomplish. In addition, the kind of coordination that is central to knowledge activism requires an enabling context. In the next chapter, we focus on how such a context can be created, especially through the implementation of organizational structures that are a good match for a company's strategy and vision.

·8·

ENABLER 4

Create the Right Context

It might sound a bit strange. However, I describe it as slip-
ping into customers' minds. . . . We come to see what our
customers expect in the future, while we listen, consider
various problems, and forecast upcoming changes with
them.

— Shun Murakami, President,
Maekawa Food Process Engineering

Knowledge in organizations takes on many guises: It is partly tacit, individual as well as social; it must be nurtured and stimulated, as well as justified and effectively distributed. Throughout *Enabling Knowledge Creation*, we have emphasized that new knowledge creation begins with individual tacit knowledge, which is often difficult to communicate to others. Tacit knowledge is the most important source of innovation, yet it is often underutilized in a firm and difficult to separate out for productive work.[1] Clearly, new knowledge must be articulated and shared with others in an organization if it is to have any impact at all. The preceding chapters have focused on the need for a well-articulated knowledge vision, the importance of conversations for sharing knowledge, and the key role knowledge activists can play in this regard. Here we discuss the enabling context for knowledge creation that underpins all of these.

Our fourth enabler, *create the right context*, involves organizational structures that foster solid relationships and effective collaboration. As knowledge and innovation become more central to competitive success, it is no surprise that many executives have grown dissatisfied with traditional organizational structures. Since the mid-1980s, corporations have begun transforming themselves through a variety of alternatives. Just a quick sampling: cross-functional product development projects (Takeuchi and Nonaka, 1986); reengineering efforts that replace functional organizational arrangements with process-based ones (Hammer and Champy, 1993); virtual corporations that pursue interorganizational activities beyond traditional corporate boundaries (Goldman, Nagel, and Preiss, 1999); and the Urgent Project Team of Sharp, a "hypertext" organization that crosses small business unit lines (Nonaka and Takeuchi, 1995). Organizational behaviorist Dan Denison (1997) summarizes the recent development of such arrangements as an effort to devise new structural forms that offer an unprecedented level of flexibility and adaptability. In other words, traditional organizational charts, with their rigid hierarchies and vertical integration, can no longer coordinate business activities in a world where boundaries are fuzzy, relationships are ever more complex, and the competitive environment is in constant flux.

We explore several specific alternative structures—Sony's empowered divisions, Maekawa's independent corporations, and Toshiba's Advanced-I Group—in the company stories that take up most of this chapter. Our aim in discussing what these Japanese companies have done, however, is to link new organizational structures with the right enabling context. Every company must grapple with unique business, cultural, and interpersonal conditions; even if a cross-divisional unit, for instance, can help a firm risk resources on the creation of new knowledge, this kind of arrangement may not work for companies in other businesses or with different strategies. The key is to structure an organization so that knowledge creation throughout proceeds more effectively and efficiently, dismantling as many individual and organizational barriers as possible.

In fact, the whole process of knowledge creation depends on sensitive and aware managers who encourage a social setting in which knowledge continues to grow. Because an enabling context that is a good fit for a company's strategy and business provides a foundation for all knowledge-creation efforts, this fourth enabler influences how tacit knowledge is shared within microcommunities, the creation of concepts, and the resulting prototypes that are built. But creating the right context has the most impact on how concepts are justified organizationally— that is, whether a broad range of perspectives is used to match new concepts with a company's strategic objectives—and how new knowledge is cross-leveled throughout. In addition, new knowledge can be created interorganizationally, as the recent growth of virtual corporations and strategic alliances indicates. Therefore, where knowledge creation is concerned, organizational structures should reinforce tacit-explicit knowledge interaction across many different boundaries.

Before presenting the Sony, Maekawa, and Toshiba stories, we revisit the concept of enabling context—or *ba*—paying particular attention to how this enabler can help unlock the tacit knowledge of individuals. We delineate four kinds of interaction that influence the ways knowledge can be generated and shared in an organization, and the knowledge spiral that combines all of them into an overall enabling context. We then discuss how to align context, strategy, and structure. The company stories indicate how firms can structurally respond to international competition in their industries, whether their strategic focus is on creating new knowledge or disseminating existing knowledge.

A CLOSER LOOK AT BA—
THE "PLACE" FOR KNOWLEDGE CREATION

From our perspective, an enabling context is what drives knowledge creation, and *ba* refers to the *right* context—one that fosters emerging relationships within microcommunities, across group boundaries, throughout an organization, whatever it takes to unleash tacit knowledge. *Ba* is essentially a shared space that serves as a foundation for knowledge creation, one that is often defined by a network of interactions. This context is not confined to the physical space of an office or face-to-face meetings, since interactions with people may happen through e-mail or other virtual means of communication. Rather, the concept of *ba* unifies the physical spaces, virtual spaces, and mental spaces involved in knowledge creation. More to the point of this chapter, the various knowledge-creation contexts that inevitably overlap in a diverse organization—the "cyber *ba*" of a company intranet, the particular context of a project team, the market environment—can be connected to form an overall enabling context or *basho*.[2]

Not every organizational context is right for knowledge creation, of course; if that were the case, every knowledge-creating company would be performing at its peak. Unfortunately, knowledge enabling is a difficult art to master. Far too many firms are enmeshed in the hypercompetitive context described in Chapter 3, and all companies are bound to confront an array of individual and organizational barriers. While many of these barriers are a natural part of complex human activities, what distinguishes an enabling context from ordinary interaction is that it provides a social context for advancing individual and/or collective knowledge creation. Indeed, the power to create knowledge is embedded not just in one person but in the interaction of that person with others and the environment. Therefore, a particular individual's knowledge can be shared, re-created, and amplified when he or she is part of that context.

Take the activities of Kleiner Parkins Caufield and Byers (KPCB), one of the most successful venture-capitalist firms of Silicon Valley. KPCB has helped many entrepreneurs focus on the Internet to create new business. Its clients include America Online, Netscape, @home, and Amazon.com. According to recent information on its Web site,

> One of the most important elements within KPCB's concept of value-added investing is access to a network of shared information and knowledge referred to as the Keiretsu. The term "keiretsu" describes modern Japanese

networks of companies linked by mutual obligation. The companies in the KPCB Keiretsu consistently share experiences, insights, knowledge and information. This networking resource, comprised of more than 175 companies and thousands of executives, has proven to be an invaluable tool to entrepreneurs in both emerging and developing companies.[3]

This firm does not directly refer to "enabling context," but its network of mutual obligations and shared experiences certainly corresponds to what we mean by *ba*. (Interestingly, KPCB also offers a virtual twist on the more conventional meaning of *keiretsu*—the consortiums of Japanese companies and their suppliers.) The companies in the KPCB Keiretsu and their executives constantly interact via e-mail or face-to-face meetings. They also interact directly or indirectly with KPCB partners. We believe this enabling context has helped those involved create new business frontiers. In fact, this firm's ability to create such an enabling context is its most important competitive advantage. Given the quickly evolving realm of Internet-related businesses, the knowledge generated by the KPCB Keiretsu can be shared, re-created, and amplified quickly and effectively.

An enabling context can be built intentionally, as with the KPCB Keiretsu. Top management and knowledge producers can facilitate knowledge creation by providing appropriate physical spaces (meeting rooms) or cyber connections (computer networks), or by promoting interactions among organizational members through task forces, teams, and retreats. Yet enabling contexts are also spontaneously created, and care-based relationships provide the foundation for the trust, support, and commitment required to nurture such unplanned occurrences. In this case, managers must recognize and shape spontaneously formed instances of *ba*, which can change or disappear very fast. Leaders have to understand how organizational members are interacting with one another and the outside environment in order to quickly capture naturally emerging *ba*.

Even so, recognition and understanding are not enough to manage the dynamic knowledge-creation process. The enabling context must be energized so that individuals or the organization can create and amplify knowledge. For that purpose, managers need to provide the following conditions: the right amount of autonomy for participants; a certain level of creative chaos, redundancy, and variety to make the environment stimulating; and, again, a high-care organization—one that fosters mutual support and commitment, along with indwelling, the process first described in Chapter 3 in which participants "live" with a concept together, converting tacit knowledge into effective social knowledge.

Note that our concept of an enabling context may seem similar to the "community of practice" developed by other researchers (Lave and Wenger, 1991; Wenger, 1998). A community of practice implies that members of a group learn through participating in the practices of that group and by gradually memorizing jobs—as in an apprenticeship system. However, there are important differences between this concept and an enabling context. While a community of practice is a place in which members learn knowledge that is embedded there, an enabling context helps create new knowledge. The boundary of a community of practice is firmly set by the task, culture, and history of that community, but an enabling context is determined by the participants and can be changed easily. Membership in a community of practice is fairly stable, and it takes new members time to become full participants. But the many organizational members who interact in an enabling context come and go. Instead of being constrained by history, an enabling context has a here-and-now quality—and it is this quality that can spark real innovations.

CREATING A SHARED KNOWLEDGE SPACE: FOUR KINDS OF INTERACTION

An enabling context, then, is a shared knowledge space, one that encourages and nurtures participation on many different levels. This is the space that fosters indwelling in a high-care organization; it is the shared space that knowledge activists help shape in their role as catalysts or energizers of knowledge creation. Yet the interactions that are at the heart of *ba* can happen at a department meeting, during a brainstorming exercise at a company retreat, via the Internet, or when two professionals talk over drinks after work. It is useful to break this down into different kinds of interaction to get a handle on the various ways managers can create the right context. Table 8.1 shows four interactions that all contribute to an overall enabling context: originating, conversing, documenting, and internalizing. The simple grid of this figure involves two dimensions: one indicates the type of interaction (individual or collective); the other refers to the interaction medium (face-to-face contact or through "virtual" media like books, manuals, e-mail, and teleconferences).

The knowledge spiral depicted here indicates how closely connected these interactions are; the knowledge originated through individual face-

Table 8.1. Interactions in a Knowledge Spiral

	Individual Interaction	Collective Interaction
Face-to-Face Interaction	ORIGINATING Sharing tacit knowledge between individuals	CONVERSING Having group conversations to form concepts
Virtual Interaction	INTERNALIZING Making explicit knowledge tacit once more	DOCUMENTING Converting knowledge into explicit forms

to-face contact, for instance, can be conceptualized through collective conversations or dialogues, then converted into explicit documents, then internalized once more as tacit knowledge. More important, the whole process keeps spiraling onward—from originating to conversing to documenting to internalizing to originating—as the new knowledge created continues to evolve.

Originating interaction is how individuals share feelings, emotions, and experiences. Individual face-to-face interaction is the only way to capture the full range of physical sensations and emotional reactions that are necessary for transferring tacit knowledge. Individuals sympathize and/or emphasize with others, actions that inspire the care, trust, and commitment that allow for knowledge sharing. Although people may describe what they know through words, originating interactions include other means of expression as well; these include physical gestures, jokes, scribbled drawings on a napkin—all the ways people communicate when they meet in real time and space.

Conversing allows a group of people to share the mental models and skills of individual members. This reinforces the conversion of tacit knowledge into explicit knowledge, and here conversational skills and the use of a common language come to the fore. Individuals discuss the mental models of others, analyzing their own at the same time. Conversing lets participants benefit from the synthesis of rationality and intuition that produces creativity. As such, it needs to be more consciously fostered than originating interactions. Selecting individuals with the right mix of specific knowledge and capabilities is essential, since knowledge is created through peer-to-peer interactions. When knowledge activists help form microcommunities, for instance, they encourage effective conversing as well as originating interactions.

Documenting is both collective and virtual. Because explicit knowledge can be transmitted to a large number of people through written documents, this kind of interaction mainly involves the combination and presentation of existing explicit knowledge. It is most efficiently supported by a collaborative environment, one that in many firms is now based on information technology like on-line networks and groupware.

Finally, *internalizing* is individual and virtual. When somebody reads company documentation or sees a video, the next step is for him or her to internalize the explicit knowledge presented there. In other words, individuals internalize knowledge that has been communicated throughout their organization or relevant group via manuals, e-mail, videos, or other media. The fact that new knowledge begins with the tacit ideas of individuals and eventually becomes tacit again—internalized to the extent that organizational members share certain values, can know a variety of things without having to refer to documents, and acquire skills and capabilities that are no longer conscious—indicates that the process does not move in one direction. Rather than pinning down every piece of knowledge in explicit form, managers need to recognize the power of tacit knowledge and the importance of enabling its use.

As these descriptions imply, the four interactions reflect the knowledge-creation steps we have described throughout this book. Originating, for instance, is closely connected with the sharing of tacit knowledge within microcommunities; conversing is related to concept creation and justification; documenting is part of prototype building; and internalizing is connected to cross-leveling of knowledge. But according to our knowledge spiral, the knowledge generated through each kind of interaction is eventually shared and forms the knowledge base of an organization. In other words, it all adds up to something larger than the sum of individual efforts.

Moreover, these different interactions exist at many levels of experience, all of which may be connected to form the larger enabling context. You might think of these four kinds of interaction as "baby *ba*" or subcontexts for knowledge creation. Individual interactions are the basis for teamwork, which in turn can provide the enabling context for an organization. The market environment provides another kind of context, and the natural interactions among these different levels will expand the entire knowledge-creation process.

CHOOSING THE RIGHT STRUCTURE FOR THE RIGHT CONTEXT

Depending on the company and its knowledge vision, an enabling context may emphasize originating over documenting—or rely on e-mail rather than face-to-face meetings. At a basic level, originating, conversing, documenting, and internalizing are a part of all knowledge-creation processes. But each company has an interaction style of its own and will use different kinds of experiences to form its networks of mutual obligation and trust. So how do companies create a coherent enabling context, one that fits both their knowledge vision and business strategy? Our short answer: The right context must be accompanied by the right organizational structure.

Let us point out first that context and structure are not the same thing. Again, an enabling context can either be consciously constructed or arise spontaneously. Setting up an appropriate organizational structure certainly falls under the purview of management, and this chapter details a variety of ways to construct knowledge-intensive interactions. But as we have emphasized repeatedly, knowledge enabling means more than conscious planning. An enabling context is not just established with a new organizational chart; how managers implement a new organizational structure—and their ability to allow such structures to shift and grow and evolve, depending on business circumstances and the people who are part of the process—is what really matters. If an enabling context is largely defined by the quality and depth of participants' interactions, an organization's structure can arrange for these interactions to happen or it can hinder them. As with so many aspects of management, the most creative reorganization will accomplish nothing if personal relationships are poor, or if executives focus only on short-range facts.

Yet strategy, the planning arm of corporations, is closely connected with structure. Described from this angle, an enabling context should provide an organization with the strategic ability to acquire, create, exploit, and accumulate new knowledge continuously and repeatedly in a cyclical process. Once again, flexibility is key—or more specifically, the proper balance between flexibility and corporate control. Most business organizations have several objectives for their sustainable growth. They need to pursue operational effectiveness at the same time that they pursue innovation. They should create knowledge for the current market while preparing for the knowledge they may need in the future. Since these objectives sometimes compete with one another, it is not appropriate to pursue all of them by means of the same management or structure. Therefore, organizations should develop specific structural arrangements that can provide the right contexts for various objectives.

What that may come down to, in practice, is different structures for different units, divisions, or businesses of a company. A firm may have an overall advancement strategy, one that emphasizes future success and innovation, yet still need to maintain and support an existing business. The existing business, after all, may provide the resources for creating new knowledge that leads to future innovations. As we noted in Chapter 4, most knowledge-creating companies focus on advancement rather than survival strategies; our point there was to underscore the importance of looking to the future. Executives need to consider knowledge creation as the means for developing sustainable competitive advantage. It is a process that requires companywide commitment and must be seen as something that pays off over the long term, not a series of one-shot initiatives suggested by various groups or consultants, which often have little connection to a larger knowledge vision. However, no company, except perhaps for an Internet start-up in its first few years, can live entirely in the future. Balancing survival and advancement is essential, and this managerial goal is related to finding the right match between strategic objectives and enabling context.

Let us further categorize strategic or operational challenges by distinguishing between new or existing knowledge and new or existing business. In doing so, we can point to four different strategic objectives—risky new businesses, new product development, a new business platform that may involve alliances with other companies, or process innovations—each of which requires a different structural approach for enabling knowledge creation. Table 8.2 depicts how these objectives are related.[4] One axis separates a new business from an existing business. The other distinguishes between the creation of new knowledge and utilization of existing knowledge.

For existing businesses that depend on utilizing existing knowledge, the basic strategic objective is process innovation or cost efficiency and time-based competition. The point is to improve operations and processes so that existing knowledge is used most effectively and efficiently. Given that the strategic direction for these businesses has been clearly spelled out by corporate headquarters, in structural terms, empowered divisions (or small business units) make the most sense. Divisions with the authority to proceed on their own will create the kind of enabling context that leads to process innovations. Empowered divisions are more efficient at distributing and exploiting existing knowledge when corporate executives do not interfere or impose their will from above.

Existing businesses that need to develop new knowledge, however, must bring together representatives from a number of different functions and areas in an intensive yet flexible way. A case in point is new product development, often the main strategic objective in this category. Here task forces or project teams are the structural arrangements that enable knowledge creation. New knowledge always stems from individuals; thus, individual knowledge should be explicitly stated and shared with other organizational members. A task force provides the right context for sharing this individual knowledge. Through conversations that involve each member, tacit knowledge can be articulated and shared among participants, then developed into new concepts and prototypes.

For new businesses that are developed from existing knowledge, a firm's strategic objective may be to create a new business platform for various companies. It is increasingly difficult for a single company to develop a new business by itself without forming alliances or partnerships with others. Witness the KPCB Keiretsu of Internet-related players. Participation in a new business platform should be carried out by subsidiaries of a com-

Table 8.2. The Relationship Between Strategic Objectives and Knowledge

	New Business	Existing Business
New Knowledge	Risky but strategically very important	New product development; innovation independent of everyday operations
Existing Knowledge	New business platform; depends on alliances or partnerships	Process innovation

pany, which can be operated with less interference from corporate head-quarters and may more easily form strategic alliances with other key players. The platform or virtual-network structure that this implies will provide the appropriate enabling context for interorganizational new business.

Finally, if part of a company's strategy involves creating new businesses based on new knowledge, participants need to be able to explore fields that are completely new. This exploration process is highly uncertain but strategically very important for any firm emphasizing advancement. Structurally, a cross-divisional unit with strong corporate support is an effective approach. A unit that directly reports to top management should have full responsibility for the new businesses developed. Most task forces are temporary, and using the knowledge they generate may not be easy, especially once their given task has been completed. A cross-divisional unit, however, can be longer lived, and the responsibility it has for sharing, documenting, and distributing knowledge is fueled by corporate interest. Knowledge creation will be conducted more systematically and consistently, providing a better enabling context than that of a task force.

Note that none of these structural approaches conforms to a traditional hierarchy. Even when corporate executives are involved, it is their commitment, encouragement, and coordination of diverse efforts that are required for knowledge enabling, not a rigid adherence to business planning or micromanagement. Given the rapidly changing business environments of Sony and Toshiba, for instance, it has become crucial for such diversified companies to realize economies of scope. Economies of scope require the sharing of tacit and explicit knowledge—that is, the resources, skills, know-how, and technologies often generated by two or more otherwise distinct divisions. The company stories that follow all describe some form of cross-divisional structure or task force, but the ways their specific structural approaches have evolved depend on their strategies. (See Table 8.3.)

In the first story, Sony exemplifies both the use of empowered divisions for process innovation and the ability to create new businesses by developing new business platforms involving its subsidiaries and other firms. Maekawa focuses on the task force structure—or what it calls independent corporations—and its close interaction with customers to create the

Table 8.3. Four Organizational Structures That Encourage Knowledge Enabling

	New Business	Existing Business
New Knowledge	Cross-divisional unit (Toshiba)	Task force (Maekawa)
Existing Knowledge	Platform/virtual network (Sony)	Empowered division (Sony)

right enabling context for new product development. Finally, Toshiba's version of a cross-divisional structure—its Advanced-I Group—provides the right context for creating new businesses and innovative concepts. As the Toshiba story illustrates, the enabling context should also encourage tacit knowledge sharing at the corporate level so that new ideas can filter throughout a large, multidivisional company. It is at this level that an overall enabling context connects the many *ba* involved, making knowledge creation a part of a firm's basic values and culture.

SONY'S ORGANIZATIONAL TRANSFORMATIONS

Established in 1946, the Sony Corporation is a leading global electronics firm. Currently, Sony covers a wide range of businesses, including electronics (video, audio, television, and computer equipment; semiconductors and electronic components), video games (Sony Computer Entertainment), music (Sony Music Entertainment), film and television production (Sony Pictures Entertainment), and insurance (mainly through Sony Life Insurance). Sony's sales during the fiscal year that ended March 31, 1999, increased to $56.6 billion. Its net income is almost $1.5 billion.[5]

Sony's name is widely recognized as a mark of excellence for trend-setting products. However, since the early 1990s, the competitive environment surrounding Sony has drastically changed. The markets for entertainment hardware and software are rapidly evolving because of new digital and networking technologies. Sony's major competitors used to be home-electronics companies like Matsushita and Philips, but now it faces fierce competition from information-technology companies like Microsoft, Intel, and Compaq. And because music and videos can now be distributed through computer networks without hard media like CD-ROMs and mini discs, these technological developments are threatening Sony's existing businesses.

In general, just as the 1980s for U.S. industrial firms was a decade of reshaping corporate strategies and rebuilding organizational structures, the 1990s have forced a number of Japanese multidivisional firms to transform themselves. Instability and uncertainty in the electronics industry have been caused by convergence of various segments, the velocity of technological changes, and globalization. The personal computer, the network, and the home electronics industry segments are all converging, although the ultimate outcome is not yet clear. For example, PCs are closely related to networks and communication because of the rapid development of the Internet. Yet to make current PCs more friendly, electronics corporations are trying to integrate computers and home electronics. Take the digital TV. A big-screen computer television like Gateway 2000s Destination, designed for the family room and aimed at people who already own a home PC, was released to the market in 1996. In the same year, large Japanese electronics firms like Sanyo and Sharp began selling Web TV boxes as consumer electronics products, allowing consumers to browse the Web on conventional televisions. These two distinct industries have already put a product on the market that tests the public appetite for interactive television, even if neither has been a rousing success to date.

Given this industry convergence, cross-divisional coordination is necessary for sharing and transferring the knowledge from different electronics industry segments accumulated in otherwise independent units. In order to survive in this environment, quick decision making and agile adaptation are indispensable. Japanese multidivisional electronics firms are notorious for their slow decision making, but the radical and rapid environmental changes that Sony now faces have impelled its top executives to take a new strategic tack. In January 1996, top management announced a new structure aimed at integrating R&D activities. The idea is to reinforce the strategic role played by its corporate headquarters unit at the same time that Sony maintains empowered divisions or companies. Sony's main focus is on using existing knowledge, either to create new businesses or to improve current operations. Its main challenge is balancing corporate responsiveness with flexibility and the ability to move fast— that is, creating the right enabling context for its diverse array of businesses.

The Company System: Sony's Empowered Divisions

In April 1994, Sony established its "company system." Nineteen small business units for specific products were reorganized into eight companies for specific markets.[6] This eight-company organizational structure was supposed to (1) create a more market-driven, market-responsive corporation; and (2) clarify lines of responsibility and increase autonomy. Each company had its own R&D, manufacturing, and sales functions in order to reduce the time spent on cross-functional coordination. That meant each company was expected to move much faster. The president of each company was empowered to make quick decisions without any interference from corporate headquarters. In addition, each company was expected to provide dividends to headquarters, giving it even more motivation to respond to environmental changes quickly and agilely. In other words, Sony's new structure was based on independent companies fully responsible for their own business performance. The slow consensus decision-making system used previously—that is, the old context or *ba* for knowledge creation—also changed, as the control exercised by Sony's headquarters weakened.

Yet this structural approach created new problems, especially in coordination and knowledge distribution. Once he became president and COO in 1996, Nobuyuki Idei revised the company system. The eight companies were reorganized to form a total of ten within the Sony Corporation.[7] The Consumer A&V Products Company, for instance, became three new companies: the Display Company, the Home AV Company, and the Personal AV Company. The Information Technology (IT) Company was established to oversee Sony's businesses in the personal computer and IT areas. Company presidents still had the authority to manage their respective businesses; individual companies were assigned their own management goals as well as clearly defined responsibilities for financial statements, but their job responsibilities were reduced in other ways.

For one thing, the marketing function of the eight former companies was consolidated. The old marketing departments from those companies were combined into three marketing groups: Japan Marketing, International Marketing and Operations, and Electronic Components and Devices. For another, new corporate laboratories were set up, encompassing some of the R&D departments from the eight earlier companies.[8] These revisions to the previous company system meant that marketing and R&D activities became more centralized again, and Sony's corporate headquarters was reinforced. An executive board was established to develop and execute corporate strategies. The board, chaired by Idei, included four newly appointed officers (from human resources, production, marketing, and communications), in addition to the chief technology and financial officers. Figure 8.1 outlines these structural changes.

The upshot was that the ten companies became part of five larger groups, all of which had autonomy but were also more closely connected with corporate strategy making. Nobuyuki Idei explains the reasons for his revisions as follows:

> The previous company system facilitated too much independence in each company. As a result, they tended to think their own business development was optimum. Therefore, in order to let each company respect Sony's corporate interest and make a good balance between company interests and corporate interests, we made these revisions."[9]

The revised company system essentially involved the empowered-division structure already described, and the enabling context became more coherent in two important ways: integration of knowledge about research and development; and clarification of the role corporate headquarters plays in formulating strategy.

Under the previous system, each company pursued its own R&D activities. However, as the threats posed by new technologies increased, the localization of R&D activities was less effective. By integrating the intel-

Outline Chart of Organizational Changes (as of April 1, 1996)

Note: The individuals indicated after the company are their respective presidents

Policy Board

Chair: Norio Ohga

Executive Board

Chair: Nobuyuki Idei

Executive Board Members:

Tsunao Hashimoto
Vice Chairman of the Board and Representative Director, Chief Human Resources Officers (CHO)

Minoru Morio
Executive Deputy President and Representative Director, Chief Technology Officer (CTO)

Kozo Ohsone
Executive Deputy President and Representative Director

Yoshiyuki Kaneda
Executive Deputy President and Representative Director, Chief Production Officer (CPO)

Tamotsu Iba
Executive Deputy President and Representative Director, Chief Financial Officer (CFO)

Kiyoshi Yamakawa
Senior Managing Director

Junichi Kodera
Senior Managing Director, Chief Marketing Officer (CMO)

Kenji Tamiya
Senior Managing Director, Chief Communications Officer (CCO)

Home Entertainment & Information Group
Directors in Charge:
Minoru Morio (Exec. Deputy Pres. and Rep. Director)
Junichi Kodera (Sr. Managing Director)

Display Company	Suehiro Nakamura (Managing Director)
Home AV Company	Katsumi Ihara (General Manager)
Information Technology Company	Kunitake Ando (Director)

Personal Entertainment & Communications Group
Directors in Charge:
Kozo Ohsone (Exec. Deputy Pres. and Rep. Director)
Hideo Nakamura (Managing Director)

Personal AV Company	Shizuo Takashino (Director)
Personal & Mobile Communications Company	Masao Morita (Counsellor)

Image Creation & Communications Group
Directors in Charge: Kiyoshi Yamakawa (Sr. Managing Director)

Broadcast Products Company	Masayuki Takano (Director)
Image & Sound Communications Company	Takeo Eguchi (Director)

Electronic Components & Devices Group
Director in Charge:
Yoshiyuki Kaneda (Exec. Deputy Pres. and Rep. Director)

Semiconductor Company	Seiichi Watanabe (Director)
Components & Computer Peripherals Company	Teruaki Aoki (Director)

Director in Charge: Kozo Ohsone (Exec. Deputy Pres. & Rep. Director)

Recording Media & Energy Company	Akiyoshi Kawashima (Counsellor)

Director in Charge: Junichi Kodera (Sr. Managing Director)

International Marketing & Operations	
Japan Marketing	Sr. General Manager: Katsuhito Hayashi (Managing Dir.)

Electronic Components & Deluxe Marketing Sr. General Manager:
Nobuyghi Watanabe (Counsellor)

Research Center	Director: Toshiyuki Yamada (Director)
Architectural Lab.	Director: Alkazu Takeuchi (Sony Computer Science Lab.)
Product Development Lab.	Director: Katzuaki Tsurushima (Director)
Systems & LSI Lab.	Director: Shigeyuki Ochi (Counsellor)

Corporate Laboratories

D 21 Laboratory	Director: Toshitada Doi (Director)

Corporate Support Functions

Figure 8.1. Organizational Changes at Sony (April 1996)
(*source:* www.world.sony.com/CorporateInfo/News-E/199601/99–004E/)

lectual assets nurtured and developed in different companies at the corporate level, Sony's executive board hoped to be better prepared for new business development as the electronics industry converges. Idei points out that Sony is well positioned to generate close interactions between its companies and subsidiaries—providing a platform for new businesses that rely on strategic alliances—and thus creating unique value in the digital era for Sony's worldwide customers. Indeed, by revising its previous company structure, Sony executives decided to pursue "value-creation management" with its companies and subsidiaries.

In the old system, each company developed its own strategy while pursuing operational effectiveness. But each company soon realized that accomplishing these two assignments was not easy, and changes in the market were so drastic that none of the previous eight companies were able to conduct long-term strategic planning. Therefore, the revised system made the executive board responsible for such strategy. Idei compares Sony's corporate headquarters to a computer operating system and its companies to applications software (Idei, 1996). Just as the operating system is the most important software on a personal computer, a corporate headquarters unit should be strong and have the best intellectual capabilities. Meanwhile, like an "empowered" applications program, each company should develop its unique competence but remain in close contact with corporate plans and strategies.[10]

Overlapping Enabling Contexts

Sony's organizational changes establish a clear division between the individual companies responsible for operational management and the corporate headquarters unit responsible for strategy making and oversight. Another way to interpret the firm's recent structural transformation is that, in an effort to develop competitive advantages not only for today but also tomorrow, Sony has implemented a different enabling context-for-different-strategic-requirements approach. In a diversified corporation like Sony, its overall enabling context often amounts to many subcontexts or baby *ba* that overlap. If an enabling context constitutes a network of interactions, then such interactions will shift according to the business, division, or company.

Existing Sony businesses that depend mainly on existing knowledge—such as audiovisual equipment like Walkmans and TVs—rely on the empowered-division approach for process innovation. You might call this *ba* at the company level. Meanwhile, new businesses based on existing knowledge are carried out by Sony's subsidiaries. This, in turn, calls for another context at the subsidiary level—the *ba* of Sony Music Entertainment, the *ba* of Sony Pictures Entertainment, and so on. More to the

point, these subsidiaries have been generating new business platforms—
that is, another enabling context for new business that involves strategically
important partners such as Square (a Japanese video game manufacturer)
and Toshiba.

Although we are focusing on Sony's utilization of existing knowledge,
its executives are also interested in developing new products and extending its business range to encompass broadcasting and other forms of electronic distribution. Like the task forces of Maekawa and many other
manufacturing firms, Sony's project teams include members from across
its companies so that existing businesses can develop new product concepts. In order to pursue corporatewide planning, Sony has also established a cross-company project, creating yet another enabling context that
moves beyond traditional boundaries. Currently, Sony has a cross-company project for its fledgling Digital Network Solutions business, which
aims to create an integrated network system for customers that provides
movies, music, and financial services.

The Transformation Continues: Unified Dispersed Management

It may be more useful to think of a company's enabling context as a knowledge space that is always shifting, overlapping, and transforming. In March
1999, Sony executives announced plans to realign its group architecture
yet again. The new architecture will strengthen the electronics business,
privatize three Sony subsidiaries,[11] and increase the management capability of its business units. Here we briefly touch on the corporation's efforts
to realign its electronics operations, since this relates most directly to the
development of a platform structure for new business opportunities.

The 1999 organizational revision consolidates the previous ten companies into the following four business groups: Home Network Company
(digital televisions for the network-centric era); Personal IT Network
Company (unified telecommunications products); Sony Computer
Entertainment (video games); and Core Technology and Network
Company (developing recording media and devices in collaboration with
other business units). Figure 8.2 shows this next round of changes. By the
second revision of the company system, Sony executives made clear that
they wanted to create a "value chain" across companies and subsidiaries
to focus on the emerging networking business. Therefore, new enabling
contexts were created to support these new strategic objectives.

To help each business unit operate autonomously, essential support
functions and R&D laboratories have been transferred back to them from
corporate headquarters. Authority will be delegated to a board and management committee within each company. To provide a flexible system for
pursuing new business opportunities in networking, these companies can

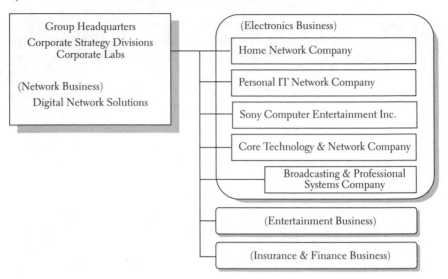

Figure 8.2. Organizational Changes at Sony (March 1999)
(*source*: www.world.sony.com/CorporateInfo/News-E/19903/99-0301)

spin off new business platforms of their own—for example, they can create new companies—a system that allows for full utilization of the technologies and expertise available within each unit. Meanwhile, Sony's
headquarters has been divided into two distinct functions: Group
Headquarters and business-unit support.

The size of Group Headquarters will be kept to a minimum. It will oversee group operations, organize business units, and allocate resources
speedily. Many of the support functions will be transferred to the appropriate companies, enabling them to operate autonomously. Corporate support functions like accounting, human resources, and general affairs will
be separated from Group Headquarters to improve the quality of their service and to develop their own business with companies other than Sony in
the market. While immediate and short-term projects will be transferred
to the relevant companies, long-term R&D projects carried out by the corporate labs and those related to future network businesses (in the separate
Digital Network Solutions division mentioned above) will remain a part
of Group Headquarters.

Big competitive threats call for big organizational changes, of course,
although you may be wondering if it is necessary to undergo such structural transformations every other year. Consolidating telecommunications, computer, and home-electronics devices—that is, offering new
products that combine access to the Internet, telephone service, other
office functions, even music and video—is the competitive frontier of the
consumer electronics industry, and Sony means to be ahead of the game.

Yet developing such new businesses calls for more coordination across the entire value chain of companies, subsidiaries, and other partners. Note that the Digital Network Solutions division is under direct corporate control, which means that headquarters strategists and other top executives can lend more support to emerging new business.

With this latest transformation, Nobuyuki Idei, who is now CEO, has declared that Sony will pursue "unified dispersed management." Its new group architecture includes self-contained, autonomous business units along with a headquarters that plays a strong coordination role. Although it sounds paradoxical, unified dispersed management characterizes Sony's overall strategy of creating a value chain across companies at the same time that each company and subsidiary remains financially independent. Unified dispersed management is a structural approach for the network-centric era, one that allows for quick decision making and flexible coordination. As the Sony CEO says, "We are committed to creating new lifestyles and providing new forms of enjoyment to people in the network-centric society of the twenty-first century." We would add that such evolving organizational structures reflect the evolving enabling contexts for knowledge creation in the postindustrial economy—one that is more virtual than ever but still relies on the *ba* of many workers and groups, as well as the oversight of managers.

MAEKAWA'S INDEPENDENT CORPORATIONS

Since its inception in the 1920s, the Maekawa Manufacturing Company has also gone through many organizational shifts.[12] Like Sony, it currently strives to balance flexibility with corporate unity, although Maekawa's approach to that never-ending paradox is different. We focus on Maekawa's efforts to develop new products through task forces—or its independent corporations. What makes this structural system unique, however, is that the entities involved have more autonomy and authority than the standard task force. In previous chapters, we have briefly discussed Maekawa's Toridas project. This fourteen-year effort was initiated and carried out jointly by different independent corporations, producing an automated chicken deboning machine that is one of the company's most successful innovations. In this section, we look at how Maekawa structures its independent corporations and approaches the issue of tacit knowledge sharing with customers.

While Maekawa has continued to strengthen its position in the field of industrial freezers, the company has also been responding to what its customers say they want: applying freezing systems and heat-transfer technologies to other fields. As a result, Maekawa has broadened the spectrum of its activities to services and technologies in the fields of energy, food processing, and extremely low-temperature equipment. It now manufactures several hundred types of freezers for industrial use. The Maekawa brand name is well known, and these account for more than 90 percent of all industrial freezers exported from Japan. The company now has about a 30 percent share of industrial freezers in the world market. Although the entire industry has suffered from the Asian economic slump of the 1990s, Maekawa has continued to make a fair profit. In 1998, Maekawa had sales of $931 million and a net income of $16 million.[13]

Surprisingly, Maekawa's headquarters unit has only about seventy employees. Their functions are limited to tasks such as providing its independent corporations with necessary information, financial goals, and technical support. The headquarters unit of Maekawa, located in the southeastern part (Koto-ku) of Tokyo, is in a renovated condominium, which also houses the offices of various independent corporations. It looks as if corporate headquarters is just another tenant. In the entrance hall, name plates of the independent corporations and headquarters' departments appear on a wall with no differentiation. The physical space itself symbolizes Maekawa's unique organizational structure, in which the headquarters unit is subordinate to the independent corporations. Maekawa began implementing this management system in 1970 in order to allow each independent corporation to respond fully to the needs of regional markets without any interference from headquarters.[14]

The corporations, classified by product and market type, operate on a self-supporting accounting system. Currently, Maekawa has eighty such independent corporations in Japan and twenty-three in other countries. Since Maekawa has approximately 2,500 employees, the average number of employees in each independent corporation is about twenty-five. At any other company, these corporations might be viewed as branch offices or subsidiaries, but not at Maekawa. The company's employees share similar corporate values and believe that each independent corporation is a constituent of Maekawa. In this sense, Maekawa exists only as a collective entity, in which each of the approximately hundred independent corporations participates in an overall enabling context.

Each independent corporation has complete responsibility for its own management, with the ultimate goal of responding to the local needs of a given region. The functional domains of each—such as design, manufacturing, sales, marketing, service, general affairs, and accounting—are covered by a limited number of employees, and each member is responsible for two or three functions. This way, an entrepreneurial corporate culture has been fostered at Maekawa, meaning all employees working for independent corporations are active entrepreneurs at the same time that they are mutually dependent on one another. This entrepreneurial culture extends to the relationship among independent corporations as well. While each is an autonomous organization, they are also closely connected to the others. Maekawa's corporations are grouped into several blocs according to regions and industrial markets. Each bloc comprises several independent corporations, whose presidents meet together regularly.[15] Shun Murakami, president of Maekawa Food Process Engineering, explains:

> When you become a director of an independent corporation and devote yourself to responding to the needs of a particular region, you realize the limitations of your independent corporation. Then you start thinking about which other corporation(s) could complement your capabilities. In other words, you try to cooperate with other corporations in order to achieve your objectives.[16]

In some cases, an independent corporation has its own market, appropriate for its size and within which it alone works. However, in practice this is not the way many of Maekawa's independent corporations operate. Since a local independent corporation has a limited number of employees, sometimes it cannot respond to the needs of customers by itself. A typical example is when it has to develop a new product to solve customers' problems. Then the local independent corporation determines which other Maekawa corporations might help satisfy a customer's needs and actively asks for their support. Throughout the history of this unique management system, the members of each independent corporation "instinctively" (Murakami's word) know that they cannot fully respond to customer needs without concentrating all the efforts and resources of Maekawa. Consequently, the number of joint projects by different independent corporations has greatly increased. (See Figure 8.3.)

With these local independent corporations "separate and united" at the same time, knowledge built up at each corporation can be easily shared with others, ultimately becoming the knowledge of the entire company.

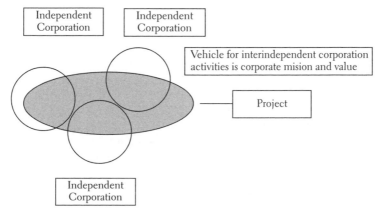

Figure 8.3. Independent Corporations: Separate and United

It is very common for the corporations to exchange human resources. For instance, there is only one employee working at the Tokyo head office of Maekawa Meat Planning, one of its metropolitan independent corporations. The rest of its employees (approximately fifteen people) work at other local independent corporations scattered throughout Japan. They do business by keeping in close contact with local meat suppliers while also cooperating with the staff members of these local corporations. Or consider the *Toridas* project. About a hundred people were involved from different independent corporations, such as the Ford processing company for plant engineering, the MMS independent company for manufacturing automation, and several local independent corporations for sales. Various independent corporations whose businesses were closely related to chicken-meat processing jointly created the *Toridas* task force. And its members were constantly offered necessary information, knowledge, and resources from their various independent corporations.

Connecting Structure with Vision and Strategy

Maekawa's use of independent corporations reflects an unusual sense of mission and corporate values. In general, there should be consistency between a firm's structure and its knowledge vision. Maekawa focuses on making unique contributions to customers; this, in turn, requires solid understanding of customers' enabling contexts or *ba*, which can be achieved only by working closely with them so that knowledge will be created, captured, or capitalized on—resulting in a kind of "co-innovation" with customers that depends on sharing tacit knowledge. Automating chicken deboning, in which Maekawa engineers worked with employees at its customers' plants, yielded such a co-innovation.

This encompassing knowledge vision has been repeatedly conveyed to all employees through slogans like "the realization of society with no competition" or "doing business within one's own territory" by company chairman Masao Maekawa. Through these messages from top management, all employees decide the direction of their organizational activities. According to Shun Murakami, "Suppose sales of our freezers are slowed due to fierce price competition in the market. If we are involved in that price competition, we will be gradually losing our unique value added, since tight competition means that our competitors are also able to respond to our customers' needs. Then we will try to create a new market by developing a new product that responds to customer needs and which no other competitor can produce."[17]

Each independent corporation is evaluated on the level of innovations they have achieved. Moreover, such an evaluation is made not by the headquarters unit but by other independent corporations that are familiar with the business of the corporation under review. Murakami says, "When you become the leader of an independent corporation, you feel extremely defenseless, being watched and examined by the independent corporations around you." The relationship among independent corporations is, however, respectful rather than antagonistic. Each is ready to help others accomplish Maekawa's main strategic objective: to react to customer needs more rapidly than competitors by developing a new system or product without being involved in price competition.

Thus, Maekawa's management system, inseparable from its mission, facilitates the field-based activities of its independent corporations. The term *field* refers to areas where the company can achieve competitive advantage and growth (Maekawa, 1994). More precisely, it means a certain business domain or market in which each independent corporation of Maekawa can provide its own unique values—that is, innovations that cannot be quickly copied or described by competitors.

Emphasis on Tacit Knowledge

Given this knowledge vision and strategy, sharing tacit knowledge has been critical to Maekawa's success. For one thing, the enabling context of customers is not easily conveyed by verbal descriptions. Even when customer satisfaction becomes the paramount goal of a manufacturing company, many executives complain that they have a difficult time finding out what their customers want. Now that the age of mass production has passed, it is commonly understood that explicit, verbal, or well-articulated information about customer needs is scarce. Maekawa is no exception here. According to Chairman Maekawa, his company's customers seldom make specific suggestions like, "We want to do this using this and that." What they actually utter is "a very vague anxiety or image." In fact, words may express only 10 percent of the image a customer has in mind. However, when any member of a Maekawa independent corporations grasps such tacit knowledge or *ba*, there is in-depth communication and mutual understanding between the customer and the company, the kind that leads to development of an innovative product. In this way, Maekawa's mission is closely related to one of its main corporate values: emphasizing tacit knowledge. (See Figure 8.4.)

Tacit knowledge is embodied in or possessed by people; it cannot be separated from individuals. Therefore, Maekawa acquires tacit knowledge in a field through committed interactions with customers. Chairman Maekawa literally calls them "interactions in the world of tacit knowledge." Such interactions, however, cannot be accomplished overnight. To see into this world, employees must gain a wide spectrum of knowledge about not only customers' businesses but also all relevant social, economic,

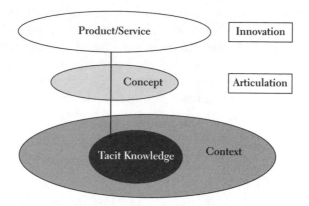

Figure 8.4 Innovation in Context

and environmental factors the company may be dealing with. It is vital for them to foster and accumulate high-quality knowledge. In this regard, Maekawa encourages training personnel with a long-term horizon in mind. Yet the company has no specific training programs as such. Instead it emphasizes self-learning on the job. At each independent corporation, even young staff members frequently visit the actual job sites of their customers. The company believes that "young staff members can be enlightened through interactions with customers when they have opportunities to participate in the activities in *ba*" (Maekawa, 1995). Their bosses never give them specific instructions for interacting with customers. Rather, staff members are supposed to learn about a customer's enabling context for themselves through repeated visits there; to foster their own views of the world; and to mature enough to interact with customers professionally, creatively, and with care.

Engineers at Maekawa's independent corporations are also strongly encouraged to develop an "ability to talk with customers." This is considered an indispensable aspect of their participation in that enabling context. Engineers who can recognize the technical needs of customers by observing their production lines with them are trusted more than those focusing only on technical specifications.

Moving People to Facilitate Knowledge Sharing

In order to be united, of course, Maekawa's independent corporations need to share information with each other. Unless all corporations grasp what information, skills, and specialists exist throughout the company, a bloc of related corporations cannot come up with the appropriate actions to take; the *Toridas* project, for instance, never would have come to fruition without such sharing of resources among all the separate players.

Knowledge sharing at Maekawa is facilitated by a number of supporting systems, including the single-page business plans discussed in Chapter 6. Here we focus on two mechanisms for moving Maekawa's people around its organizational structure: (1) linking independent corporations through conferences and bloc steering-committee meetings; (2) shifting personnel between corporations to respond to business changes, which encourages the development of knowledge activists.

Linking Independent Corporations

In each bloc, the presidents of the member corporations get together once a month for the bloc's steering committee meeting, in which information about the needs and activities of customers is exchanged, and market trends and general views are discussed. At such meetings, the participants establish strategies for the bloc, by which they decide how to deal with the existing markets or cultivate new markets. They then lays out a plan for exchanging human and technical resources within the bloc to achieve their objectives, and draw up the bloc's business plan for the year. Each of the participating independent corporations lay out specific plans for their activities in compliance with the business plan set at this meeting. That way, different corporations both share the same information and strengthen the foundation for their cooperative relationship.

In addition to these bloc steering committee meetings, there are business conferences to facilitate information exchange and cooperative relationships between independent corporations; development conferences; and technical conferences. At business conferences, problems and solutions related to the establishment of certain independent corporations are discussed. Conferences for developing new products and systems start from the early planning stages of a project and are held until the commercialization of resulting products. At technical conferences, each participating corporation makes its own technologies open to the others, information on relevant problems is exchanged, and the results of research on new technologies are presented. In addition to technical conferences, technology-related information is conveyed to each independent corporation via various communication mechanisms such as e-mail, fax, phone, letters, and face-to-face meetings to further facilitate information sharing within the group.

These meetings and conferences, held within the blocs or among different blocs and corporate headquarters, are effective mechanisms for concentrating Maekawa's resources and capabilities. Furthermore, they are important opportunities for participants to have face-to-face interactions with people outside their own independent corporation. Such face-to-face interactions make Maekawa employees feel that they live under the same roof, even if they work in widely dispersed locations.

Shifting Personnel Between Corporations

Knowledge sharing is also facilitated by personnel rotation among the independent corporations. This often takes place when the size of a certain corporation's business is about to be reduced or enlarged due to changes in the marketplace. The company's independent corporations constantly adapt themselves to comply with the management philosophy of Masao Maekawa: "The corporation can survive only when it changes itself spontaneously, giving itself up to changes in the business environment."[18] Thus, the number of employees at each independent corporation is always changing. Personnel rotation between different corporations is carried out at the discretion of the appropriate managers, without interference from headquarters, reflecting the full autonomy of each corporation. "We place the greatest importance on the opinions of independent corporation employees," Chairman Maekawa adds, "those who actually sense and experience changes in the business environment."[19]

At the managerial level, shifting personnel in such a flexible and spontaneous fashion can help develop knowledge activists. As we made clear in the last chapter, managers who spread the word about knowledge throughout an organization must be intentionally developed. For example, an incentive system that encourages knowledge activism could be based on how well managers recognize, shape, and participate in an enabling context for knowledge creation—that is, how well they collect information, interpret it, share their knowledge with colleagues, establish caring relationships, and ultimately contribute to the growth of knowledge-based competence in firms.

To enrich managers personal experiences, the source of their individual knowledge creation, a system of job rotation can also be implemented so that managers are faced with different kinds of information, contexts, and employees. This is essentially the situation at Maekawa, where personnel regularly rotate among independent corporations, depending on changing business conditions.

The company has plenty of knowledge activists, scattered throughout its corporations and ready to take on a leadership role in developing knowledge-based competence. This redundancy of potential command enables it and other such firms to be very agile in a turbulent environment. At Maekawa, knowledge activists are trained on the job; there is no specific training program for how one becomes a catalyst, coordinator, or merchant of foresight in this company. Yet just as every staff member is expected to develop his or her own abilities to interact with customers and share tacit knowledge, Maekawa's knowledge activists hone their skills through various mechanisms, particularly during active interaction with colleagues in meetings.

TOSHIBA'S ADVANCED-I GROUP

From independent corporations or task forces, which generate an ongoing series of innovations, we now turn to a cross-divisional unit under more direct corporate control. Toshiba, like Sony, confronts a rapidly changing competitive frontier, in which the old rules of the electronics industry no longer apply.[20] One of Toshiba's strategic objectives has been to create new multimedia businesses based on new knowledge, no easy feat. In order to develop knowledge-based competence in diversified firms, creating an enabling context in which people who belong to different divisions share knowledge is critical. And to make better use of the tacit knowledge that resides in a certain division, this context should encourage tacit-knowledge sharing at the corporate level; otherwise, the knowledge generated will not be used in other divisions. Therefore, a cross-divisional unit like Toshiba's Advanced-I Group is of fundamental importance, because it provides the right enabling context for knowledge creation across divisional boundaries.

Toshiba's early history has two strands. In 1875, Tanaka Engineering Works, Japan's first manufacturer of telegraphic equipment, was born. Hisashige Tanaka, its founder, was well known for inventions that included mechanical dolls and a perpetual clock. Under the name of Shibaura Engineering Works, his company later became one of Japan's largest manufacturers of heavy electrical apparatus. In 1890, Hakunetsu-sha & Company opened as Japan's first plant for electric incandescent lamps. This company subsequently evolved into a manufacturer of consumer products. By 1899, it had been renamed the Tokyo Electric Company. In 1939, these two strands came together when the two companies merged to form an integrated electric-equipment manufacturer: Tokyo Shibaura Electric. It was soon popularly known as "Toshiba," which finally became the official corporate name in 1978.[21]

In 1983, Toshiba announced "E&E" (Electronics and Energy) as a new corporate concept. The goal was to consolidate the company's expertise and knowledge in virtually all areas of electronics and electric products. Top management believed that the synergy created among E&E fields would be crucial if Toshiba was to cultivate new business opportunities, since the company could apply a wealth of expertise and knowledge in these areas to pioneer new products and technologies. Toshiba currently manufactures a wide range of products, which are developed through four major business groups: information and communication systems (computer systems, telecommunications equipment, automation systems, medical electronics equipment), information media and consumer products (personal computers, word processors, copiers, storage devices, audio and video products), power systems and industrial equipment (industrial apparatus, power-generating plants, transportation equipment, elevators and escalators), and electronic components and materials (semiconductors, electron tubes, optoelectronic devices, liquid crystal displays, batteries, printed circuit boards).

Diversification has enabled Toshiba to achieve sustainable growth. For example, despite a steep drop in semiconductor memory prices and lower sales in power stations and equipment, Toshiba's consolidated net sales in the fiscal year that ended March 31, 1998 are $41.3 billion.[22] The decline in the semiconductor and power station business has been compensated for by the growth of the company's personal computer and peripherals business. Diversification at Toshiba has provided security against rapid and drastic environmental changes, even as the company has faced the same industry convergence challenges that Sony has.

Indeed, Toshiba has also begun to transform its strategies and structures to deal with converging technologies, although its path differs from Sony's. The ultimate goal of the transformation at Toshiba is for its diverse business activities to be structured so that each division is based on products that rank among the world's best. For that purpose, Toshiba has classified its various operating divisions as either a high-growth, a mainstream, or an emerging business. In 1997, Toshiba publicly announced that it would allocate a large share of its resources to businesses classified as high-growth or emerging.[23] Toshiba's headquarters unit examines the competitiveness and growth opportunities of each division and decides divisional profit performance targets accordingly. Strategically important businesses for Toshiba are now information infrastructure, information services and software, and advanced information and communication systems and equipment. As of this writing, concentration and focus on the most competitive and promising divisions characterizes Toshiba's new organizational arrangements.

From Project I to the Advanced-I Project

In 1984, as part of its E&E vision, Toshiba launched "Project I." This was a cross-divisional task force with the ambitious strategic objective of extending the company's knowledge in the realm of advanced information and communications systems. (The "I" of Project I stands for information, integration, and intelligence.) By launching Project I, Toshiba executives wanted to develop their advanced information systems and products business by integrating Toshiba's intelligence—that is, the knowledge that already existed in various divisions. But Project I also ended up creating new knowledge for new business opportunities. Its early successful products were the T-1000, Toshiba's first notebook computer, and the T-3100, which was released in the United States and Europe in 1986.

Before that time, Toshiba had produced neither mainframe computers nor desktop PCs. Yet because so many other electronics manufacturers were already competing in the fast-growing desktop PC business, Toshiba focused on the untapped notebook computer market in the 1980s. Focusing on a new business in this way turned out to be a smart move, differentiating Toshiba from the rest of the pack, although the strategy posed a number of challenges. Because very few companies were interested in the development of notebook PCs, Toshiba had to develop systems and devices (such as a 3.5-inch floppy disk drive) for notebooks by itself. For that purpose, talented engineers from other parts of the company, especially those who worked in the power systems and industrial equipment group, were asked to help the information systems group tackle this tough job. Since the power systems and industrial equipment group represented Toshiba's core businesses at the time, these were the best engineers at the company. Through this knowledge transfer across divisions, the development of Toshiba's notebook PCs eventually resulted in enormous success.

In April 1994, Toshiba launched a successor to Project I. The activities of the Advanced-I Project include developing and promoting emerging multimedia businesses; implementing cross-divisional planning and coordination; leading cross-divisional projects for new product development; creating new businesses with alliance partners; and allocating special funds to accelerate business development in divisions. To date, this cross-divisional project has resulted in successful products such as digital videodisc players, a mobile personal digital assistant, and a smart TV (that is, an interactive broadcasting system). Released in the market are several models of DVD players, and Data Slim is one personal digital assistance product. The interactive TV is not released yet, but it will be on the market in two years. In general, the Advanced-I Project currently includes nine business areas—interactive TV, video on demand, information on demand, personal digital assistance, DVD, information provider business for consumers and corporations, multimedia software, and information infrastructure and equipment—with an overall strategic focus on emerging multimedia businesses.

Structural Support for the Project

Like Project I, the whole point of the Advanced-I Project is to move knowledge across divisional boundaries, mixing human resources and technologies as necessary to create new knowledge. This is the enabling context or *ba* for such cross-divisional efforts, one that requires a management system to keep it going. (See Figure 8.5.) Toshiba formed the Advanced-I Group in July 1994 to structurally support the Advanced-I

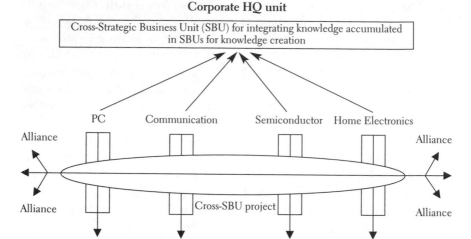

Figure 8.5. A Cross-Divisional Unit for a Multidivisional Electronics Firm

Project. The Advanced-I Group has four subdivisions—which cover marketing, planning for new business initiatives, system LSI planning, and multimedia—and includes approximately ninety dedicated staff members. The Group, as part of Toshiba's corporate headquarters unit, is led by a senior executive vice president, with three directors appointed as deputy executives. The involvement of directors (a total of four board members) suggests the Advanced-I Group's strategic importance. Creating new businesses based on new knowledge is very risky. If such initiatives are handed over to divisions, the divisions may shy away from jeopardizing their own performance, and an attempt to create an innovative new business area may only go halfway. At Toshiba, the risk of pursuing various initiatives under the Advanced-I Project has been shouldered by its corporate headquarters.

The Advanced-I Group holds a management committee meeting every two weeks. At this meeting, important decisions about new business plans, investments, and alliances are quickly made. The role the Group plays as a cross-divisional strategic unit is well reflected in the membership of its management committee. In addition to the four board members and the Group's dedicated members, the chief technology executives of Toshiba's nine divisions are regular members of this committee. In committee meetings, they can share business and technological updates from each division and also develop insights into the strategic direction of their own divisions based on these updates. If coordination is necessary for new projects, chief technology executives can easily name people in their respective divisions who should be involved. In other words, the tacit and explicit knowledge of separate divisions, as embodied by each chief technology executive, can be shared in an enabling context that is driven by corporate interest in emerging businesses.

Once the management committee agrees to form a cross-divisional project based on such face-to-face knowledge sharing, the Advanced-I Group's dedicated staff members coordinate the project's activities. The management committee also holds a one-day meeting every three months to conduct a progress check of the projects approved at previous meetings. Last, the Group organizes another meeting every three months to which all of Toshiba's board members, including the chairman and CEO, and representatives from its divisions are invited. About 120 attendees review the activities initiated by the Advanced-I Group and intensively discuss the future direction of the Advanced-I Project.

The Advanced-I Group receives approximately 0.5 percent of sales from each division, which comes to a total of about $200 million in the fiscal year 1998 to fund its activities. The financial support from each division emphasizes that the Advanced-I Group's mission is to lead the entire company of Toshiba into new business opportunities by coordinating efforts across divisions. In return for this financial support, the Advanced-I Group takes the lead in capturing new business opportunities, integrating the knowledge and expertise generated in different divisions. In other words, the Group as a whole plays the knowledge-activist role at Toshiba.

The advantage of the Advanced-I Group as an integrating mechanism is threefold. First, coordination between interdependent divisions is easier and faster. Knowledge accumulated in each division is shared through intensive face-to-face communication among chief technology executives, thus reducing the kind of uncertainties about the true value of knowledge that can impede collective activities (Hill, 1994). Second, corporate headquarters can reduce the performance ambiguities inherent in cross-divisional activities by directly facilitating them (Govindarajan and Fisher, 1990; Gupta and Govindarajan, 1986). Third, corporate initiatives for cultivating new business opportunities are more directly communicated by a cross-divisional unit like the Advanced-I Group, which receives the strong support and commitment of Toshiba's board members, than they are by empowered divisions and task forces.[24]

CORPORATE CONTROL VERSUS FLEXIBILITY: A CONSTANT PARADOX

In the face of rapid industry shifts, facilitating organizational knowledge creation consistently and intentionally through an overall enabling context can keep a company on the cutting edge. The impact of environmental changes cannot be ignored as a key factor in Toshiba's establishment of the Advanced-I Group. If the business environment is complex, uncertainties about cross-divisional activities are many, and the risk of such activities is great, strong coordination from corporate head-quarters provides the necessary glue. Business historian Alfred Chandler (1994) argues that in industries in which new product development is a critical component of interfirm competition—where R&D expenditures are high, state-of-the-art facilities are costly, and marketing requires spe-cialized skills—the corporate office needs to concentrate on the entrepre-neurial (value-creating) function. Borrowing Chandler's argument, we would add that corporate headquarters needs to concentrate on knowledge enabling, which can involve everything from designing a new physical work space, to creating a virtual network of information alliances, to form-ing microcommunities, to coordinating relatively autonomous divisions.

Of course, the complexity of integrating mechanisms for cross-divi-sional coordination will vary depending on the extent of interdependence (Hill 1994); sometimes a simpler version of a task force is quite appropri-ate. At Maekawa, a belief in the value of tacit knowledge is shared by all employees. Rather than using a corporate headquarters group as a coordi-nating mechanism, this company's strategy, management system, and organizational structure have been formulated so that its mission will actu-ally be carried out by diverse independent corporations. In other cases, a company like Sony keeps revising the level of control its corporate head-quarters exercises over autonomous companies and subsidiaries. Meanwhile, Toshiba's Advanced-I Group is a sophisticated horizontal structure that provides the right context or *ba* for cross-divisional coordi-nation and collaboration, as well as for interfirm collaboration.

The right enabling context, after all, adds up to the interactions that inspire knowledge creation. It is a constantly evolving knowledge space defined by the depth and quality of the relationships that emerge. Managers cannot force knowledge creation or sharing to happen, but they can encourage collaboration and the kind of organization that values knowledge from many sources. Triggering and coordinating the move-ment of knowledge across organizational boundaries is what turns local knowledge into a sustainable competitive advantage—one that will increasingly determine the fate of multinational companies with disparate global operations. The next chapter focuses on globalizing local knowl-edge, the last of our five enablers.

· 9 ·

ENABLER 5

Globalize Local Knowledge

*If you force ice cream into a kid, she will probably spit it
out, even if it's good, because you are trying to get it in
there. But if you place it on the table and put something
red on top, it becomes extremely interesting.*

— Leif Edvinsson, Vice President, Skandia

It goes almost without saying that many midsize and large firms are
no longer contained within national borders. Companies continue
to globalize their operations for several compelling reasons. By locating manufacturing operations where factor costs are low, firms can gain
a cost advantage over competitors. By working closely with advanced
and demanding customers in some countries, firms can acquire valuable
information for future product development, thereby gaining a differentiation advantage. By setting up business operations abroad, companies
can focus on growing foreign markets. And by locating R&D facilities in
a country with a well-developed educational and scientific tradition,
they get access to new expertise, technologies, and product concepts.
Sometimes executives may also choose a foreign location to exploit a
business opportunity with a local partner. At other times, locating business operations abroad can be driven by the need to attract the best managerial talent.[1]

Whatever the motive, companies increasingly distribute tasks over an
expanding geographic, sociopolitical, demographic, and cultural area.
Tasks become dispersed in two ways. First, they uniformly distribute
themselves over a large geographic area, leading to the parallel buildup
of local knowledge in different places. This parallel buildup may be necessary, as it is for acquiring accounting and sales expertise; local innovation and best practice may also offer the best approach to transferring
knowledge under certain collaborative arrangements. Still, highly spe-

cialized knowledge development within a particular discipline, such as microbiology or hydrodynamics, is costly. Some multinationals build "centers of expertise," in which a team of experts develops specialized knowledge for solving local tasks and appropriately distributes it across a worldwide organization. In practice, however, this is not always the best solution, especially when local managers resist having changes forced on them.

Second, tasks can be dispersed throughout a system of business operations. A company might build up a competitive advantage by creating knowledge and developing products locally with a cutting-edge customer. A resulting product might be so successful that it has the potential to do well in other countries, but then the company will need to distribute such sources of competitive advantage throughout its system of global business operations (Bartlett and Ghoshal, 1986, 1990). Top managers of diverse multinationals must not only pay attention to local knowledge but also set up the means for making it accessible and easy to accumulate. Other authors have recognized that local business operations need access to those areas of a company's knowledge that might provide local competitive advantages (Gupta and Govindarajan, 1994, 1991). One by one, as various units use such knowledge and adapt it to their own circumstances, the competitive advantage of the entire organization can grow.

This may seem like a good idea, but establishing give-and-take in global knowledge transfer is much easier to talk about than to practice. As the company stories of the last chapter illustrate, multinationals like Toshiba and Sony keep revising their organizational structures, shifting the balance between corporate control and local flexibility as business conditions change. Globalizing local knowledge is, indeed, a major challenge; it is one of the most important responsibilities of the corporate headquarters manager and those local managers who must cooperate in order to make it happen. As such, executives need to address a number of issues: How should knowledge be globalized? Can knowledge be transferred like any other commodity? Can knowledge be packaged? Who maintains control of knowledge in the new location?

Globalize local knowledge is the final enabler we discuss in this book, and it is closely tied to cross-leveling, the last step of the knowledge-creation process. The 5 x 5 Grid from Chapter 1 reappears once more (see Table 9.1) to underscore the connection between the two. Our fifth enabler has a positive impact on the formation of microcommunities, especially in target sites for the knowledge created. However, globalizing local knowledge does not directly affect the sharing of tacit knowledge within microcommunities, concept creation, concept justification, or prototype building, since these are generally self-contained processes.

Table 9.1 The 5 x 5 Grid: Globalizing Local and Cross-Leveling

KNOWLEDGE-CREATION STEPS

KNOWLEDGE ENABLERS	Sharing Tacit Knowledge	Creating a Concept	Justifying a Concept	Building a Prototype	Cross-Leveling Knowledge
Instill a Vision		√	√√	√	√√
Manage Conversations	√√	√√	√√	√√	√√
Mobilize Activists		√	√	√	√√
Create the Right Context	√	√	√√	√	√√
Globalize Local Knowledge					√√

The main reason for this enabler is to spread knowledge organization-ally. In fact, all the enablers strongly influence the fifth step of the knowledge-creation process: a knowledge vision focuses organizational attention on key concepts and values; conversations, by their very nature, are a medium for knowledge transfer; knowledge activists help coordinate disparate initiatives and can spread the news across many boundaries; and the right enabling context will establish how knowledge should be shared, balancing corporate strategy making with creativity at the local level. But while these four enablers also affect the other knowl-edge-creation steps to varying degrees, globalizing local knowledge is all about cross-leveling. It emphasizes breaking down the physical, cultural, organizational, and managerial barriers that often prevent effective knowledge transfer in a multinational corporation. It is the cherry on the ice cream described in Leif Edvinsson's opening quote—the process that makes the knowledge of other far-flung divisions appealing to a local operation, rather than threatening, irrelevant, or too "foreign."

In this chapter, we start with a new perspective on knowledge trans-fer—or what we call *knowledge re-creation*—offering an alternative to more conventional notions of control and completeness. Next, we out-line a process for globalizing local knowledge that includes three phases: triggering, packaging/dispatching, and re-creating. A detailed story from Adtranz, which began as a joint transportation venture between Asea Brown Boveri and Daimler-Benz, follows. Here we focus on how one of Adtranz's customers, Indian Railways, effectively re-created technology for high-speed locomotives. The chapter concludes with a more general discussion of enabling knowledge re-creation through public presenta-tions about its benefits.

KNOWLEDGE ACROSS TIME AND SPACE:
THE ISSUE OF CONTROL REVISITED

Imagine you are the editor of a comprehensive, 60,000-reference dictionary of the English language intended for worldwide distribution. The editorial policy of your company is to keep the dictionary's definitions as easy to understand as possible to enable any user to speak the English language correctly. With a team of English-language experts, you go to great lengths to explain the use of the book, define words, give them their proper grammatical connotations, provide various forms of each word, and even offer examples of how words might be used in daily speech. You are lured by an ideal: an explicit document that contains all knowledge of its subject and therefore allows a user to control all aspects of language production. If your dictionary is sufficiently comprehensive and the instructions clear enough, you believe, it should be possible to distribute knowledge of the English language globally, thereby controlling its use everywhere.

Such control, however, remains only an ideal and not a very good one when it comes to a constantly evolving enterprise like language. Some philosophers of language adhere to cognitivist beliefs, asserting that the function of a language is to adequately represent the world. The word *vase*, for instance, directly corresponds with the physical object of a vase; even when word and object are indirectly connected through the use of analogy, for instance, their relationship can be logically analyzed.[2] Yet as anyone who can talk knows, such relationships are not necessarily logical or easily described. Take double entendres. Even when English is one's mother tongue, a word or phrase can be open to two interpretations. In fact, once people master a language, they will likely play with the double meaning of words. At the very least, nonexpert speakers will create new meanings as they go along in order to communicate. So, in a tavern in Paris, a Danish and Spanish owner of your dictionary converse in English, the only language they share. But their use of words is too creative to fit any dictionary, and their grammar too pragmatic to be accepted by an English language instructor. Given this particular set of local conditions and a commitment to understanding each other—that is, a belief that achieving mutual understanding matters—they are perfectly capable of solving the problem of communication.

Similarly, the subject of knowledge transfer as previously dealt with in the literature of international business (Gupta and Govindarajan, 1991) entails an ideal of control that is not realistic. A brief look at the typical knowledge-transfer description reveals what we mean. A local business operation develops a new product or improved manufacturing process. This process or product is documented in minute detail, through engineering drawings, performance specifications, manufacturing specs, even a physical prototype. A team of experts compiles the final documents, packages them, and ships the package off to another part of the world. At the recipient's end, the package is unwrapped, the specifications read, the innovation understood, and the process or product is implemented exactly as specified. The experts remain in control of local implementation, partly because they can be held accountable for any problems that result, partly to maintain their expert status. As with the dictionary, perfect completeness is related to perfect control. Through complete documentation and direct instruction, experts assume control over their products and processes, even over their final use, across all dimensions of time and space.

Inspired by the writings of philosopher and sociologist Nico Stehr (1994), we suggest that this underlying assumption turns knowledge into a kind of commodity, something that supposedly can be captured and transferred through documents, by instructions, or in a physical form. The expert team act as "corporate intellectuals," forming an elite whose publicly sanctioned function is to create and cultivate knowledge that is comprehensively documented (Merton, 1957; Aronowitz, 1990). In doing so, corporate intellectuals have to define a need for their knowledge and services, and they continuously search for locations throughout an organization in which their expertise, knowledge, and innovations can be used. Yet according to sociologist Robert Merton (1957), if one merely implements knowledge received by such corporate experts, one is simply "a cog in the transmission belt of communicating ideas forged by others" (p. 210).

Here is what often happens in practice. In coming to terms with the knowledge transferred—some of which is probably still tacit, no matter how thorough experts believe their documentation is—a local subsidiary may experiment with new and unconventional solutions, going beyond or violating the instructions issued by the corporate team. Sometimes this works, even if the experts do not know what local managers have done; other times, it does not. But regardless, failure to implement an innovation accurately almost always has negative repercussions for the local managers responsible. The experts, especially if they believe the innovation is truly necessary for the local recipient, will assess the seriousness of the anomaly and then suggest appropriate sanctions.[3] Beyond active resistance, local management will likely come to terms with partly covert expectations by closely mimicking the language and actions of the experts, sometimes pretending to understand what is required when they do not.

In addition, when local adaptations are necessary to make the innovation work, covering up and secrecy are possible tactics. The dialogue might proceed as follows:

EXPERTS: We know what is best for you. (Covert: Because you are either too provincial or downright incompetent.)

LOCAL MANAGERS: Yes, you know what is best for us. (Covert: Although we don't know what you know—and we don't want to know.)

EXPERTS: Then why have you failed to implement what we specified?

LOCAL MANAGERS: We know how to deal with what you think is best.

EXPERTS: What do you mean? Just implement what we send you!

Under these unfortunate but all-too-realistic conditions, everyone practices a little bit of ignorance. Such ignorance may maintain the status quo, which can feel more comfortable than making changes, but it does not lead to effective communication or implementation. The difference in knowledge between a corporate team of experts and local organizations is the engine that drives conventional knowledge transfer. But this engine will only sputter and stall if corporate experts insist on the completeness of their specifications and local managers do not understand what is expected of them.

As we detail in the Adtranz-Indian Railways story, one of our colleagues, Carla Kriwet, found that implementation of an innovation and further local innovation are linked. Knowledge received by a local subsidiary has to be adjusted to fit with the local skill level, customer requirements, and manufacturing technologies. Pragmatism and a willingness to experiment are key factors in a successful transfer of knowledge and technology. Hence, Kriwet (1997) calls for a process that better describes the nature of knowledge transfer, one that is based on a new set of assumptions.

We heartily concur. Let us first reiterate that knowledge is not a well-defined commodity. In global terms, it results from a creative process of pragmatically defining and solving local tasks to accomplish a larger knowledge vision.[4] By changing this assumption, we see clearly that the simplistic model of knowledge transfer, in which completeness and control are key levers, has shortcomings. The ultimate goal of globalizing local knowledge must be to enhance the capacity for social action, competence, and successful task performance. More specifically, the local knowledge of one unit should lead to competitive advantages for other local units, such as through lowering manufacturing costs, sharing data on selected customers, distributing a common product, or employing similar training programs.

For each local business operation, knowledge should increase the capacity for acting on local business opportunities and avoiding local business threats. Since local conditions are specific to each operation (market structure, customers, technologies, suppliers), knowledge received from corporate headquarters or another division will have to blend in with local knowledge, existing practices, and experience. It should also be possible to refine and change the knowledge received. Such knowledge will be shaped by local expectations; it will be justified according to local values.

Documents will be reinterpreted, certain sections intensified, and others downplayed. Rather than speaking of knowledge transfer, then, think of this as a process in which knowledge is globalized through re-creation—not mere imitation—at the local level.[5]

Does that mean corporate intellectuals or centers of expertise should vanish? No, but the roles and locations of such experts need to change. The emphasis on control and completeness is a far cry from the process-oriented work of an effective knowledge activist. Activists catalyze and coordinate local efforts; they do not plan or control them. Therefore, knowledge should no longer be considered an abstract commodity that can be sent from one part of the organization to another. Nor is knowledge simply a representation of a product or technology. Knowledge can never be perfectly controlled. No group is privileged in terms of intervening and directing correct implementation of an innovation (Radhakrishnan, 1990), and every unit must assume the intellectual responsibility for creating and nurturing knowledge at the local level.

From an enabling perspective, knowledge that is transferred from other parts of the company should be thought of as a source of inspiration and insights for a local business operation, not a direct order that must be followed. Control of knowledge is local, tied to local re-creation. Knowledge re-creation, in turn, happens through a continuing dialogue among experts of equal status who represent their local business operations. The local unit uses the received knowledge as input to spark its own continuing knowledge-creation processes.

Given this new understanding, how should globalization of knowledge through local re-creation be carried out? Figure 9.1 depicts three phrases—triggering, packaging/dispatching, and re-creating—that should help managers break down the process into practical pieces. The following sections explain each phase in detail.

PHASE 1: TRIGGERING

The first step in globalizing local knowledge is to trigger the process through recognition of a business opportunity or need. For instance, a

Figure 9.1. Transmitting Explicit and Tacit Knowledge

group or unit within the global company has developed a new product or technology. They believe this has potential for other parts of the organization and initiate a systematic search in which knowledge re-creation might lead to business benefits. Alternatively, a group or unit search for an innovation, technical solution, or data that may help in performing a local task. In other words, those who have created knowledge must come to the attention of those who seek knowledge creation, and vice versa.

This may seem like a hopeless task in a company with geographically and culturally dispersed business operations. There are always search costs for knowledge exchange—the costs of identifying needs and opportunities; of teleconferencing, meetings, and airplane tickets; of the time required to dwell on engineering drawings. High search costs may lead local business operations to create the knowledge they need themselves, rather than first seeking out sources of knowledge in the larger company that can be of use. To be sure, search costs can sometimes be so high that they exceed the costs of creating knowledge locally. But there are plenty of good reasons for not replicating knowledge-creation activities in a large company. The managerial challenge is to find cost-effective mechanisms for triggering knowledge exchange, and we suggest three here: bulletin boards, regular knowledge conferencing, and the use of knowledge activists.

Bulletin boards, the most common mechanism for knowledge exchange, can be distributed electronically or on paper. Most internal bulletins provide information about opportunities, ongoing projects, signed contracts, new products, new technologies, new employment, and so forth. Such information should be supplemented with the concrete needs of local business operations under the heading "Wanted"—new manufacturing technologies, expertise, a new product, data on selected customers. When care is high in organizations, these announcements will be seen and heard by people who have made a commitment to the larger goals of the company. Caring for knowledge means that organizational members actively seek from, and provide information to, bulletin boards. Care also implies active questioning about why one needs particular kinds of knowledge.

While bulletin boards are easy to implement and relatively cheap, we offer a few caveats. First, it may be difficult to give an accurate and short description of a particular area of expertise. In a global company with several thousand product groups, in which knowledge is very complex and specialized, it may also be hard for someone to recognize the value of knowledge presented in this manner as an opportunity. Reading a short description in isolation is not the best way to achieve more fundamental understanding of another's knowledge and possible contributions. Sometimes only lengthy conversations and instruction will convince a local unit that the knowledge of another is of value to its business operations. Second, a bulletin board may not always capture the latest knowledge-creation initiatives, because information on the board may lag far behind what people are actually doing. Just a quick glance at many Web sites indicates how often information is out of date. Third, it can take awhile for a global company to develop an effective bulletin system, discouraging those who first try one out. Local business operations need immediate success stories with bulletin boards to trigger globalization of local knowledge; otherwise, they will pay little attention to them.

Regular knowledge conferencing is another way to bring needs and opportunities to the attention of different groups throughout a company. The General Technology Conference and other R&D conferences at Sharp, for example, keep organizational members posted about the company's various innovations and provide an excellent forum for discussing knowledge needs. By focusing on the tasks, challenges, and goals related to creating the science of optoelectronics, participants gain a sense of direction in which they can discuss their own needs for knowledge. The format of such conferences should be relatively open to allow for both "need pull" and "opportunity push." For example, each operation is given a conference slot to assess its recent important knowledge-creation initiatives and what its concrete needs for future knowledge creation might be.

The discussion can be further facilitated by letting each representative present his unit's local knowledge vision or understanding of the overall company knowledge vision. Such a conversation about vision will help to communicate what organizational units within the company might expect of each other in terms of future knowledge creation. The only danger is that a conference format may be somewhat passive, or even myopic, for enabling knowledge creation and knowledge re-creation. Note, however, that customers and suppliers can be valuable participants in such triggering conferences. Sometimes an outsider's point of view can identify hidden sources of knowledge that other participants may have ignored or forgotten. Too much certainty about one's own knowledge — like the exercise of too much control — can paralyze the process of identifying new needs and opportunities. A global customer, for instance, may have done business with a geographically remote subsidiary of a large company, based on a particular product concept developed by local engineers. In this case, the customer's point of view and experience can provide useful knowledge to the rest of the company.

Finally, the *use of knowledge activists* can trigger globalization of local knowledge. As we detailed in Chapter 7, activists catalyze knowledge creation, coordinate knowledge-creation initiatives throughout a corporation, and communicate a larger vision to everyone they meet. The task of coordinating knowledge creation in the global organization can be complemented with an open search for knowledge needs and opportunities. The activist's task as a merchant of foresight is to envision and communicate possible areas of cooperation. Since good activists are agile and open-minded, and often have a broad network of contacts, they can be commissioned by a local business operation to discover expertise throughout the company or, alternatively, a need for knowledge. The knowledge activist can also be a mediator in the local knowledge re-creation process, helping to ensure quick wins.

Aside from these three mechanisms, triggering can happen more indirectly through internal comparative performance systems. In comparing the performance of different local business operations, managers can become aware of substantial differences. For example, differences in profitability levels may indicate that various operations have different levels and sources of competitive advantage. Although industry conditions are often the culprit here, identifying such performance differences can be a trigger for dismantling certain barriers or for exchanging knowledge with other parts of a company.

There are various types of reference points for comparing one company's or business operation's performance with another's. Performance refers to a wide range of indicators: turnover, profitability, manufacturing and quality costs, return on investments, market share, average life span of products, and average age of products currently sold in the market. For internal comparison, managers refer to the performance of comparable units — such as other sales organizations, a product-development team, or a manufacturing operation in another country. Research has shown that when the current situation that managers face is satisfactory, meaning that their unit's performance exceeds that of a reference point's, they tend to react negatively to changes. It is when the current situation is unsatisfactory that managers are more open to change, embracing new initiatives, new solutions, and more flexibility in strategic planning (Feigenbaum, Hart, and Schendel, 1996).

Even the best-in-class performer, however, may need new knowledge to implement advancement strategies. For example, a manufacturer in one country may benefit from a new logistical system from a unit in another, even if the latter is a lower performer overall. Using reference points, as with the other triggering mechanisms, has its downside and can increase organizational barriers to new knowledge. The not-invented-here syndrome, reinforced by narratives of great competitive success, can make knowledge exchange difficult, and complacency may blindfold managers to future possibilities and threats. Therefore, such performance systems should be coupled with a managerial focus on finding and using new, valuable, and rare knowledge throughout an organization. This can be enhanced through companywide participation in triggering conferences, as well as participation in creating a company knowledge vision.

PHASE 2: PACKAGING AND DISPATCHING

The second step in the process of globalizing local knowledge is the packaging of knowledge. The only kind that can be truly packaged for shipment is explicit social knowledge. Tacit individual knowledge is more "sticky"; it usually remains with its local business unit, unless the individuals who hold it travel to another local operation (Szulanski, 1996). The packaging process is essential to moving knowledge across organizational boundaries, but it also depends on the knowledge that is packaged. Still, we can offer some general advice for knowledge packaging. Note that we also discuss how the package is dispatched, since the two activities are closely connected in this phase.

First, *the managers involved must decide on what knowledge needs to be packaged*. Explicit knowledge comes in the form of engineering drawings, product specifications, prototype specs, performance specs, manufacturing specs, a list of possible suppliers and purchase directives, and so forth. For the business operation that dispatches the knowledge, this represents the end state of a long knowledge-creation process, but the resulting documentation will not and should not include a description of everything required to get there. The original participants' tacit knowledge helps to structure and order the various pieces of explicit knowledge; that is, the socialization of participants allows them to interpret the material for use by others. A counterintuitive drawing of a technical solution is associated with a particular difficulty the team faced at a certain moment; a specific way of presenting the technical information is mainly driven by the peculiar needs of a local customer's manufacturing director. There is nothing wrong with such approaches at the local level, but an effective knowledge package destined for other units generally will not include such material.

Only explicit knowledge that has helped the local business operation solve its tasks should be transferred; additional knowledge can be packaged and dispatched based on the experiences others have. After all, the receiving business operation has to make sense of what is sent. In order to increase the capacity for social action, the dispatchers might open a constructive dialogue with the receiving unit before sending the package. Then both sides of the process can discuss the recipient's available knowledge, what else is needed, how to sequence the transfer, and how to best enable knowledge re-creation.

Second, dispatching *managers must decide on the sequence of shipment*. Addressing the following questions will help clarify this decision. Can the receiving unit locally organize the explicit knowledge if it is dispatched in one batch? Do they need additional instructions for how to do this? If a sequence of shipments would work better, what should be the correct order? What knowledge does the receiving business operation need first?

Should we dispatch knowledge in a sequence similar to the original knowledge-creation process—for example, descriptions of the various concepts and prototypes tested, as well as the criteria used for justification of the concept? Should we send background information, then product specs, then manufacturing and purchasing specs? Or should we let the receiving unit first get an overview of the knowledge to be dispatched, then send the details according to an agreed-on schedule?

Third, *managers should assign local experts or spokespeople to the knowledge dispatched*. As mentioned above, explicit knowledge is only the end product; tacit knowledge of how a document came to be is required to fully make sense of it. The explicit elements of a knowledge package, then, should be indexed with local areas of expertise and references to groups or individuals who can help receiving units.[6] Such spokespeople obviously must be qualified to provide assistance on relevant technical details. But we recommend that spokespeople be more than technical experts; they should be trained as helpers, facilitators, and interpreters of knowledge for others.

The issues and concerns of a local business operation will be embedded in the context or *ba* that originally produced the explicit knowledge. But a receiving unit does not want to know how a particular cable, for example, should be attached to a particular generator. Recipients want to understand how that generator, given its performance specs, will interface with other technical installations and their locations, and will altogether fit into the total picture of a ship's engine room. Spokespeople therefore need to be able to shift scales; they must be able to take a generalist's view of operations as well as that of a technical expert. They should have pedagogical skills and see every conversation as an opportunity to increase the receiving unit's capacity to act rather than an irritating distraction in their own work day. In addition to the triggering mechanisms discussed above, training spokespeople is another key lever for reducing the costs of knowledge exchange.

Fourth, *managers should decide on "storage bins."* Explicit knowledge can be stored in a variety of ways. Figure 9.2 presents a typical matrix structure for storage.

Through this matrix structure, each element of explicit knowledge is connected to a spokesperson. This person (or group) provides the background for the original knowledge-creation effort, relating a particular piece of knowledge to the larger picture.

Finally, *managers can develop a knowledge-exchange policy*.[7] This policy should help to identify the rationale for the knowledge-exchange process as well as the knowledge involved and the means of packaging and dispatching. The rationale for knowledge dispatching is to provide sus-

Storage bins

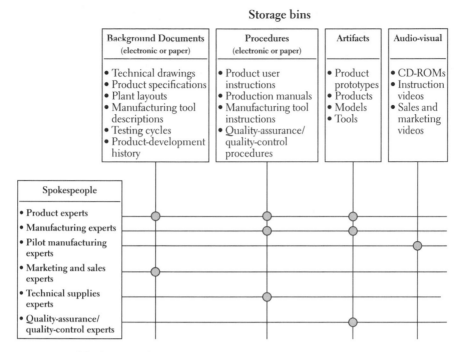

Figure 9.2. How Explicit Knowledge is Stored and Related to Spokespeople

tainable competitive advantages throughout a company. However, in a diversified multinational corporation, in which many business units operate autonomously and are evaluated as such, dispatchers should not end up losing local sources of competitive advantage. At the very least, knowledge giveaways that do not benefit the giver provide no motivation for knowledge sharing. Therefore, executives should start any discussion of exchange policy with an in-depth analysis of the competitive advantages of the units involved.

The exchange policy could be coordinated by the knowledge activist in cooperation with the dispatching and receiving units. It might take the form of a reference document that can guide the various activities and keep them on track. This document would also function as a "social contract" between the dispatcher and recipient. (See Table 9.2.)

For example, when knowledge about a competitor's innovation in technology is dispatched from Unit A to Unit B, both units profit from it. Both can gain competitive advantage through the knowledge exchange, because both units will become increasingly aware and coordinated with respect to potential competitors' moves. This knowledge exchange, for which the IT manager is responsible, happens all at once via mail and

Table 9.2. A Typical Knowledge-Exchange Policy

Knowledge from Unit A to Unit B	Competitive implications for A	Competitive implications for B	Means of dispatching
Knowledge on a new manufacturing technology adapted by a competitor	Competitive advantage	Competitive advantage	Mail and e-mail
Knowledge on a new market analysis technique	Parity	Competitive advantage	Project team
Knowledge of best practice in manufacturing	Parity	Competitive advantage	Workshops
Knowledge on a new manufacturing process for a new product	Parity	Sustainable competitive advantage	Training

e-mail within one day, and is not very costly. But budgets for different types of exchanges obviously vary, depending on the depth and quantity of knowledge, the number of people on either end, the storage medium, and the time required.

PHASE 3: RE-CREATING

The third and most important phase of this process involves re-creating the knowledge dispatched at the local level. While triggering and packaging/dispatching are quite straightforward, knowledge re-creation can follow a number of paths, depending on the circumstances and participants. The least insightful approach is for a local unit of a global company to receive input from a remote business operation and reproduce it in a 1:1 format. This is consistent with the widely accepted principles of completeness and control found in traditional discussions of knowledge transfer. Essentially, in this view, the re-creation process should strive for a copy of the original knowledge. The manufacturing tools used will have the same dimensions, the raw materials purchased will be the same, and the quality-control procedures will be implemented and the product produced in a way that is as similar as possible to that of the dispatching unit.

But just as conventional ideas about knowledge transfer are problematic, 1:1 re-creation can run into obstacles. Some objects have irreproducible features; they are *sui generis*, or in a class by themselves (Eco, 1992). For example, the quality of oil and gas from the North Sea is very different from that of the Mexican Gulf, and refineries have to adjust

Table 9.2. (Continued)

Storage and sequence of shipment	Spokepeople	Responsibility for packaging/dispatching	Time frame	Budget
Batch	Technical director	IT manager	1 day	$1,000
Sequential	Marketing director	Project manager	5 days	$40,000
Sequential Documents, procedures, experiences of participants	Project manager	Engineer Workshop facilitator	1 week	$100,000
Sequential Prototypes, models, or tools Audio-visual Training program	Human resource manager Technical director	Technical director Trainer	4 weeks	$1.5 mill.

accordingly. Japanese tuna may differ from American tuna, and the production of sushi requires local adaptations. Other products that depend on a high degree of craftsmanship—that is, practice grounded in tacit knowledge—will also have irreproducible features. Luxury watches, leather goods, and custom furniture are just a few examples. It is unrealistic to expect such skills to be easily replicated or transferred between units in a multinational company.

Furthermore, simple reproduction of a product or technology often has negative connotations. It may be considered a "forgery," "fake," "spurious," or "second-rate" by other units, especially if they had anything to do with creating the original. The ingrained pride of engineers and other creative workers can make reproduction difficult, unless the product or technology is particularly rare, unique, interesting, or challenging.

In addition, globalization of local knowledge is often an unintended consequence of knowledge-creation initiatives, not something that has been planned. In many cases, the value of new knowledge can be assessed only after its creation. As a consequence, the explicit knowledge that results may be poorly documented and not easily reproduced across time and space. In triggering and packaging/dispatching, the knowledge creators themselves will have to make numerous adjustments and improvisations. At times, the resulting explicit knowledge will appear less than credible, with numerous gaps and errors.

All these factors force local business operations to improvise. In the best possible way, they have to come to terms with any explicit knowledge that is transferred. We want to emphasize that improvisation at the local level is legitimate and necessary for knowledge re-creation. Indeed, it may help to think of re-creating as a knowledge-creation process like any other, one that involves the five steps of sharing tacit knowledge, creating a concept, justifying that concept, building a prototype, and cross-leveling. In this case, cross-leveling of knowledge is the whole point of the exchange.

Knowledge re-creation generally starts with its own version of a micro-community, a selected group of participants at the local business operation who unpackage the explicit knowledge, interpret what they see, and then share tacit knowledge about their observations, including their aspirations and hopes for re-creating the new technology or service. Uncovering local technologies and knowledge that can be of use in the creation of a concept is an important part of this step. One of the positive results of sharing tacit knowledge is that participants come to an agreement together about their goals. Another positive result is that rather than starting with concept creation, sharing tacit knowledge allows for a deeper understanding of the received technology and its potential.

Next, the group re-creates a concept that may resemble the original but in which local conditions also shape the outcome. For example, a concept for a new pump may be combined with valve technology previously created by the local business operation. During concept justification, the group pays even less attention to making the re-created concept match the original. The explicit knowledge dispatched will be pragmatically selected based on local conditions and the way in which the re-created concept eventually evolves. Justification of the re-created concept will depend on legitimate arguments grounded in local market data, supplier conditions, and production requirements

Once the concept has been justified for local conditions, a prototype can be built. Note that this may end up resembling the original product or technology, but the process of constructing it is still owned and controlled by the local business operation. In particular, the prototype will need to draw on the components and technologies at hand. Moreover, it has to fit with local manufacturing processes, supply conditions, and customer requirements.

The advantage of seeing re-creation as just another knowledge-creation process is reduced complexity. Managers will worry less about divergent local processes, allowing complexity to flourish where it is truly needed — in the richness and depth of the knowledge created.[8] In fact, "self-similar" management practices can be an effective way to simplify management throughout a company at the same time that local variety grows (von Krogh and Roos, 1995a).[9] If all managers use the same terminology for knowledge creation, communication among people from different business units and countries will be much easier. General Electric's global efforts to spread Six Sigma terminology, described in Chapter 6, exemplifies this approach.

Rather than limiting shared knowledge to a product or technology, managers can share an understanding of the process a company goes through to re-create knowledge locally. They will understand some of the preparations required, the challenges of forming a microcommunity, the need for caring relationships, and the way to envision a final prototype.

Sharing an understanding of the process should also encourage managers to treat triggering, packaging/dispatching, and re-creation with more care. They will come to respect the tremendous efforts of engineers and middle managers in re-creating the explicit knowledge received. Experimentation will be considered natural rather than an anomaly, and the focus will be on supporting knowledge creation through spokespeople and knowledge activists rather than corporate experts who impose sanctions.

Perhaps the only way to achieve this shared understanding of knowledge creation in a large corporation is through overall company training programs. Such training programs would surely benefit from cross-national, cross-functional, and cross-managerial participation. But even if it is difficult to conceive of something so all-encompassing, a company has much to gain from a commitment to moving knowledge across many boundaries. Adtranz and Indian Railways, for instance, made this kind of commitment to knowledge exchange, and the story of their activities illustrates all three phases of globalizing local knowledge. The social interaction between knowledge providers and recipients allowed technology transferred from Switzerland to be adapted to local conditions in India—a formidable task by anyone's measure.

ADTRANZ: INTERNAL AND EXTERNAL KNOWLEDGE EXCHANGE

The knowledge-exchange project we examine here was started by Asea Brown Boveri and Adtranz in the early 1993. The aim of this story is to highlight the period from 1995 to 1996 during the Adtranz project, through which researcher Carla Kriwet—as a part of a larger research program on knowledge—gained deep insights working and living with Adtranz representatives.[10] This story was written with Carla Kriwet. Our story looks at how two subsidiaries, Adtranz Switzerland and Adtranz India, worked with Indian Railways to build high-speed electrical trains in that country. It investigates both the external exchange of knowledge from Adtranz to its Indian customer, and the internal exchange between the company's European headquarters and its Indian subsidiary. Overlapping networks of interaction like this make for complicated organizational efforts, but the situation has become increasingly common in the global business arena. In this case, Adtranz benefited from ABB's experience with knowledge-and-technology-transfer (KTT) units, incorporating several diverse enabling contexts or *ba*.

In January 1996, ABB and Daimler-Benz merged their rail transportation activities to form a new venture called ABB Daimler-Benz Transportation (Adtranz). The Swiss corporate giant ABB covers a range of industries and businesses, including power generation, transmission, and distribution; oil, gas, and petrochemicals; and financial services. In 1998, it reported orders of $31 billion and employed about 199,000 people in over a hundred countries.[11] Daimler-Benz was one of Germany's leading automotive companies. In its current incarnation as DaimlerChrysler, the company's car brands include Mercedes-Benz, Chrysler, Dodge, and Jeep®, and the corporate portfolio covers aircraft and equipment manufacturing, as well as financial services. In 1998 DaimlerChrysler had revenues of about $155 billion and 442,000 employees around the world.[12] In 1999, ABB and DaimlerChrysler agreed that DaimlerChrysler would acquire ABB's share of their 50-50 joint venture and that Adtranz would be integrated into the strategic portfolio of DaimlerChrysler.[13]

When Adtranz first began operations in 1996, its corporate parents each owned 50 percent; it therefore had access to a range of resources and knowledge from both ABB and Daimler-Benz. In 1996, the new company had revenues of $5 billion, putting it ahead of competitors Siemens and General Electric. By 1998, Adtranz had revenues of approximately $3.2 billion and about 24,000 employees worldwide. Its product portfolio includes electric and diesel locomotives; high-speed trains; trams and underground trains; fixed installations, signal and traffic-control systems and infrastructure.[14]

Adtranz's corporate managers were convinced from its inception that, because of the complex demands of customers like Indian Railways, the company needed to excel in all areas of rail transportation—through reliability, availability, effective maintenance services, security, high-quality products and procedures, minimal damage to the environment, minimal product and development costs, and fast innovation cycles. More to the point of this story, the company guidelines highlight the necessity of cooperation between local organizations and worldwide technology centers in order to meet local demand at the lowest possible cost (Adtranz, 1996).

The Players

The knowledge re-creation project with Indian Railways began in the early 1990s, before Adtranz was officially formed. It started with ABB's Transportation Switzerland unit and was later folded into Adtranz Switzerland's organization. Adtranz Switzerland (CHTRA) and Adtranz India (INTRA) were wholly owned subsidiaries of the new venture. CHTRA became one of Adtranz's most important country organizations and included a center of expertise for electrical locomotives.

INTRA began as a small signaling company. ABB took it over and over the years it subsequently developed into a major supplier of tap changers and breakers to Indian Railways. By the time the knowledge recreation project got underway, INTRA had grown to 150 employees in New Delhi. However, this local Adtranz subsidiary lacked the necessary know-how for constructing high-speed electrical trains.

Indian Railways is a state-owned company and the only customer for rail technology in India. With over a million employees, it is one of the largest companies in the world, at least in terms of workforce. But in 1996, its annual revenues did not exceed $6 billion, making the annual revenue per employee only $3,680. The company has the largest railway network in the world, dating back to colonial times, when it was rolled out for the transport of tea, textiles, and other export goods. Unlike European railway companies, Indian Railways not only runs but also manufactures trains. In 1996, it had an annual production output of 100 to 130 locomotives.

Thus, this company was both an Adtranz customer and a potential competitor. Indian Railways already had a large knowledge base and the necessary infrastructure for assembly and production of locomotives. It had its own R&D department, which set the standards for railway technology in India and was a powerful institution within the organization. What Indian Railways did not have was technical expertise in high-speed trains—the kind of expertise that would prove critical to the country's transportation needs.

The Contract

In 1993, ABB Transportation Switzerland signed the most comprehensive technology-transfer contract in its history. The goal of the contract was to enable Indian Railways to build high-speed electrical locomotives in India. It also included information for purchase and assembly of non-ABB products, as well as instructions about all technical improvements critical for the production of this type of locomotive. The contract contained clauses clearly limiting the project to technology of the current generation of electrical trains and prohibiting the transfer of technology to third parties within or outside India. Even so, the risks of such an agreement are great, and it is here that managerial discussion of the kind of knowledge-exchange policy we described above came into play. Such discussions and resulting strategies always involve weighing possible competitive advantages with disadvantages.

On the minus side, India has weak enforcement of intellectual property protection. The relevant government agencies are occasionally said to be inefficient, and penalties for misconduct are too low. So why did ABB still fight for this contract? Potential advantages for this company included expanding growth in the Indian market and the chance of establishing a long-term relationship with the only railway player in that country. Table 9.3 provides an overview of the differing motives for both.

By signing the contract with ABB, Indian Railways entered a new age of railway technology. Its old fleet consisted of tapchanger locomotives. Their antiquated technology had undergone only minor upgrades since the 1960s. ABB's (and later Adtranz's) three-phase locomotives offered a necessary innovation. They are based on alternating-current technology and driven by asynchronous traction motors. Their advantages include

- speeds up to 160 kilometers an hour (and after upgrades, up to 225 km/h)
- faster acceleration resulting in higher average speed
- a very favorable weight-to-power ratio
- virtually maintenance-free operation
- up to 35 percent lower energy consumption
- a regenerative braking system that uses the momentum of the vehicle to generate power while braking

However, skeptical voices on both sides of the contract argued that the design of these locomotives was too sensitive for conditions in India. They claimed that neither the tracks nor the signaling equipment were technologically sufficient to handle sophisticated engines. The entire Indian Railway system was regarded as saturated. Problems with electrification (only about 20 percent of rail routes in India were electrified in the early 1990s) were another argument for maintaining diesel locomotives. In fact, ABB had to make many changes to adapt its locomotives to local condi-

Table 9.3. From ABB to Indian Railways: Competitive Advantages for Both Sides

Motives of ABB (Adtranz)	Motives of Indian Railways
• Saturation of European markets	• Crucial technology upgrade
• Privatization of railway companies in Europe leading to a decline of prices	• Intensive training of Indian engineers according to Swiss standards
• Immense growth potential of Indian market	• Public pressure for fast and reliable mass transportation
• Political reforms opening the Indian market for foreign goods	• Attraction of foreign investors through improvement of infrastructure
• A chance for a long-term relationship with Indian Railways; possibility of future orders	• National prestige
• Indian project as showcase for successful operations in developing and emerging countries (especially in Asia)	
• Improvement of ABB India's intra-organizational position	

tions such as frequent overload, extreme weather (monsoons and temperatures up to 48° C), and engine drivers who had no experience with high-speed locomotives. Furthermore, the locomotives had to be additionally equipped with grills to protect drivers from stones thrown during riots, "cowcatchers" at the front to prevent accidents with India's wandering cattle, and sealed copper wires to prevent theft.

Meanwhile, INTRA had a separate local service contract with Indian Railways for maintaining locomotives. INTRA's managers considered this contract worthwhile not only because it generated profits but because the local subsidiary was exposed to ABB's latest technology, thereby increasing INTRA's appeal as a business partner for Indian Railways. At the same time, INTRA benefited from an internal knowledge exchange, including training of employees in Switzerland.

The Triggering Phase

The motives of Adtranz and Indian Railways outlined above could be considered the initial triggers for knowledge re-creation. However, it would be a mistake to reduce the Indian project to a one-time incentive and implementation phase. The entire project combined many triggers, which added up to a continuous stream of communication regarding demand and supply of knowledge. For instance, an engineer working for CHTRA on the commissioning of locomotives had a specific problem with the poor condition of Indian tracks. He discussed this issue with a colleague, who, in turn, contacted a friend working for a similar Adtranz project in another developing country. This engineer provided the information requested and added a list of other information available for the commissioning process that "might be of interest for your project." This information was carefully evaluated as to its potential for increasing the capacity to act on local opportunities and to avoid local threats in India.

Because such emergent social processes created a symbiotic relationship between tasks and personal interactions (Anderson, 1992), the team assembled for the Indian project played a key role. The team was set up jointly by Adtranz's Swiss and Indian units and was responsible for transferring railway technology to INTRA and to Indian Railways. Therefore, it crossed organizational and geographic/cultural lines, consisting as it did of Swiss and Indian engineers. As knowledge activists, these team members connected knowledge creation and sharing activities throughout this overlapping network of company relationships.

Note that the external knowledge exchange between Adtranz and Indian Railways triggered knowledge re-creation activities within Adtranz's own operations as well. High-tech products such as these innovative locomotives are constructed for professional customers, and their application requires a variety of theoretical and practical knowledge. They are based on technology that is subject to continuous upgrading and must be maintained by experts. A "smart customer" like Indian Railways needs not only an upgrade of its own knowledge through an external transfer but also active and competent local support. This involves the kind of customer support a distant headquarters office cannot provide but that a competent local subsidiary can. In order to fulfill this task, INTRA depended on an internal knowledge exchange. That means the combination of external and internal knowledge-sharing activities enhanced both the development of Adtranz's Indian subsidiary and successful cooperation with its customer.

Packaging and Dispatching

As we made clear in the preceding general discussion, once the knowledge-exchange process has been triggered, the knowledge itself has to be packaged and dispatched. However, the Adtranz Indian project indicates that these terms need to be understood in a figurative sense. Even though explicit technical specifications for the locomotives were sent to India from CHTRA, the tacit knowledge for understanding their construction could not be captured in such documents. Rather, it was conveyed through social interaction between Swiss and Indian engineers. The following were key elements of this phase: defining knowledge categories, determining the relevance of knowledge for other subsidiaries, identifying the mode of knowledge dispatch, and understanding the barriers that cropped up.

Defining Knowledge Categories

Before Adtranz could decide which knowledge should be dispatched, the different elements of the knowledge had to be classified. For the Indian project, the scheme outlined in Table 9.4 proved helpful.

Table 9.4. Knowledge Categories Developed by Adtranz and Indian Railways

Category / Process	Partial technology	Overall technology	Context	Company
Knowing What	Single parts	All technical parts	Context of use	Technical competence Strategy Structure Culture Stakeholders
Knowing How	Functions	System knowledge Links	Influence of context of use	As a social system
Knowing Why	Causes	System causality	Context dependency	Reasons behind (inter-) action
Knowing Value	Importance of single parts	Technical competitive (dis-) advantage	Context matters	Strengths/weaknesses

Defining what kind of knowledge is involved refers to the pure content of a technical or social concept. This category describes the specifics but does not provide insight into their role or importance. Typical "know-what" might be a list of constituent parts or a list of all possible suppliers for a certain component. Establishing how to use such knowledge refers to the functionality and connections between single components. Know-how of this sort cannot be acquired in the classroom because it is partly tacit and not easy to articulate. Therefore, the exchange of know-how requires a "learning by doing" approach, which often implies training on the job. Knowing why it is used includes the reasons and principles behind that functionality. Causal knowledge is essential for explaining a certain technology or a social concept and is not necessarily part of the other categories. If local engineers do not know why such knowledge is necessary, the reasons for success or failure of an activity will remain incomprehensible. Finally, knowing the value of a certain part or system derives from its importance for the project. The value is often not reflected correctly by its price: certain electrical parts may not cost much, but they are an essential part of a locomotive's control system.

The horizontal categorization relates to the content of knowledge. For instance, understanding the context of use describes knowledge of all the conditions necessary to ensure efficient, fast, and safe production and manufacturing processes. Examples include an efficient purchasing and spare-part system, well-organized stocks, adequate logistical processes in the factory, and the introduction of safety standards. Shared knowledge about the context of use helped Indian Railways to understand Adtranz not only as a supplier of sophisticated technology but as a social system of human beings who shaped the *ba* for their actions through their perceptions and experiences. The overall enabling context that evolves out of such knowledge creation and exchange is based on a series of overlapping interactions and subcontexts for behavior. In some sense, achieving an enabling context means paying attention to the diverse contexts for different activities, especially in a large corporation. For globalizing local knowledge, recognizing the various organizational, cultural, and geographic contexts for behavior has to be a managerial priority. Otherwise, knowledge exchange in a complicated social setting will stall, fall apart, or happen only partially.

Relevance of Knowledge for Other Subsidiaries

The Adtranz Indian project shows that not all local knowledge can be globalized. It is important to distinguish between knowledge that is relevant for other parts of the organization and knowledge that is bound to specific contexts. Knowledge will be more or less relevant to other subsidiaries depending on how embedded it is in a particular country's circumstances or constellation of local stakeholders.

Table 9.5 represents the relationship between specific circumstances and generalizability. The vertical dimension of this matrix refers to the degree to which knowledge is embedded in the context of the country where it is created. In particular, knowledge that is linked to the cultural norms of a certain country is difficult to transfer to settings in other countries. The horizontal dimension depicts the degree to which knowledge is linked to the characteristics of certain stakeholders. For example, *generalizable knowledge* compromises insights that can be used broadly and are not dependent on geographic conditions and local stakeholders. Such knowledge may include best practices and innovative ideas that improve the quality of products or the effectiveness of production processes, new insights into technology-transfer processes, and successful problem-solving strategies. On the other hand, *deeply ingrained local knowledge* is limited not only by national boundaries but also to the relevant stakeholders of a specific project. *National knowledge* and *stakeholder knowledge* are relevant only for those operating within the same national or cultural environment. Stakeholder knowledge refers to knowledge about the organizational culture, structure, and strategies—that is, the enabling context or *ba*—of stakeholders like customers, suppliers, government agencies, and strategic alliance partners. But unlike deeply ingrained local knowledge, such insights may help corporate players to understand and evaluate stakeholders beyond the boundaries of a certain country.

In the Indian project, one manager noted, "This transfer of best practices means extra work and money, and a lot of times it might just be not worth it."[15] Kazuhiro Asakawa (1995), who has also conducted research in the field of managing knowledge processes across borders, notes that "even outstanding knowledge appropriated locally might become a loss if the cost of conversion outweighs the merit of knowledge appropriation" (p. 9). What managers need to determine for future re-creation is which part of the knowledge is too deeply embedded in the country or project organization to be usable elsewhere and which can be generalized to increase the capacity to act in other countries. From this perspective, emphasizing completeness and control of the knowledge dispatched is the wrong tac-

Table 9.5. How Generalizable Is a Given Type of Knowledge?

	Specificity of stakeholder knowledge: *low*	Specificity of stakeholder knowledge: *high*
Specificity of country knowledge: *high*	National knowledge	Deeply ingrained local knowledge
Specificity of country knowledge: *low*	GENERALIZABLE KNOWLEDGE	Stakeholder knowledge

tic; at most, providing thorough documentation and maintaining control of the process is secondary to determining who can use what—and why.

Modes of Knowledge Dispatch

Once the knowledge has been defined, participants need to agree on how to exchange it. In the Indian project, explicit knowledge of components was dispatched through documents from Switzerland to India; but more important, the partly implicit reasons for how and why the knowledge was to be used, as well as its value, was conveyed in training sessions. The training of Indian Railways engineers was divided into on-the-job and classroom work in ABB's factories in Switzerland (electrical engineering) and Australia (mechanical engineering). In addition, Adtranz engineers made visits to Indian Railways factories, where they introduced the new technology to Indian engineers and workers. The time individuals spent in training and visits depended on their position and role in the project—from three days to several months.

The Swiss engineers were spokespeople; they helped local engineers to understand why the new technology was superior, partly by telling success stories about three-phase locomotives running in Switzerland. The training comprised several modules that focused on different engineering skills (assembly, testing, commissioning, system engineering) and was generally described as a success on both sides, because through the training, the Indian engineers gained good insights into the complicated technology. They received training on the manufacturing process itself and also learned the salient principles for setting up and efficiently running a high-speed locomotive factory.

Of course, the technical documents dispatched to India were another essential piece of this phase, but not just because of their content. The documents themselves were "dead" knowledge, which had to be energized by explanation and application; yet their presence in Indian locations fulfilled an important symbolic function. They were tangible, and exchanging them was regarded as the manifestation of the project's success. As one Indian Railways manager explained, "Even if you do not understand the drawings immediately, you see that they are there, waiting for you. It somehow gives you the feeling that things are moving."[16] Also, establishing efficient document storage and retrieval systems in the chaotic offices of Indian Railways was a great challenge. Once this system was in place, it was viewed as a necessary precondition for effectively applying written information during the production process.

In addition to the formal training and dispatched documents that were specified in the contract between the Indian and Swiss partners, knowledge exchange happened more informally. In fact, relationships and personal networks can be a crucial factor in the success of knowledge re-creation projects. Because of the great importance attributed to family and friendship in India, knowledge sharing more often followed personal relationships than formal communication patterns. However, due to its sociocultural and psychological dimensions, the knowledge created and exchanged through this project was sometimes ephemeral. Formerly valuable knowledge links between experts became obsolete (for example, the originally helpful connections with experts in the fields of diesel and steam technology), or were interrupted (because of arguments among friends or other kinds of relationship fallout) and had to be replaced by new ones.

Understanding Barriers

In addition to technical and organizational difficulties with the shipment of documents and coordination of training plans, political barriers influence the globalization of local knowledge. Here we mean the kind of jockeying that often arises between organizations, as well as national political differences. The success of a knowledge exchange depends on more than how thoroughly it is documented or how easy it is to teach; in the Adtranz Indian project, in particular, the extent of the knowledge exchanged was based primarily on the willingness and ability of the individuals involved.

On the knowledge-dispatching side, Adtranz engineers and managers knew that "technology transfer and imitation are blades of the same scissors."[17] Although the contract clearly restricted Indian Railways from subsequently exporting three-phase locomotives to Adtranz's traditional markets, the question of knowledge protection remained a delicate issue. On the receiving side, some Indian Railways engineers identified themselves with the conventional technology already in place and resisted technological changes that might make their expertise obsolete. While the not-invented-here syndrome was not a companywide phenomenon at Indian Railways, it still had to be taken seriously by the project's various managers.

Another big obstacle to both internal and external knowledge exchange in India was the cultural differences between the Indian and Western partners. For instance, the different attitude toward manual work in the factory repeatedly caused problems: While highly qualified Swiss engineers considered their practical approach of "getting down to it" an essential part of the work, their Indian colleagues were eager not to be associated with the "boilersuit men" on the shop floor. In practice, this meant that concrete problems in the factories—such as inefficient logistical systems and inappropriate work clothes for employees—were sometimes not addressed, at least initially. However, this knowledge re-creation project also indicates that cultural barriers are not God-given; to a large extent, they can be overcome if the different cultural groups make an effort to do so. For example, one Indian manager mentioned that he thought most Western people live mainly for their work and are not religious; but after observing that many Swiss engineers showed deep interest in Hinduism and have religious beliefs themselves, he definitely changed his mind. Exchanging cultural and personal beliefs during a lunch break can be a first step toward overcoming prejudices.

Re-creating Knowledge Locally

The proof is in the pudding, so to speak, or in how well knowledge is re-created at the local level. Only if the receiving unit considers the knowledge dispatched helpful for addressing its business tasks can the exchange be called a success. That is why the various microcommunities and external stakeholders matter so much, as they did in the Adtranz Indian project. The re-creation of knowledge in this project was shaped in three ways: through integrating implementation and innovation activities, microcommunities, and a managerial focus on local stakeholders.

Simultaneous Implementation and Innovation

Here INTRA played an important role. The growth strategy of Indian Railways and the special requirements of the Indian market triggered new ideas for developing a robust technology in emerging markets, thereby enhancing INTRA's position within the larger company of Adtranz. Because local market orientation can inspire innovative ideas, each subsidiary should have the capability and opportunity to act as a knowledge dispatcher as well as a knowledge recipient. That way, knowledge, rather than authority or control, determines subsidiary roles within a large, geographically dispersed corporation.

In fact, branding one country organization as the "implementer" can be detrimental, since this strips the subsidiary of its responsibility for innovation and may kill the creativity of a local organization's employees. If local units view themselves only as implementers, their managers will not be involved in the organizational strategy process and will therefore lack crucial motivation and commitment to any larger strategy. This may induce individuals to transfer to other country organizations or different companies, leaving the firm with the problem of "brain drain." As business researchers Robert Moran and John Riesenberger (1994) correctly state, "The old phrase 'Think globally, act locally' is an oversimplification of the true complexities of today's global competition; 'Think globally and locally, act appropriately' better describes the real marketplace"[18] (p. 119).

A classification system that distinguishes between subsidiaries with the responsibility to act and those with the responsibility to think presents an overly broad picture of knowledge creation in a transnational company. This inappropriate division does not do justice to the complex nature of such organizational structures and to the innovative capacities of all members. In the Indian project, innovation and implementation efforts complemented and were contingent on each other. The implementation process stressed the business value of knowledge at the same time that it emphasized the importance of continuous knowledge development, partly through experimentation. While knowledge transfer may be defined as going from one unit (CHTRA) to another (Indian Railways or INTRA), in practice it rarely moves in a single direction.

For CHTRA, the implementation of this knowledge re-creation project pointed to the indisputable need for Adtranz to keep innovating and developing its knowledge. Every day CHTRA engineers and managers observed evolving business activities in a huge emerging market in which qualified Indian engineers were rapidly absorbing technical and organizational expertise. It was impossible to ignore the vulnerability of Adtranz's current knowledge base, or not to see that future competition would be knowledge-based competition and that the Swiss company would have to accelerate its innovation efforts to remain competitive. Knowledge is not a fixed asset but must be continuously developed if it is to yield sustainable competitive advantage.

The innovative context of an emerging market, the nonroutine task of knowledge re-creation, the cultural differences within the project team made experimentation and improvisation indispensable elements for both internal and external knowledge exchange. Compared with former licensing agreements, the whole process of extensive technology sharing between Adtranz and Indian Railways could be viewed as an experiment. Its aim was to reinvent an industry that had traditionally been characterized by clear boundaries between the engineering firms producing the locomotives and the national railway companies running them. At the same time, CHTRA engineers were impressed by the creative efforts of their Indian colleagues. One CHTRA manager noted, "If they do not have the correct tool, they simply take something else and bend it until it works. In Switzerland, we always look for the right tool, no matter how much time it takes." This capacity to improvise introduced flexibility and creativity into the formerly standardized manufacturing processes dispatched from Switzerland and helped to avoid unnecessary delays.

Microcommunities of Knowledge

The groups of individuals with similar or complementary expertise that informally emerged during this project were also crucial for the re-creation of knowledge. Within Adtranz and Indian Railways, these communities usually revolved around engineering knowledge. Membership was based on experience in a specific knowledge area (mechanical engineering, testing of locomotives); interest in the development of this knowledge (through contacts with the R&D department of Adtranz or other internal and external sources of knowledge); a willingness to share this knowledge within the community; and personal ties and common values regarding fairness, honesty, trust, and mutual support. Moreover, these groups were not isolated islands of knowledge but were linked to other communities by exchange relationships or common tasks. They did not have explicit boundaries or lists of members; rather, membership was determined by mutual agreement.

Perceived identity in a community like this is often indicated only through subtle signs, such as when participants share delicate information. In the Indian project, this informal structure was advantageous because it stimulated creativity and served as an efficient coordination system without adding an additional layer of organizational bureaucracy. Instead, these microcommunities provided the security and friendship necessary for bridging existing knowledge gaps. They provided forums in which even complex questions could be addressed, where the presentation of preliminary plans like work flowcharts could trigger fruitful discussions, and where constructive criticism could prevent future disappointment. Given the time pressures of this project, the work of the engineers was usually characterized by a "let's talk facts" attitude, which meant these communities provided a unique opportunity for knowledge sharing.

Local conditions in India further underline the importance of microcommunities: In the Indian Railway factories, where tools were antiquated, the work was interrupted by power outages several times a day, and telephone and fax connections to the Delhi headquarters frequently broke down. The employees on the scene had to be able to improvise, without waiting for managers in other locations to tell them what to do.

Knowledge-focused Stakeholder Management

Finally, the re-creation of knowledge in India was influenced by local stakeholders—in this case, Adtranz's customer, Indian Railways; local suppliers; and the Indian government. As the main knowledge-receiving organization, INTRA was embedded in a multitude of stakeholder relationships, which had an impact on its knowledge requirements. These stakeholders were linked by knowledge-exchange relationships, and by formal and informal cooperative agreements. A knowledge-focused approach attempts to assess the current and future knowledge of stakeholders as well as their interests and attitudes in relation to a particular technology-exchange project.

For example, politicians had a great influence on this project, since they were an important source of knowledge regarding political developments that could determine its outcome; the ongoing discussion about Indian Railways' annual budget in the Indian Parliament is just one case in point. Furthermore, they were in a position to influence public attitudes toward CHTRA and INTRA. Another important noncontractual stakeholder group was the Indian public, whose primary objective was to obtain cheap and safe rail transportation. And many smaller local suppliers were certainly affected by the contract.

Proactively managing the stakeholders in this project yielded a number of benefits. It underlined the political aspects of knowledge exchange by allowing for a detailed analysis of the power positions and options of different interest groups. Perhaps most important, it depicted the partners in this project as members of a larger knowledge network. The identification of stakeholders and the links among them is the starting point for such an effort. It not only balances different demands but also tries to integrate them into a proactive, future-oriented exchange strategy.

MAKING THE CASE FOR KNOWLEDGE RE-CREATION

As the Adtranz story illustrates, an effective exchange of knowledge depends on both the specifics of the interaction and the larger context. Two general enabling approaches should not be forgotten in globalizing local knowledge. First, the spokespeople or knowledge activists responsible for a knowledge re-creation project should make a case for why the dispatched knowledge matters and present it publicly. Second, managers can use narratives to convey the importance of knowledge exchange, especially when workers need to be motivated to break down a variety of barriers.

Making a case for knowledge re-creation is crucial, because explicit knowledge packaged and dispatched is lifeless; on its own, it has no passion, vigor, or vision. Only when this explicit knowledge is internalized, when it is transformed into shared tacit knowledge, does it contribute to a local business operation's capacity to act. At that moment, it becomes alive. To facilitate the process of internalization, the global company must make a business case for knowledge exchange, both with the local receiving unit and the larger organization. This can be carried out by spokespeople or knowledge activists at the very beginning of the re-creation process. The main idea is to demonstrate the concrete benefits to be gained from the dispatched knowledge. For instance, a corporate or local event can be planned in which the final process or product is presented, its potential benefits for the customer and firm described, its position as cutting-edge technology lauded, and the particular challenges involved in setting up manufacturing or production of such a product honestly addressed. Furthermore, providing a global overview of the knowledge dispatched, the sequence or proper arrangement of that knowledge, a list of appropriate spokespeople, and the importance of improvising when necessary should help the receiving business operation know exactly what is involved.

Such events can be repeated at various intervals, encouraging local microcommunities and others involved in re-creation. They should also be coupled with direct feedback to the dispatching unit. A local subsidiary might, for example, come up with new ideas for improving product quality or reducing manufacturing costs—just as Indian engineers in the Adtranz project experimented with the standardized Swiss specs they received. Table 9.6 lays out several useful approaches to making a business case.

As for constructing narratives, this is a natural part of how human beings come to terms with the world. In previous chapters, we have pointed out that company stories, or individual tales about success and failure, can sometimes constrain knowledge creation, setting up expectations before the process has begun or narrowing the boundaries too quickly. Yet stories about why and how people do things are also a necessary component of learning. Narratives preserve impressions and distribute them to others. Some narratives are historical, referring to particular incidents in the past; others capture the quality of different experiences—say, humorous misunderstandings between groups, or the sense of purpose and intense "high" experienced in another collaboration. The latter might be thought of as a means for distilling common sense or for conveying the tacit emotional knowledge that underpins such activities. For globalizing local knowledge in particular, some narratives will have an instructive character, generally explaining to individuals how to deal with the knowledge they receive.

You could say, in fact, that knowledge is located in a web of narratives that offer individuals moral and ethical direction. Take this story about a young engineer named Jim. He ended up leaving his company because he was overly ambitious. Jim was smart but extremely pushy, and he rarely paid attention to other people's ideas. Jim kept trying to tell his bosses, Carl and Bob, about the new methods he had been taught in graduate school, sending them reams of research papers. When Carl and Bob tell this story to

Table 9.6. Presenting the Benefits of Knowledge Re-Creation

Event/Approach	Benefits to Demonstrate	Timing	Location	Who is Responsible
Conference	Reduced costs	1 day	Recipient	Knowledge activist
Demonstration	New markets	2 days	Dispatcher	Spokesperson
Workshop	New products	1–2 days	Customer	Business-unit manager
Lecture	New services	1–2 days	Supplier	Technology staff
Project	New processes	1 week	Partner	Marketing

another young engineer over beer at the local tavern, this engineer quickly learns how to deal with what she knows. She understands without the bosses explaining their preferences—which are, in any case, largely tacit—that she has to be careful not to suggest too many new solutions too fast.

Now consider this story told to Bob when he was first starting out at the company, which helped him get his bearings and influenced his later management style. Just before Bob's arrival, a young engineer received a quick promotion to plant manager because he had been able to locate a bottleneck in the process that dramatically decreased production lead-time. By mobilizing the workers on the shop floor, the engineer removed the bottleneck. But instead of tooting his own horn, he gave credit to his boss, who, in turn, was promoted to manage a larger factory with similar problems. The moral of the story? Pay attention to the development of others at the same time that you work hard on technical problems to discover new and unconventional solutions.

Narratives and knowledge creation go hand-in-hand. Knowledge re-creation based only on documentation that can be packaged and dispatched happens in a vacuum of stories. The web of narratives is incomplete; there are no historical reference points, no recipes for action or commonsense rules of thumb. One way to overcome this vacuum is to construct a storyboard, which can be dispatched with the explicit knowledge. The storyboard can combine small pieces of data, a rhyme or proverb, pictures, or statements from the original knowledge-creation participants. Its themes can range from success stories focused on sections of an engineering drawing to biographies of the people in a given microcommunity. Storyboards can provide guidelines for how to deal with complex issues in re-creating knowledge, such as calibrating a sensitive instrument or conducting joint engineering with an outside consultant.

Managers can also equip knowledge activists with appropriate storylines. Good activists, who are often charismatic and people-oriented, are likely to infuse the story with more life, encouraging and stimulating participants at the receiving unit. In addition, stories can be told and retold by the spokespeople who provide help with technical details. Here a storyboard or handbook that compiles what happened when the original knowledge-creation initiative was first attempted—the thrill of victory, the agony of a thousand defeats, the renewal of confidence when participants tried again—will be a source of emotional and creative inspiration as well as a technical reference.

Sometimes the whole point is to empathize and recognize the difficulties others will face. Exchanging knowledge across many borders, especially when those borders constitute organizational and individual barriers to understanding, is no easy task. But globalizing local knowledge starts at the moment of local knowledge re-creation; it can be tied to a variety of activities and creative minds, and need not be based on a comprehensive company training program or a huge investment of resources. Too much control from above, after all, can quash the constantly evolving innovations of those who deal with demanding local customers, meddlesome politicians, and quirky environmental conditions. Microcommunities should always focus on creating knowledge that others can use—if not in its totality, at least as a source of inspiration. In our next chapter, a consulting firm's activities illustrate many of these enabling ideas, as this company dismantles an array of barriers that often prevent knowledge creation and re-creation.

·10·

KNOWLEDGE ENABLING
IN ACTION

Dismantling Barriers at Gemini Consulting

> *The elusive and personal character of knowledge turns every aspect of knowledge creation into a real fight, and like most wars, this one cannot be left to knowledge military only: the whole organization must be designed and managed for and around knowledge.*
>
> — Pierre Hessler, Chairman of Gemini Consulting

Although all companies create, adapt, interpret, and trade in knowledge of some sort, the business of a management consulting firm is knowledge creation. Consultants rely on tacit, explicit, individual, and social knowledge to serve their clients. The service they provide is knowledge about a particular area, and that knowledge is created and exchanged through various enabling processes—good conversations, re-creation of local knowledge for better insights, even knowledge activism if consultants are hired as change agents. As such, knowledge enabling is at the heart of the management consulting industry. In this chapter, we describe one consulting firm's activities to show what knowledge enabling—the many overlapping interactions, the barriers that must be overcome, the corporate culture that supports knowledge sharing—looks like at its best.

Management consulting firms, of course, are often defined by their "product"—that is, the value-adding advice they give management/-owners of companies in particular areas like strategy, operations, and information technology. From a customer perspective, the essence of these services lies in the creation and exchange of specific knowledge whose implementation leads to superior performance. Clients do not pay for external know-how but for knowledge they can use and act on; otherwise, why pay another firm to create it for you? For such knowledge to be usable, clients need an understanding of how to enable it in their organizations: how to align business strategy with structure, how to reinforce effective enabling contexts or *ba*, how to re-create and internalize knowledge so that it can be acted on. Sometimes communicating insights about application of knowledge matters more than the content itself. That means the exchange of knowledge between consultants and clients requires an enabling context of its own, one that allows for multiple interactions and tacit-knowledge sharing; it certainly constitutes more than a report on paper.

From their own strategic perspective, management consulting firms can differentiate themselves through specialization (industry, functional, issue-based); cost of services; speed; and/or the probability of implementation success. But note that successful implementation is likely to matter most in generating continuing business and a sustainable competitive advantage for a consulting firm. Once again, the depth of the knowledge provided, as well as the efficiency and effectiveness of the operational process through which it is exchanged and created, plays an important role. In an economic model of management consulting, knowledge enabling is strongly correlated with bottom-line performance. Figure 10.1 shows the impact of knowledge enabling on various profit and loss (P&L) items at a typical consulting firm.

Gemini Consulting is a leading management consulting firm with, as of 1998, a staff of about 2,300 located in more than thirty offices on five continents. Most of the story we tell here is based on the work of Bernd-Michael Rumpf, a consultant at Gemini's corporate headquarters.[1] Since its inception in 1991, Gemini Consulting has grown through a series of more than ten mergers, building a platform for integrated consulting services ranging from strategy to market-oriented business transformation to Information Technology (IT)-enabled implementation. Gemini Consulting is the sister company of French-owned Cap Gemini IT service companies, which, with over 38,000 employees, comprise one of the

Figure 10.1. Knowledge Enabling and a Consulting Firm's Profit and Loss

Profit & Loss items ...	... and how they are affected by knowledge enabling
Fees	Knowledge/insights created and speed of generating those as basis for project sale
Direct Consultant (Labor) Cost	Time spent to identify, share, and (re)create necessary knowledge
Market Expenses	Speed/cost of building project proposals using worldwide experience and hit rate
Unbillable Consultant Cost	Effectiveness of measures to capture and create knowledge outside of client projects
Indirect Cost	Integration and ease of use of knowledge systems, cost of support staff
= Earnings before bonus and taxes	

largest information-technology services organizations in the world. In 1998, the whole Cap Gemini Group had revenues of U.S. $ 4.4 billion.

Gemini Consulting supports clients in many industries, including telecommunications, financial services, chemicals, and life sciences. Although consulting firms rely on the talents of individual employees—consultant "gurus" who are self-motivated—making use of the Cap Gemini Group's combined abilities has been essential to the success of Gemini Consulting. Indeed, Gemini has a very strong corporate culture that supports knowledge enabling. Its core values are excellence, openness, trust, teamwork, and mastery. Thus, knowledge sharing has always been important at this firm,[2] and the implementation focus of its projects has made cooperative and mutually supportive behavior a necessity. These values, in turn, have been reinforced by Gemini's leaders, performance-evaluation systems, and corporate stories—adding up to an effective enabling context or *ba*.

This chapter crystallizes the specifics of knowledge enabling in a service industry that thrives on knowledge creation. We start by examining Gemini Consulting's structure and core processes, illuminating the overall enabling context of a quasi-virtual, project-based organization. We then address the strategic challenges Gemini faces as a consulting firm and discuss how it has overcome a variety of knowledge barriers. Understanding such barriers is central to knowledge enabling and will help businesses to succeed in the marketplace. More than anything, consulting firms need to be like the "knowledge cities" envisioned by Helmut Volkmann of Siemens: places where consultants and their clients put knowledge into practice.

GEMINI'S ENABLING CONTEXT:
ORGANIZATIONAL STRUCTURE AND CORE PROCESSES

Unlike most firms in the consulting industry, Gemini is not a partnership organization but a group of traditional corporations. Gemini is organized according to two knowledge dimensions: customer industries in the form of global market teams (GMTs); and functional expertise areas or "disciplines." This structure is repeated on the country and regional level (see Figure 10.2). While the global market teams are responsible for market development in general and financial results in the country organizations, the disciplines build and manage the consulting staff pool—that is, the mix of skills offered by the company's consultants.

The formal organizational structure, however, provides only a framework for what consultants actually do. Consulting is project work. For each assignment, a specific project team is pulled together, one that will vary in size and type of expertise. This means a Gemini consultant operates in

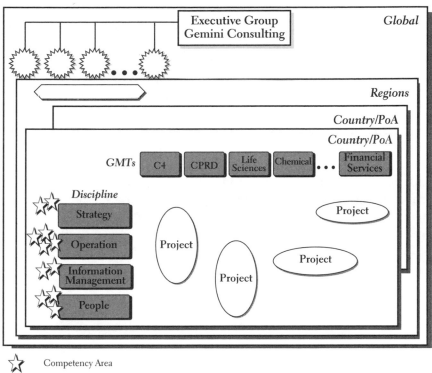

Competency Area

Shop/Information Center

Global Service Offerings (Center of Excellence)

C4 = Computing, Communication, Content, Consumer Electronics
CPRD = Consumer Products, Retail, Distribution
PoA = Point of Affiliation

Figure 10.2. Gemini's Organizational Structure (Schematic)

ever-changing project organizations with only virtual affiliations to the overall organizational framework—for example, as a member of a specific office or "Point of Affiliation" (PoA), or as a content expert in a "Competency Area."

The project character of consulting work is also reflected in Gemini's core processes (see Figure 10.3). Note that many of these processes are performed on a regional or even global level. Gemini Consulting is in this sense more globally organized than many of its competitors. When a business-development process has been successfully completed—that is, a client has agreed to a proposed project—the right project team then needs to be identified.[3] The project manager, in cooperation with Gemini's "staffing" or human-resources function, does so by accessing the firm's global people database, which includes information about specific skills and individual levels of expertise. A team can also be formed through personal references from and communication with other managers, on the regional and global levels. In effect, an internal labor market exists in which Gemini seeks to balance demand and supply on a weekly basis. In order to have a pool of available people with the right talents and skills, recruiting and global training are core processes at this consulting firm, and are linked with its service offering and knowledge needs.

The selected team—typically between five and fifteen consultants—takes responsibility for the delivery of the project, attempting to satisfy Gemini's clients. This becomes the basis for further business development. Although such projects are time-limited, the group activity of the consultants mirrors that of microcommunities. In fact, the relationships established during specific projects will carry over into others, especially when teams are formed around similar interests and areas of expertise. Such tacit knowledge of group interaction is invaluable for a consulting firm's continuing business. Because consultants work on a sequence of projects, Gemini has to ensure the career or "people development" of its employees. Consultants often hop from firm to firm, and high turnover means

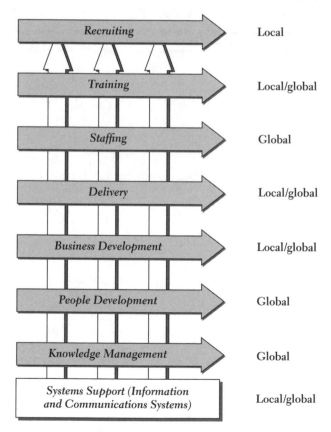

Figure 10.3. Gemini's Core Processes

that fragile and unarticulated knowledge about how groups interact is easily lost. With industry attrition rates of about 25 percent, keeping and developing talented consultants is crucial for the knowledge base, and thus the competitiveness, of any consulting firm.

HOW GEMINI CONSULTANTS CREATE KNOWLEDGE

Knowledge enabling at Gemini Consulting occurs in two ways. First, the firm has a specific process for creating new knowledge or using existing knowledge—that is, the way its consultants go about capturing, filtering, putting into databases, accessing, and finally re-creating knowledge in other situations. Second, Gemini's overall enabling context interweaves other processes, organizational structures, and systems within the firm to reinforce knowledge-creation activities.[4]

We can examine how the specific process works through a hypothetical example. Gemini Norway has just finished a project in the purchasing department of a large multinational client. The project team has accumulated a wealth of knowledge about the best-in-class purchasing process, key performance indicators, the best approach to pursuing such an effort at a multinational, best-in-class supplier partnership management, and so on. All well and good, but what happens to this knowledge? At Gemini, it is the responsibility of the project manager—in this case, Peter Project—to ensure that it is captured. He does that by compiling a standardized electronic "project book" that contains a description of what is involved: the client's organization, issues, work streams, benefits generated, the name of the Gemini work team. In addition, he puts together brief presentations about best-in-class work that the team has performed. The project book is put on local Gemini servers immediately; the presentations, however, are screened for quality before they can be included on the global database of the purchasing competency area. The documents will be categorized for restricted access and/or "sanitized," depending on confidentiality requirements. Françoise Purchase, head of this competency area, decides whether to include them in the database.

Three months later, Peter's colleague, Raoul Rover, has the opportunity to sell a similar assignment in South Africa. Rather than starting from scratch, he accesses Peter's project experience. First, Raoul scans the global database for purchasing. Then he gets in touch with Françoise (via the intranet, Lotus Notes, voice mail, or a direct phone call) to "pick her brain" about Gemini experts and experience. In addition, he scans the Gemini "People Yellow Pages" to find colleagues in South Africa with specific knowledge in this area. All of this happens within twenty-four hours. Raoul brings together a virtual network of functional and industry experts to write an excellent proposal. The contract is awarded, and now he works with his staffing colleagues to find the right people mix for a new team. When this team is on the ground, the cycle of knowledge identification, exchange, and re-creation is reiterated on a more detailed level.

To support its many projects, Gemini has sought to align all its other core processes. Recruiting is linked with perceived industry and functional knowledge gaps. Training curricula tie in with the Gemini competency areas in each discipline. Annual bonuses and promotions are keyed to the contributions consultants make to Gemini's knowledge base and innovation as well as their personal support of projects/sales proposals.

The competency areas are organized around functional needs — for example, purchasing, supply-chain management, leadership development — or business issues like growth. These competency areas are regionally based but coordinated globally. In essence, they are virtual groups led by a regional expert; consisting of three to ten members, they combine seasoned practitioners with younger, topic-focused consultants. They support projects from the outside, proactively ensuring knowledge capture and its quality, monitoring external developments, generating new insights, and joining the global marketing teams in their sales efforts. The competency areas play the knowledge-activist role within the firm, and Gemini underscores their importance by providing each group with adequate support staff.

In addition to the competency areas, Gemini's corporate level includes groups called "Global Service Offerings" (formerly "Centers of Excellence") that focus on new strategic business areas — such as client-relationship management.[5] They operate globally and are run by full-time consultants known as "product managers." Regional information -and-analysis centers called "shops" also act as full-time information specialists to support the global market teams and projects with existing external and internal information. The shops deliver value-added analysis work to internal clients through market studies, financial information, and the like. Each shop generally consists of both experienced and younger consultants, and is another training ground for Gemini.

Organizational support of knowledge creation contains one other key component: the information-technology and communication-systems infrastructure. At Gemini, this is extensive and includes laptops for individual consultants, a global intranet (groupwide system called Galaxy), Lotus Notes, and a voice mail system. In a project-based organization with many virtual connections, sophisticated information technology can link remote knowledge flows and reinforce an effective enabling context. In this sense, it provides an electronic knowledge space or cyber *ba* for the firm.

STRATEGIC CHALLENGES AT GEMINI CONSULTING

Knowledge enabling is the core product that Gemini sells. The firm's main business objective is to excel in knowledge exchange and creation, benefiting its clients, employees, and shareholders. Yet Gemini, like many consulting firms, faces several formidable strategic challenges in meeting this objective.

First, its knowledge is created around the world by more than 1,800 consultants every day. The enabler discussed in the previous chapter is crucial to Gemini's operations, because the company's major challenge is globalizing local knowledge: identifying, packaging, and capturing what the firm knows, then distributing and re-creating it locally for any specific assignment. Most of the time, the speed of this process is as important as the quality. Thus, the firm has to continuously strengthen its knowledge-creation and innovation potential. Innovation on specific projects has to be combined with companywide knowledge creation and reapplied to other projects.

In designing its knowledge system, Gemini's top management also had to balance effectiveness and cost. Finding the optimum balance is difficult, and to do a helpful approach is distinguishing between two types of knowledge—supply-driven and demand-driven. Supply-driven knowledge encompasses explicit knowledge that has been gathered in the past through other projects, previous work experiences, available market studies, and so on. Demand-driven knowledge, however, is created on demand for customers; in many cases, it is based on already available supply-driven documents, but it is highly dependent on the tacit knowledge of Gemini's consulting staff, who work closely with customers. Ideally, supply-driven and demand-driven knowledge are generated in equal amounts. In practice, this is never the case, since client situations diverge, knowledge becomes quickly outdated, and explicit knowledge cannot substitute for experience. Therefore, investments in supply-driven knowledge have to be carefully managed—too much is potentially a waste of resources and too little means higher cost of delivery and potential loss of assignments in time-pressured sales situations.

A further strategic challenge lies in the conflict between the individual view and the organizational perspective. This conflict dogs many management consulting firms, as well as law firms, health-care facilities, academic settings, or any organization in which individual professionals are largely in charge of their own activities. For an individual consultant, knowledge means market value, which is measured in relative terms. Sharing her knowledge might actually decrease this consultant's personal market value. From the organizational perspective, however, Gemini

Consulting needs to leverage such individual knowledge in order to train other consultants with it and apply it to new projects. Since most of its consultants stay only three or four years, the company must ensure the translation of tacit knowledge into explicit knowledge, as well as the socialization of tacit knowledge within the firm, as this dissemination is crucial to its long-term success.

GEMINI'S KNOWLEDGE BARRIERS: BREAKING DOWN THE WALLS

These strategic challenges are closely connected to the knowledge barriers a consulting firm like Gemini confronts. Although companies differ depending on their particular businesses and markets, Gemini's emphasis on dismantling barriers is a good illustration of how a knowledge-creating company approaches the problem.[6] Rather than ignoring such barriers, a productive knowledge-creating company starts by identifying them. And understanding knowledge barriers will help a company define a balanced set of measures that can deal with the inherent challenges of knowledge enabling.

In this section, we summarize the barriers—strategic, organizational, process, infrastructure, cultural, and individual—that Gemini Consulting has faced in the past few years and, in some cases, still faces today. This inventory does not refer to any specific point in time; it is also not a status-quo description or chronological report of events. Instead, we stress Gemini's understanding of these barriers and how the firm has overcome many of them. Dismantling barriers must be undertaken actively and on a variety of levels. Such measures cannot be devised as isolated actions but must be part of a holistic management system and overall enabling context.

Dismantling Strategic Barriers

Gemini Consulting's original position was a difficult one, since it had to integrate many companies with totally different corporate visions, knowledge-management systems, and knowledge cultures. Thus, for the first half of the 1990s, Gemini emphasized the operational side of integrating basic management processes and technical systems. A strategic view of knowledge and its importance for business success was not developed further on the corporate level. At that time, Gemini lacked a clear, focused, and widely communicated knowledge vision. What role does knowledge play for Gemini overall? What knowledge areas should Gemini build, which strengthen, and which maintain at their current level? What role should individual consultants play in creating new knowledge and transferring it? All of these questions were relevant to the firm's core business, but they went unanswered.

This led to a situation in which Gemini had up to fifty competency areas operating without clear strategic objectives. The vital alignment between supply-driven and demand-driven knowledge was incomplete; individuals questioned whether their personal efforts to create and exchange knowledge would be effective and rewarded; and all employees were insecure about the relative importance of such knowledge-enabling processes compared with billable project work.

Although many parts of the current management system were in place, the lack of a knowledge vision and absence of a knowledge map of Gemini resources were definite barriers to creating a more effective enabling context throughout the company. Knowledge was not yet fully a part of the management perspective; rather, it was an implicit factor that affected individual work but was not explicitly connected with the larger organization. Moreover, these barriers were accentuated by Gemini's continued fast growth. Every resource went into project delivery and was stretched to the limit; all internal work—including knowledge-creation activities—tended to be questioned and sometimes postponed. In this case, short-term project delivery needs could have endangered long-term competitiveness.

Fortunately, once the major integration tasks of the many mergers had been completed by Gemini's top management, the firm focused on the future development and strategic use of knowledge. A knowledge vision was developed; the competency-area structure was streamlined—from fifty centers down to around twenty competency areas and five global service offerings; and the expert career track was strengthened. Knowledge was emphasized in vision statements like "Thought and action leadership," and it became an explicit element in many executive communications.

Gemini's knowledge vision has also been reinforced by a change in its overall management structure. In 1998, the chairman of Gemini Consulting, Pierre Hessler, was given responsibility for the long-term development of the Cap Gemini Group as a whole, and the effective use of knowledge became a strategic priority. In this position, he has actively promoted knowledge innovation, internal knowledge-enabling efforts, and knowledge enabling as a service offering—on a global and groupwide scale. Moving in this direction also helped to counterbalance the resource-constraining effects of company growth.

By 1999, Gemini's top management had taken on the next step, rolling out the knowledge vision to all employees, and refocusing individual behavior on companywide knowledge creation and sharing. A second measure involves installing a continuous knowledge vision/strategy process, by which knowledge portfolios can be defined, implemented, monitored, reviewed, and adjusted.

Dismantling Organizational Barriers

When Gemini Consulting was created in 1991, the organization went through a cycle of globalization, localization, and selected globalization. As we discussed in Chapter 8, different organizational structures can either facilitate knowledge enabling or hinder it.[7] A structure with global responsibility and similar local processes in dispersed units—and which provides an active exchange of information and people—makes knowledge flow not only deeper but also faster. Yet even with such a structure, Gemini discovered that global coordination can create local control vacuums. Why should the German subsidiary care about investing in local knowledge creation when corporate responsibility for that competency area is located in the United States?

In a local organization structure, processes and IT systems may not be compatible with the rest of the firm. Furthermore, performance-measurement systems may create disincentives for local leadership to share its knowledge for the good of the overall company. Cap Gemini IT services, even while enjoying tremendous success in the marketplace experienced this kind of dysfunction. For years, Cap has had a strong country/regional focus. Effective knowledge creation and exchange was considered a local responsibility. But when the need for integrated knowledge-enabling efforts increased, this structure became a barrier. Cap people in different countries and regions did not know each other; there was little central intelligence about individual consultant skills and know-how; and knowledge-enabling processes had developed in entirely different ways in local offices—some insisted on personal sharing between consultants, others used electronically accessible documentation, and still others depended on relevant information stored in private file cabinets (or laptops).

Because Gemini Consulting is essentially a virtual organization that conducts very little company work in a headquarters office, it faces another kind of knowledge barrier. Its project organization requires a more indirect means of control. Thanks to the motto "The client comes first," the power that project managers exert over team resources makes it difficult to develop a new knowledge area. Consultants are assigned to specific projects, and they usually only work part time on internal efforts; they may even see internal knowledge creation as a distraction. In extreme cases, only the CEO can order somebody to work on a specific internal assignment. In addition, the virtual character of the organization and the absence of a real boss can interfere with the efficiency and effectiveness of knowledge-capturing and creation activities. Innovation is an everyday agenda item within projects, but how this approach is to be extended organizationally remains an issue for continuous improvement.

Of course, working in a project-based structure also provides an effective enabling context in many ways—by developing a staff that is used to excelling across regions and functions, for instance, and by providing the organizational freedom that allows individuals to pursue innovative ideas. Recently, Gemini has strengthened local/regional responsibilities while maintaining certain global processes that positively affect internal knowledge sharing and creation. In addition, its disciplines have gained more organizational power, reflecting their importance as home bases for competency areas. The global service offerings now report directly to Gemini's Executive Group (see Figure 10.2). Locally, Gemini has significantly built up additional support staff to alleviate some of the clerical strain on consultants, providing them with more time for knowledge innovation.

Dismantling Process Barriers

Since 1993, Gemini Consulting has worked intensively on standardizing its processes for knowledge capturing. These describe how knowledge developed in projects is to be captured, collected, put into knowledge databases, maintained, and retrieved. In practice, however, this knowledge-capturing process had shortcomings. First, it was not universally understood throughout the company. Most project managers knew about it, but not all did. It was not an explicit topic in training for new consultants. Second, the quality-assurance loop was broken. Project managers did check the quality (and degree of confidentiality) of documents; but when a document had to be put into Gemini's databases, responsibility for doing so was often not clear, or the check simply was not performed. Third, the feedback loop was not fully institutionalized. People retrieved knowledge but rarely gave direct feedback to the consultants who had created it or to the heads of competency areas. New documents were fed into the database, and other consultants were left to figure out their usefulness. Fourth, the process for knowledge innovation throughout the company was not described as a whole, although innovation did occur every day on the projects.

Gemini has reworked the knowledge-capturing process in two main areas: (1) ease and speed of use; and (2) quality assurance. In the first area, the following measures have been planned and mostly implemented: technical improvements; further standardization of knowledge-capturing formats; more involvement of knowledge specialists; more active internal marketing by competency areas and global service offerings; and introduction of Internet-like search capabilities. The databases have been restructured according to the phases of the consulting process. Knowledge had been organized in categories like projects, presentations, or competitors; now it is structured according to the application situation—such as the business-development phase (sales material), analysis phase, or implementation phase. As for quality assurance, responsibilities for document checking have been clarified, and the process now incorporates more direct feedback from users. Finally, Gemini's knowledge-creation process has been redesigned to tie in with its knowledge vision, the needs of individual projects, market demands, and a variety of overlapping contexts.

The need for such alignment in a globally dispersed company, of course, increases the possibility for other barriers. Due to the tacit nature of much of consulting knowledge, all other core processes like human resources and staffing policies need to facilitate the knowledge flow. At Gemini, cross-project, cross-discipline, cross-marketing, and cross-national staffing have always been relatively easy due to the company's global organizational structure, revenue-transfer system, harmonized evaluation and personal-development systems, and globally integrated staffing process. The challenge here is to identify the best fit among project-skill requirements, consultant skill profiles, and the personal needs of consultants. This potential barrier has been well managed, since Gemini's staffing department categorizes the firm's consultants in a skill and development-needs database, which is searched to handle staffing requests.

But providing appropriate incentives for knowledge sharing and creation is a more complex issue. At Gemini, the general rule is that these activities are part of the normal job of each consultant. To reflect this, "people development" and "thought and innovation leadership" are two explicit performance-evaluation criteria. In addition, work outside of projects—such as in a competency area—is rewarded in the year-end bonus. However, two questions remain unresolved, forming a significant barrier. How can individual knowledge work and its value be measured? And should the lack of it be sanctioned? In the past, Gemini Consulting focused only on the sheer amount of knowledge input; the impact of such knowledge was not evaluated. This led to a situation in which some consultants just filled the databases with low-quality documents, or affiliated themselves with a competency area without participating in any substantial knowledge-creation efforts. As a result, more active contributors became frustrated and sometimes reduced their own efforts.

As you might expect, specific problems with the knowledge-capturing process and Gemini's incentive system were related. It has become increasingly important to train consultants in the art of knowledge enabling, especially as this concerns how they personally can and must contribute. During training of new consultants, good practice is demonstrated and later reiterated by a knowledge "champion" on each project. Correspondingly, Gemini's incentive system has been realigned. While knowledge-creation activities are now more completely and transparently recorded, their impact is assessed through performance evaluations similar to those for consultants' performance on project assignments.

Nevertheless, measuring knowledge performance remains an issue in this virtual organization. Gemini has introduced several rewards to acknowledge innovation excellence, such as a groupwide innovation and a publication prize. The next step might be evaluating knowledge-creation efforts on the basis of sustained contribution. In general, the size and type of reward must reflect the importance of an innovation to clients and the company, and these rewards have to be balanced with rewards for market activities such as sales support.

Dismantling Infrastructure Barriers

In the first half of the 1990s, Gemini made substantial investment in upgrading its information-technology capabilities in order to help integrate its merged companies. In addition to a laptop for each consultant, a worldwide voice mail system and a globally linked net of data server were installed. Lotus Notes was also introduced and loaded with Gemini's knowledge databases. At the time, this technological platform was quite advanced, but the use of Lotus Notes on a Macintosh/ Apple technology platform did not deliver acceptable performance. It simply took too long to get on Notes and to replicate or retrieve documents. All too soon, employees went back to relying on personal relationships; they used voice mail to communicate and exchanged documents via the server structure. Even there, however, it soon became clear that the system lacked necessary search engines and communication features that allowed virtual "chatting." In other words, Gemini's IT platform did not yet provide the right enabling context (or cyber *ba*) for the exchange and creation of knowledge. In some respects, it actually became a knowledge barrier.

In 1997, Gemini changed its IT environment to a DOS/Windows platform. This move alone drastically improved the performance of Lotus Notes, leading to a more efficient use of its knowledge databases. In a next step Gemini has created a state-of-the-art intranet solution based on the group wide intranet called Galaxy. It provides increasingly sophisticated Internet searching and interactive communication abilities. It also tackled the challenge to intergrate Gemini Consulting's IT system with Cap Gemini's. In 1998, each system required separate access, but in 1999 the entire Cap Gemini Group plans to have over 38,000 employees contributing, exchanging, and creating knowledge on one IT platform.

A lack of physical meeting spaces and training opportunities could have posed another barrier at Gemini Consulting, as it does at many global companies. However, Gemini operates and has invested heavily in a significant number of such spaces: more than thirty offices, Gemini University, 2 week global [on boarding] training of new consultants, other regional/local training, industry (GMT) meetings, competency area meetings, and so on. Gemini University, for instance, is a virtual university in the sense that it is not a fixed location. Its training courses are held four to six times a year for one week, and as of this writing, training is taking place in Princeton (New Jersey) and Paris. All consultants have the right to enroll for one of these weeks. When it first started in 1995, the university was a pure classroom-type training facility and emphasized knowledge sharing rather than knowledge creation. But over the last few years, it has been transformed into a networking space tied more closely to the context of Gemini's global operations. Regardless of the physical location, Gemini consultants meet from all over the world; they not only enroll in training courses and get to know each other but also have started to use Gemini University to create new knowledge.

In addition, Gemini Consulting has recently revitalized its office culture as a way to foster knowledge flows. Typically, consultants spent four out of five work days at a client's site. Many were starting to spend the entire week away from their company office, which severely hindered internal knowledge exchange and creation. In 1998, Gemini's top managers decided to enforce the four-day rule, requiring consultants to come to their offices on Fridays. Virtual offices sometimes still require physical training and meeting places. Although effective use of information technology is a real boon to globally dispersed companies, firms cannot rely on it to generate knowledge or innovations—that is, cyber *ba* can be part of a coherent enabling context that focuses on knowledge innovation, but it should never be considered the driving force.

Dismantling Cultural Barriers

All management consulting firms face a potential conflict between client needs and knowledge innovation. Some clients have clear ideas about what the results of a consulting project should be; otherwise, their willingness to change is limited. In these cases, client expectations can constrain true innovation. On the other hand, only innovative solutions that are put into practice are valuable contributions. Therefore, it is a neverending challenge to nurture a corporate culture focused on creating innovative, value-enhancing, *and* practical solutions.

Closely linked with corporate culture is corporate language. As we have pointed out in earlier chapters, a common language—the way employees communicate and write presentations, the words they use, how they facilitate meetings—is the basis for good knowledge flow. Gemini Consulting has its own language or "Gemini slang." During their first two weeks, new consultants receive training in Gemini methodology; they even receive a vocabulary list of Gemini words. Codifying this common language has been instrumental in integrating the corporation's merged companies. The firm also trains client staff, where appropriate, in use of its common language. Note that a uniform language takes on special importance in a global company, where the issue is not just agreeing on terminology but communicating across national language barriers. In Gemini's case, English is its official language. By communicating across the corporation in one language, knowledge capturing, sharing, and creation often happens more quickly and effectively. At the same time, a diverse consulting firm needs to preserve some local nuances, especially to serve particular clients. At Gemini, all documents are not automatically translated into English; rather, they are filed in their native tongue, along with an English abstract.

Cultural barriers do not exist only between a consulting firm and its clients; they can also arise between company divisions and local units. Consider Gruber, Titze, and Partner, the German company Gemini acquired in 1993. Gruber, Titze worked on a "closed shop" principle, reinforced by a partnership company structure. Therefore, knowledge remained in its different units, and exchange was limited. The barriers came down only after the "old" and "new" Geminis began working together on assignments, learning from each other and delivering and implementing transformation projects. Today the German office is as good an example as any of a Gemini office.

Indeed, Gemini Consulting's culture, common language, and conversations constitute knowledge enablers rather than barriers. The individual consultant must understand his or her role within this system. Everybody has to contribute, and specific incentives are given only for extraordinary contributions. But lack of contribution is sanctioned—in the community as well as through individual career tracks. Such a culture has to balance knowledge innovation, market success, and project excellence. While it is easier to measure contribution to the sale of a new project, knowledge creation must be equally valued. The culture should create more "knowledge heroes," consultants who are celebrated for their leadership in this regard. That means intellectual confrontation as well as cooperation must be actively encouraged. Because of its implementation focus, Gemini has traditionally valued cooperative behavior. Its current challenge is to allow for more intellectual competition at the same time that it ensures partnership in implementation.

Dismantling Individual Barriers

Even with a strong knowledge-sharing culture like Gemini's, successful consulting firms depend on the work of individual professionals.[8] In fact, consultants are often considered a special breed: bright, intellectually curious, self-confident, hard-driving. They tend to be fast learners who live for their jobs and good financial payoffs. Getting a group of people like this to share and create knowledge, which determines their personal market value, requires a thorough understanding of what motivates them. For each consultant, managers must discover what makes her tick: money? learning? a promotion? Does she view consulting as a mere step into industry, or do a combination of things drive her work? Enabling knowledge creation depends on the right use of individual motivation. Gemini makes a special effort to deal with these factors in an extensive personal-development process, through frequent and formalized conversations about personal expectations with consultants, and during the hiring process.

"Gurus" are important for continuous innovation within a consulting firm. They push the boundaries of conventional thinking. Yet their self-image can also make knowledge enabling more difficult. Gurus seek to protect their status, since this gives them considerable prestige and room to move. They are rarely inclined to create internal "competitors," which obviously curtails knowledge sharing and collective knowledge creation. In practice, gurus may take young consultants under their wings, but they are generally reluctant to do so with experienced peers. A related barrier involves project and account managers, who also want to protect their status and consequently have a hard time dealing with failures. Since learning from failures is as important as having successes, a company needs to objectively judge and document individual performance to benefit all consultants. Gemini counteracts this barrier through its culture and management system: failure is sanctioned only when the person does not reach out for help early enough. In addition, independent surveys (the "partners-in-quality program") are conducted with clients, in which they can discuss how they perceived the project. And Gemini "content experts" (its name for gurus) are also responsible for developing two or three new experts as part of their daily tasks.

Another significant individual barrier is limited accommodation, something that Gemini and most knowledge-creating companies will always grapple with. Ideally, a consultant incorporates all documented internal and external knowledge; discusses solution options with experts, clients, and colleagues; forecasts possible implementation paths; and proposes the right solution. But in practice, not all these activities are performed, and only a part of the knowledge available is used. No consultant can process all knowledge. However, it is easy for individuals to fail if they feel threatened or overwhelmed. When the difference between a consultant's current knowledge and the knowledge required for a new task is too great, he or she may not be able to make an appropriate personal stretch. A healthy stretch is good for consultants, but they should not be assigned to tasks that are beyond them.

Furthermore, there may not be sufficient time for a consultant to digest available knowledge. At the beginning of a project, all sources are tapped, and material, ideas, and support from colleagues come pouring in. But if the time pressure is too high, a beleaguered worker may choose the first knowledge source to cross his desk, not the best one. To avoid this, Gemini Consulting has optimized its technical infrastructure, making its knowledge databases easy to use and establishing "help-me" networks of experts/practitioners. Even so, one other factor can lead to limited accommodation: experience itself. As in any job, proven solutions tend to hinder innovation—"if it ain't broke, don't fix it." Both consultants and their clients can be blinded by this attitude, especially when time pressures are intense. It is therefore critical to provide consultants with continuous challenges. Gemini does so through its training programs, frequently shifting team compositions, explicit evaluation of thought and innovation leadership activities, client evaluations of projects, and so on.

As with any enabling context, the measures that dismantle knowledge barriers overlap. Optimizing Gemini's IT platform and its databases, for instance, improved the firm's infrastructure and has helped reduce limited accommodation. The firm's strong corporate culture breaks down the walls between consultants and clients, as well as local divisions, and also influences the motivations of individual workers. To be sure, consultants are not the standard employee. But they are knowledge workers *par excellence*, and the barriers that crop up with them reflect the larger challenges of knowledge creation. In a knowledge economy that depends on an ever-increasing number of knowledge workers—and in which all workers must become more entrepreneurial—management consultants may have something to say to everyone.

STEPS TOWARD KNOWLEDGE ENABLING

The Gemini Consulting story indicates that understanding knowledge barriers will help a company meet its objectives and specific management challenges. From our perspective, understanding these barriers is the first step on the knowledge-enabling path. Combined with a clear knowledge vision and effective knowledge activists, it is the basis for setting priorities and designing specific management tools. Whether a company is a consulting firm or not, supply-driven and demand-driven knowledge must be balanced to ensure long-term competitiveness. A company must continue creating new knowledge to fuel an advancement strategy at the same time that it uses existing knowledge for survival.

Good knowledge-enabling systems cannot simply be engineered. People are key: their motivations, their skill levels, their behavior. Therefore, recognizing organizational and individual roadblocks and focusing on the conditions that build an overall enabling context—a culture that emphasizes innovation, high levels of care, a knowledge-sharing mentality, supportive core business processes, sophisticated information-technology and cyber *ba*—are essential for enhancing knowledge flow. Quality, cost, and speed all have to be brought in line, which is why creating the right context matters.

The Gemini story makes clear how fragile the knowledge-creation process is and the crucial role that tacit knowledge plays. Employees are free to leave their companies, and when they do knowledge is easily lost. Therefore, socialization of individual tacit knowledge must be managed on a corporate level to allow both continuity and innovation. This will not happen on its own. Aside from creating the right context and instilling a knowledge vision, our other enablers affect the process. Conversational skills are crucial for knowledge exchange; people have to talk with one another to unleash knowledge, and actively managing conversations in business settings is often required to counteract hypercompetitive tendencies. Mobilizing knowledge activists is another way to coordinate disparate knowledge-creation activities and to form the microcommunities that encourage tacit knowledge sharing. Finally, globalizing local knowledge will ensure that the right knowledge gets to the right people or groups in a large company—and that the original knowledge is re-created in new ways, perhaps sparking yet another round of innovations.

The point is, you are never there. By its very nature, knowledge enabling has to be part of a dynamic system. With any change in an organization, its objectives, or its environment, new knowledge barriers may arise. That, in turn, may call for new approaches to dismantling them. We would never claim that this path is easy. But knowledge enabling—a way of being, so to speak, that does not let a rigid need for control interfere with a company's creativity—is the right path for most firms in the quickly evolving global economy. Our next and final chapter provides some practical tips for the journey ahead.

· 11 ·

EPILOGUE

The Knowledge-Enabling Journey

A journey of a thousand miles begins with a single step.
—Chinese proverb

A chieving a coherent enabling context, one that relies on all five enablers to spark and generate knowledge creation, is obviously a long journey. *Enabling Knowledge Creation* concludes with what it means to take the first steps and why managers need to start down this path. The journey to transform your organization into a knowledge-creating one will surely be marked by obstacles and pitfalls. But we firmly believe that the business benefits provide a definite payoff. Now that we have reached the end of this book—if not the knowledge-enabling process itself—we can sketch what the journey might look like.

Before we describe the steps, however, let us summarize the main reasons that so many contemporary companies have embarked on this journey. We believe fallout from the management principles, systems, and techniques of the 1980s and 1990s have pushed many firms in a new direction. Complex organizational matrix forms surely created isolated islands of knowledge around the world, with redundant knowledge-creation efforts. Forward-thinking managers have thus responded by creating processes and mechanisms that allow knowledge to flow more freely among these islands. Just think of the knowledge-and-technology-transfer units at ABB and Adtranz, which ensured seamless and dynamic flow of knowledge between various country organizations. In addition, the popularity of R&D, manufacturing, and marketing alliances among companies in the 1990s has created serious concerns about unwanted knowledge spilling over to partner companies. Executives interested in knowledge enabling have responded by professionalizing interface management and defining clear roles to control the flow of knowledge and technology between partners.

During the 1980s and 1990s, there has also been a rapid increase in the rate of new product introductions and in the evolution of customer preferences. Take the shift in customer preferences in the recorded music industry. While the 1980s essentially was dominated by "global" artists like Janet Jackson performing in the English language, the 1990s saw a growing number of regional customers preferring local artists, performing in their own languages. This, in turn, has allowed the rapid growth of new and relatively unknown companies, such as Rock Records of Taiwan and Rodven Records of Mexico, into substantial industry players. Knowledge-enabling managers have responded by engaging in a deeper investigation of customer knowledge — not only the stated needs of customers on survey forms, but also their unarticulated needs and tacit knowledge.

The 1990s saw traditional industry boundaries vanish as well. Consider the emergence of neutraceuticals, which we described in Chapter 6. This new industry combines knowledge from pharmaceuticals and foods to create products that have a healing effect. Here knowledge-enabling managers responded to shifting industry boundaries by creating a vision of what knowledge to develop for the future to prepare their companies for such innovative, unexpected, even previously unimaginable developments.

And through the 1990s, there was a growing discrepancy between market value and book value in many industries — now commonly referred to as the value of intangible assets. A knowledge-enabling approach has allowed organizational members to visualize the value of various components of these intangible assets to make them more manageable, even if they cannot be controlled like physical assets. Think of the effort Skandia put into the development of the IC-Navigator to visualize the development of its knowledge. Many companies have invested heavily in management techniques like total quality management and business process reengineering. The question, however, is whether these have made companies more profitable than others in the industry. Because of the high diffusion of such techniques and approaches, the answer may very well be no. Since knowledge can be valuable, dynamic, and partly tacit, it can also be unique to a company and difficult to imitate. Therefore, it can become a source of superior profits for the firm compared to the average industry level. Last but not least, the downsizing wave of the 1990s, coupled with increasing employee mobility, has in some instances led to the loss of such intangible but valuable company knowledge. Knowledge-enabling managers have responded by trying to capture this valuable knowledge before it is too late.

So, back to the journey. Figure 11.1 illustrates the evolution of knowledge initiatives as we have observed them in practice. Companies have

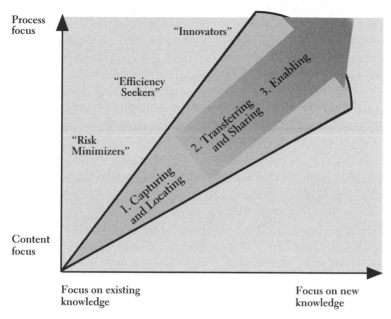

Figure 11.1. Company Development in Knowledge Creation: A Model

many different motives for starting knowledge initiatives, but based on our observations, these initiatives develop into one of three broad types: risk minimizers, efficiency seekers, and innovators. From our perspective, of course, the innovators have traveled farthest along the knowledge-enabling path. Still, most managers go through the other steps first, and there are some very sensible and understandable reasons for why they do so. For every successful entrepreneur who has leapt to the fore with a great innovation, there are a hundred who have gotten nowhere.

First, many firms start off as risk minimizers: "Oh gosh, find out what we have and hold on tight before it is too late." Such firms begin their knowledge initiatives by trying to locate and capture valuable company knowledge. Typically, they focus on the contents of knowledge, or what is known by key individuals and groups within the organization. These companies tend to emphasize existing knowledge that is of use for solving various operational tasks in marketing, finance, manufacturing, and so forth. There are several tools available for capturing knowledge, ranging from data warehousing to knowledge audits that assess the location of knowledge and its business value to rule-based systems that capture the knowledge of experts. For a list of such tools, see Figure 11.2.

The second step is characterized by efficiency seekers: "Make what we have easily accessible to the organization—and find new uses for existing knowledge." Although these companies do not put knowledge creation on their management agendas, they tend to search for new knowledge being developed throughout their organizations, as well as the existing knowledge held by individuals and groups. Their main goal is to transfer experiences and best practices throughout the organization to achieve some cost advantages by avoiding replication of knowledge creation. But even as they focus strongly on the more conventional approach of knowledge transfer, their managers frequently come to realize that technology is only the tiniest tip of the iceberg. People need to be motivated locally to give their knowledge away as well as to use the knowledge that comes from another group or organizational unit. Managers of these companies become increasingly alert to the tacit aspects of knowledge, and they start emphasizing the anatomy of knowledge-transfer processes rather than just specific technological solutions for capturing existing knowledge. Several tools are available for this stage, ranging from best-practice transfer programs to knowledge-and-technology-transfer units (Figure 11.2).

The third step, and the one that puts companies firmly on the knowledge-enabling path, is taken by innovators: "The knowledge we have is not sufficient for creating a knowledge-based business: We need to enable the creation of new knowledge for successful innovations!" Innovators focus both on new knowledge and on knowledge processes. As knowledge activists, they constantly engage and motivate their people, creating the overall enabling context for new knowledge creation that we have described throughout this book. These managers take a strategic view of knowledge, formulate knowledge visions, tear down knowledge barriers, develop new corporate values like care and trust, catalyze and coordinate

Capturing and Locating	Transferring and Sharing	Enabling
• Data warehousing	• Internet	• Instill a knowledge vision
• Datamining	• Intranet	• Manage conversations
• Yellow pages	• Lotus Notes/Groupware	• Mobilize knowledge activists
• IC-Navigator	• Networked organization	• Create the right context
• Balanced scorecard	• Knowledge workshops	• Globalize local knowledge
• Knowledge audits	• Knowledge workbench	• Professional innovation networks
• IC-index	• Best practice transfer	• New organizational forms
• Business information systems	• Benchmarking	• New HRM-systems
• Rule-based systems	• Knowledge gap-analysis	• New corporate values
	• Knowledge sharing culture	• Project management systems
	• Technology transfer units	• Corporate universities
	• Knowledge transfer units	• Communities
	• Systems thinking	• Storyboards

Figure 11.2. Examples of Enabling Tools

knowledge creation, manage the various contexts or *ba* involved, develop a strong conversational culture, and globalize local knowledge. In the words of Ian Ritchie, senior technical member of Unilever's Culinary Category Team, "Knowledge creation means to adopt new ways of working and of working together." Some of the tools available for this stage, including the five knowledge enablers, are presented in Figure 11.2.

From this broad view of the journey, we then come to particular actions managers can take to get their companies moving in a knowledge-enabling direction. In reflecting on your company's position, you might start by listing some of the challenges you want to address through a knowledge initiative. These may well overlap with the ones we have mentioned, but also extend this list to other possibilities, threats, and competitive scenarios. Next, you might consider what is most important and urgent for your business—to capture knowledge, to transfer knowledge, or to create new knowledge? Although we have depicted the evolution of knowledge initiatives as a sequential process, you might decide to do many of these activities simultaneously. Just keep in mind that knowledge creation and re-creation do indeed require a substantial managerial commitment to analyzing processes, ways of working, organizational culture, and knowledge enablers. Otherwise, you cannot achieve the kind of overall enabling context that encourages tacit knowledge sharing and innovation.

Discuss two key items with people on your management team and in other parts of the organization: the five-step *process* of knowledge creation, from sharing tacit knowledge to cross-leveling of knowledge; and the five *knowledge enablers*, from instilling a knowledge vision to globalizing local knowledge. Create some common understanding of the opportunities provided by knowledge creation and enabling, as well as some of the pitfalls inherent to the process. With respect to knowledge enabling, try to find out how you are doing compared to other relevant companies (perhaps including some of the firms we have described in this book). Where are you better at enabling knowledge, and where do you need to improve?

Allocate substantial time to think carefully through the types of knowledge you have in your business and where it resides. Is the critical knowledge for doing business kept in instructions, procedures, documents, and databases? Or is it tightly connected to the skills of individual professionals, deeply rooted in their years of experience? If the answer is yes to the second question, do these professionals operate according to care-based values, allowing younger team members to acquire their skills through mentoring processes? If yes to this question, do you recognize the role of these people in the organization, and have you given them incentives to keep contributing to the company's overall knowledge?

Do not forget that knowledge is not just held by experts, "gurus," knowledge workers, and professionals; it is tied to most working environments in your organization, and in use by everyone. The knowledge-creating company benefits from a broader mobilization of creativity and innovation among all organizational members. Once again, you cannot create the right enabling context or *ba* if knowledge is seen only as the job of a privileged few.

Even for risk-minimizers and efficiency seekers, it makes sense to figure out why the company needs knowledge-management systems and architectures. Technical solutions can help you to structure information and effectively retrieve documents, but it is the *use* of information that matters at the end of the day. Because of increasing familiarity with Internet protocols and the effective application of search engines on the World Wide Web, groupware and work-group computing technologies now allow users to deal with an increasing amount of on-line information at their desktops. Through such technologies, users can search for and retrieve information beyond local databases and file systems. "Spiders," "crawlers," and other "fuzzy search" tools are designed to make everyday work life efficient. This is all fine, but in the enthusiastic rush to embrace technological solutions, it is easy to forget that sharing tacit knowledge—much of which cannot happen through computer connections—is the key to work effectiveness, and that knowledge-creation processes are tremendously fragile. Cyber *ba* can certainly support knowledge work in a postindustrial, rapidly evolving global economy; but technologies should not drive out the process of human interaction and relationhip building that we have advocated throughout this book.

The company stories in *Enabling Knowledge Creation* cover only some of the many firms we believe have embarked on the right journey. Others worth mentioning here are 3M, Daimler-Chrysler, Nokia, Sencorp, Eli Lilly, Intel, IBM, Hewlett Packard, Lotus, PricewaterhouseCoopers, Hoffmann-La Roche, and Glaxo Wellcome. Such companies not only emphasize the value of explicit knowledge but also recognize the real potential tacit knowledge has for long-term advancement and business success. They nurture this tacit knowledge; they enable its sharing and use; they get it out of individual minds into a social environment; they turn individual creativity into innovations for everyone. In short, they engage in unlocking the mysteries of tacit knowledge—to their advantage.

NOTES

CHAPTER 1

1   Reich (1998), p. 138.
2   Nonaka and Takeuchi delineated the processes of knowledge creation in *The Knowledge-Creating Company* (1995); von Krogh and Roos expanded on theories of knowledge in organizations in *Organizational Epistemology* (1995). Also see von Krogh and Roos (1995a), von Krogh and Roos (1996a), and von Krogh, Roos, and Kleine (1998a).
3   Interview conducted by Dirk Kleine and Georg von Krogh, Munich, June 1997.
4   There are many informative sources on knowledge in organizations. We recommend the following books for an introduction to the field: Argyris (1992), Sparrow (1998), Boisot (1998), Eden and Spender (1998), Nonaka and Nishigushi (1999), Kolb (1984), Wiig, (1995), and Ruggles (1997).
5   This definition originated in *The Knowledge-Creating Company*. Nonaka and Takeuchi (1995) based their definition on Plato's discourses in the Meno, Phaedo, and Theaetetus. See p. 21.
6   Nonaka and Takeuchi (1995) emphasize "beliefs" and "justification" rather than "truth" to differentiate themselves from the cognitivist tradition, in which a belief is considered more or less true based on its similarity to an external reality. Cognitivists, especially groundbreaking researchers like Herbert Simon, Allen Newell, Warren McCulloch, and Marvin Minsky, have generally assumed that the world consists of a number of objects or events, and that the key task of the brain (or any cognitive system) is to model these as accurately as possible. In cognitivist terms, knowledge is universal, and two cognitive systems should achieve the same representations of an object or event.
7   Our "constructionist" perspective is based on recent research in neurobiology, cognitive science, and philosophy. The constructionist views cognition not as an act of representation but as an act of construction or creation. Note that the constructionist perspective is sometimes associated, and even used interchangeably, with terms like *creationist perspective, constructivism,* and *social constructivism.* Space does not allow for a fuller treatment of the difference among these terms. Interested readers can turn to Flanagan (1991) and Goldman (1986) for constructivism in cognitive science; to Rosenau (1992) for constructivism in social science; and to Clegg, Hardy, and Nord (1996) for constructivism in organization and management studies.
8   Some authors have referred to tacit knowledge as "tacit beliefs." See, for example, Churchland (1986).
9   The five phases were originally defined by Nonaka and Takeuchi (1995). See, in particular, pp. 83–89.
10 According to the cognitivist, sharing tacit knowledge is a matter of holding shared and complete representations, and there should be no doubt about the correspondence of these representations to reality. In a team, if one member is somewhat slow in making a representation, the "funnel model" can be used—that is, other team members provide sufficient information that the slow member eventually shares the same reality as the others. The constructionist, of course, has a different point of view.

Every team member has unique, personal knowledge, much of which is tacit. In order to share knowledge in a team, each individual must publicly justify that personal knowledge.

11 See von Krogh (1998).

12 Quoted by D.H. Smith in a speech entitled "Competing with Knowledge" at the Second Conference on Comparative Studies of Knowledge Creation, St. Gallen, Switzerland, June 1998.

13 Interview conducted by Ikujiro Nonaka, Kazuo Ichijo, and Georg von Krogh, Tokyo, July 1996.

14 Interview in *Business Insights*, Winter 1995, p. 77.

15 See *Nikkei Business*, October 3, 1994, p. 69, where Masao Maekawa is quoted. We will also detail the Maekawa story in Chapters 6 and 8.

16 Interview conducted by Philipp Käser and Georg von Krogh, Zurich, June 18, 1997.

17 We first coined this term in von Krogh, Nonaka, and Ichijo (1997).

18 For more on this, see Brand (1998).

CHAPTER 2

1 Personal interview with Ikujiro Nonaka, Georg von Krogh, and Philipp Käser on May 29, 1997.

2 For an overview of cognitive science and its conceptualization of experience, see the excellent work by Flanagan (1991).

3 Piaget (1960) here talks more specifically about "schemes" as the structures that are formed through experience. Every sensory input is organized into cognitive schemes. A scheme is a kind of general form of a specific knowing activity.

4 See also Camman (1988). This essay discusses the need for an external consultant, or change agent, to know himself in order to be effective in an organizational transformation. Transformation of an organization requires that the consultant undergo a "self-transformation in knowledge." This means that the consultant has to change his perspective on the change task as well as his skills at helping the organization conduct the change process. Moreover, the consultant needs to reflect on the adequacy of his skills given the challenges at any moment in time.

5 The idea of the self as a series of narratives has been proposed by Daniel Dennet. See, for example, Dennet (1988), as well as Dennet and Humphrey (1989).

6 As noted by Cave (1995, p.112), there is a strong relationship between the way we socially bring forth our identities as human beings and the stories we tell: "[W]e are not free, in these everyday narratives, to construct any identity at all; but it is both possible and normal to give more than one account of the same segment of life and of the identity of the character or characters who figure in it. Not only my different people give different accounts of my behaviour and of what kind of person I am; I am also perfectly capable of telling my own story in different ways."

7 This is a paradox of group life in general. See Smith and Berg (1987). For additional information on conflict in groups, also see Deutsch (1973).

8 Several authors have outlined barriers to knowledge creation. The barriers listed here have their roots in the work of Berger and Luckmann (1967).

9 One interesting idea in this regard is that stories that belong to an organization's stock of knowledge will influence the way organizational argumentation is carried out. In other words, certain claims can be enhanced and legitimized if you have good "company war stories" to back them up. For more on this, see Weick and Browning (1986), as well as von Krogh and Roos (1995a).

10 A formal procedure captures learning but can, over time, become full of "core-rigidities" which prevent new innovations in the company. For more on this, see Leonard (1995).

11 The ultimate quest of the cognitivist is to create information-processing machines that would resemble human intelligence. These machines would, like the brain,

manipulate symbols and thereby solve predefined problems. See, for example, Block (1990).

12 Space does not allow for a full overview of the cognitivist perspective. If you are interested in further readings, turn to the seminal work of Gardner (1985). To many observers, the cognitivist perspective originated in a paper by McCulloch and Pitts (1943). This was the first attempt to conceive of the nervous system as a logical structure. Later cognitivist work applied to human cognition includes Newell and Simon (1972) and Simon (1989). Contributions to artificial intelligence include Minsky (1963). A very comprehensive overview of artificial intelligence is provided by Kurzweil (1990). This book is instructive for understanding the fundamental idea that knowledge is expressible in language. Although the cognitivist charter at the outset was to advance a scientific rather than a psychological or philosophical study of the mind, contemporary philosophers frequently debate the contribution of the cognitive revolution to philosophy. See, for example, Goldman (1986). Because of its implications for a fundamental understanding of behavior, the cognitivist perspective has also had a strong influence on the organizational behavior literature, especially in the ways the organization has been described as an "information processing mechanism" or problem-solving entity. The most notable works here are by March and Simon (1958) and Cyert and March (1992). For more information on cognitivism in organizational and management studies, see also the essay collection by von Krogh, Roos, and Kleine (1998a) and von Krogh and Roos (1996a).

13 This well-known quote from Bateson can be found in the seminal volumes of Bateson (1973) and Bateson (1979).

14 Here our discussion of the chief knowledge officer (CKO) moves beyond his or her more traditional roles and responsibilities, grounded in human-resource management, legal counsel, information technology, or strategic planning. Many companies do conceive of their CKOs, however, as closer to what are called knowledge activists. In a recent article, Bob Guns proposes that the future roles of CKOs will be more like activating knowledge creation and carefully facilitating knowledge sharing and transfer throughout the organization. But for this to happen, a new skill set is required. In fact, Guns says the "New CKO" needs to integrate social skills, collaborative skills, skills at championing change, strategic-thinking skills, communication skills, business understanding, and passionate, visionary leadership (Guns, 1998). Given such ambitious requirements, we believe there is a need for new training programs that can equip people with the competences needed to meet these demands. As of today, however, we have not seen such programs in place.

15 For an overview, see von Krogh, Roos, and Slocum (1994). Pioneers of the constructionist perspective include, among others, Nonaka and Takeuchi (1995), Leonard (1995), Hedlund (1994), and Brown and Duguid (1991).

16 This case was developed by Georg von Krogh, Ikujiro Nonaka, and Philipp Käser. The interviews were conducted on May 29, 1997, June 20, 1997, and February 9, 1998.

17 These figures are based on the annual report 1998/99 of Phonak (loaded from the internet page http://www.phonak.ch on 15 July 1999) and on the exchange rate 1 swiss franc=$0.64.

18 ISO stands for the "International Organization for Standardization," a worldwide federation of national standard bodies from some 130 countries, one from each country. The mission of ISO is to promote the development of standardization to facilitate the international exchange of goods and services, and to develop cooperation.

19 Occasionally guidelines are determined by the market. Ideal time spans for a fast product launch are from February until April, or from September until November. During these time spans, every year the two worldwide leading hearing congresses take place—namely, the American Academy of Audiology (AAA) congress in the United States at the end of April and the German Congress for Hearing Instrument Acoustics

in the middle of October. Media presence provides an ideal setting for communication, advertising, and marketing activities. In contrast, the market is rather slack in December and January, and the closer they get to summer vacations, the less people will read press releases.

CHAPTER 3

1 For more on cognition in organizations, see, for example, Eden and Spender (1998).
2 From M. Mayeroff (1971).
3 For an introduction to this broad body of research, see Gilligan (1982), Helgesen (1990), Moss Kanter (1977), Rosener (1995), and Tannen (1994).
4 A.N. Whitehead quoted by Price, 1954, p. 16.
5 This term is borrowed from Banner and Gagnè (1995).
6 The Narvesen information is based on workshops that Georg von Krogh conducted at the company during 1997/1998.
7 For more on the type of work that fits with a group rather than individual structure, see Hackman (1977).

CHAPTER 4

1 For more on this discussion, see Harris and Helfat (1997); Castanias and Helfat (1991).
2 See, for example, Kalthoff, Nonaka, and Ueno (1997); Nonaka and von Krogh (1999).
3 Although Davenport and Prusak (1997) do an excellent job at identifying knowledge-management approaches, their discussions related to strategy are quite rudimentary. One exception to the rule is the special issue of the *Strategic Management Journal* entitled "Knowledge and the Firm" (December 1996, 17) as well as the special issue of the *International Business Review*, "Knowledge in Organizations, Knowledge Transfer, and Cooperative Strategies" (1994, 3, no. 4).
4 According to Prahalad and Bettis (1986), management holds a "dominant logic" that to a large extent is historically influenced. Historical conceptions of resources and the environment are embedded in rigid cognitive structures. The dominant logic is particularly manifest when making resource allocation decisions within the corporate portfolio. See also Bettis and Prahalad (1995) as well as von Krogh and Roos (1996b).
5 Although there are several possible ways to measure company performance, profitability is one of the key measures in the literature on strategy. For more on this see, for example, Banker, Chang, and Majumdar (1996).
6 This information is based on the keynote speech of Ollila at the Community of European Management Schools (CEMS) Conference in St. Gallen, Switzerland, in February 1996.
7 We choose to talk of "cost and/or differentiation" rather than just one or the other. There are several grounds for such claims — some residing in empirical studies of successful companies like IKEA and Swatch, others in theoretical arguments. For more on this, see, for example, Hamel and Prahalad (1994).
8 See documents from the Grace Commission (1980–1984).
9 The Maekawa story is drawn from a case in von Krogh, Nonaka, and Ichijo, 1997.
10 For more on "narrative knowledge," see Lyotard (1984).
11 This example is based on Knowledge Inc. (1997) and a 1997 presentation by Buckman Laboratories.
12 This short Intel case is found in "The Education of Andrew Groove" by Hof (1995).
13 It would be wrong to assume that the company "owns" individual knowledge (see, for example, Edvinsson and Malone, 1997). The company owns its "organizational capital," reflected in social knowledge, routines, documents, a language, relations, and so forth. When proposing that individual knowledge is available to the company, we

assume that such knowledge is applied to organizational tasks at the individual's own discretion.

14 This is what Berger and Luckmann (1967) called secondary socialization. Primary socialization occurs when the child is first socialized into the family, extended group, and society.

15 The idea that we can maintain a high degree of freedom of expression comes originally from Wittgenstein (1958). This idea is consistent with the constructionist perspective, in which a particular word does not necessarily entail a direct correspondence to an externally given reality. Wittgenstein's main claim was that we create our realities by the ways in which we play language games.

16 This term is borrowed from Ludwig Wittgenstein. See Tilghman (1991).

17 This story is based on a personal interview with Leif Edvinsson, conducted by Philipp Käser on June 18, 1997, in Zurich, and on an interview conducted by Philipp Käser on March 31, 1998.

18 For more details, see Edvinsson and Malone (1997); Roos, Roos, Edvinsson, and Dragonetti (1997).

19 See Nonaka (1998) for more discussion of enabling context or *ba* in this sense.

20 These ideas about brainstilling come from Professor S.K.Chakraborty, leader of the Indian Institute of Management in Calcutta. The waltz-rhythm example comes from the California Heart Math Institute which is running training programs against stress. Based on medical research on heartbeat rhythm, they found that music plays a crucial role in influencing it. Research done by Professor A. Marcus at the Celeste Institute in Stockholm, Sweden, added further evidence that the Heart Math Institute was right. He discovered a medical relation between the sound waves and the rhythm of the brain. Based on these insights, experiments in the SFC revealed that listening to a waltz rhythm calms the frequency of a stressed human brain from 40 MHZ down to 8 HZ.

21 This quote comes from an interview with Tidhut, conducted by Philipp Käser, April 8, 1998.

22 This quote comes from a speech Petersson gave at the SFC, May, 1998.

CHAPTER 5

1 We are very sympathetic to the suggestions of Hamel and Prahalad that any "strategic intent" should provide for new operational measures. See Hamel and Prahalad (1994).

2 This argument was also made by Markus Venzin (1997).

3 The information about Shiseido and Ayura is based on interviews with Yoshiharu Fukuhara, conducted by Ikujiro Nonaka, Georg von Krogh, and Kazuo Ichijo at the headquarters of Shiseido on September 7, 1996, and with Yukiko Ishikawa, conducted at the headquarters of Ayura Laboratories in September 1996 as well as at Shiseido.

4 The conversion of the yen figures to U.S. dollars is based on an exchange rate of 118.10 yen to 1 U.S. dollar of March 3, 1999.

5 *Nikkei Business* (May 6, 1996, pp. 36–39). Although Shiseido might still sell a certain amount of its major product through its counseling system, the company believes there is room for improvement in the counseling system. Its cold consultation sales system, which tended to ignore one-to-one marketing approaches, was disavowed. Shiseido intends to launch new consultaion sales that are focused on individual unique preferences and needs. In some cases, Shiseido does not hesitate to sell its products without any consultation if customers prefer.

6 Generally speaking, the decision to address skin and beauty problems is apparent from the reforms of the research and development system. In 1994, for example, Shiseido established the "life science research department." At the same department, the issues of the aging society and increasing stress levels were recognized; using skin research as a starting point, research considering the whole body was pursued, and

the brain and nerves were included in the general human scientific field of research. Developments are also being made in the beauty-science research department, where research on human bodies, consciousness, sensitivities, and actions has been approached from a more holistic perspective that includes artistic and philosophical issues, and considers humans as members of society. From there, research proposals have responded to the demands of individual customers for new ways of life.

7   A substantial amount of thinking has been done about such narratives of the future. See, for example, Wilson (1998) and Thomas (1998), as well as Schwartz (1996). For an overview of various scenario techniques, see Venzin (1997). For more on the scenario process as a learning process, see de Geus (1998).

8   In order to get started with the narration process, consider certain issues of *Time* magazine (1997/1998), in which the results of a number of expert interviews have been used by the editorial staff to create a narrative of future knowledge development.

8   Such horizons of expectation are formed by the sociocultural context of any group of readers of a text. This idea was borrowed from Just (1972).

10   In this way, the vision process unfolds iteratively. Some messages are sent out, reactions are received, a revised vision is sent out, new reactions received from other organizational members, and so forth. The organization can operate with several versions of the knowledge vision. See also Gioia and Chittipendi (1991).

CHAPTER 6

1   This information is based on a case study conducted by Georg von Krogh and Urs Neumair in 1995. See Neumair (1998).

2   Personal interview with Ikujiro Nonaka, Georg von Krogh, and Philipp Käser on May 29, 1997.

3   From Gurevitch (1995, p. 97)

4   See 1996 Time Warner Annual Report, "Even Better Together."

5   This information is based on a guest lecture at the university of St. Gallen, conducted by Wolf Dietrich Schutz on May 5, 1997.

6   Interview with Shun Murakami conducted on March 16, 1995.

7   This story is based on interviews with Masao Maekawa about Maekawa's corporate history and management system, conducted by Ikujiro Nonaka and Kazuo Ichijo on November 11, 1994, and by Ikujiro Nonaka, Georg von Krogh, and Kazuo Ichijo on September 17, 1997; on an interview with Yoshio Iwasaki about Maekawa's corporate history and management system, conducted by Ikujiro Nonaka and Kazuo Ichijo on March 16, 1995; and on an interview with Shun Murakami, president of Maekawa's Food Processing corporation, conducted by Ikujiro Nonaka and Kazuo Ichijo on March 16, 1995.

8   See Weber (1998, p. 46).

9   The sources for the description of GE's Six Sigma activities are GE's Annual Report 1997; "GE Races Ahead to Quality Improvement," *Nikkei Business* (September 8, 1997, pp. 34–41), and interviews with GE's Corporate Leadership Development manager Satoshi Hotta on September 8, 1998.

CHAPTER 7

1   Michel Foucault (1986) described a poet in this way.

2   Many seasoned knowledge activists who have experienced knowledge creation in practice would share this view. See, for example, Kenyon (1997).

3   For more on KTT, see, for example, Bartlett and Ghoshal (1992).

4   Studies of middle managers in Western companies show that this is not always the case. In fact, middle-level managers might exert quite limited influence in strategic discussions, which, in turn, would hamper the dissemination of strategies throughout the organization. See Westley (1990). In general, Henry Minztberg (1994) also

notes that the literature of strategic management displays little interest in the role of middle managers.

5   When speaking of organizational elites, management researchers tend to mean "top managers" (see, for example, Pettigrew, 1992). This tends to divert our attention from the key role middle managers can play in the sharing of tacit knowledge.

6   The information about Volkmann and his ideas is based on a personal interview, conducted by Georg von Krogh and Dirk Kleine, Munich, June,1997, and on Knopf (1996), Liebig (1993), *Der Spiegel* (1996), Volkmann (1994), Volkmann (1995), Volkmann (1996), and the information brochure of Siemens AG: "Knowledge Cities as Meeting Places."

7   These figures come from http://w1.siemens/de/en/investor-relations/annual. report/index.html (checked on May 12, 1999). The conversion to U.S. dollars is based on the average exchange rate of the period from October 1, 1997, to September 30, 1998. The resulting exchange rate is 1.791 deutsche marks to 1 dollar.

8   This initiative has been supported by the Zentralabteilung Technik of Siemens AG.

CHAPTER 8

1   Teece (1981) has specifically discussed how difficult it is to separate out tacit knowledge for sale in markets—that is, how an organization takes what talented individuals know and converts this into products. For those who want further details, Nonaka (1991, 1994) has also written extensively on the difficulty of converting tacit knowledge into usable innovations.

2   Nonaka and Konno (1998) refer to this "greater *ba*" as *basho*. For the sake of simplicity, in most instances we use the term *ba* to cover both levels in this book, although we do distinguish an overall enabling context from other levels of *ba*.

3   Taken from www.kpcb.com/keiretsu/, on March 27, 1999.

4   Horoyuki Morimoto of Sony kindly provided useful informaton that stimulated our ideas about the relationship between structure and knowledge described in tables 8.2 and 8.3.

5   This story is based on an interview with Nobuyuki Idei about Sony's new company system, conducted by Kazuo Ichijo on June 19, 1996, and on an interview with Toru Terakawa about Sony's corporate transformation since 1992 conducted on October 8, 1998.

6   The eight companies were the Consumer A&V Products Company; the InfoCom Products Company (InfoCom is short for information communication); the Mobile Electronics Company; the Components Company; the Recording Media & Energy Company; the Broadcast Products Company; the Business & Industrial Systems Company; and the Semiconductor Company.

7   The other companies are the Components & Peripherals Company (formerly called the Components Company), the Recording Media & Energy Company, the Broadcast Products Company, the Image & Sound Communications Company (formerly called the Business & Industrial Systems Company), and the Semiconductor Company.

8   The previous research and development structure, comprising the Research Center and the R&D divisions of each company, was reevaluated and resulted in three new laboratories: the Architecture Laboratory, responsible for research and development of software, network, and other IT-related technologies; the Product Development Laboratory, which oversees research for product development in audiovisual businesses; and the System and LSI Laboratory, which conducts research and development for LSI and system design, the backbone of hardware products. These laboratories, in addition to the Research Center established before, were called the Corporate Laboratories. In addition, the recently established D21 Laboratory will conduct long-term research and development geared toward future new products.

9   Taken from a personal interview conducted by Kazuo Ichijo with Idei on June 19, 1996.

10 By May 1997, the strategic role of Sony's Executive Board increased even more when the number of participating directors was reduced to nine members. It was composed of the President and Chief Operating Officer, the newly appointed Chief Human Resources Officer, Chief Production Officer, Chief Marketing Officer, and Chief Communications Officer, in addition to the existing Chief Technology Officer, the Chief Financial Officer, and other two executives. Sony also reorganized its Board of Directors and created a new management position called "corporate executive officer" in an effort to distinguish those individuals responsible for oversight from those responsible for management. Sony will make a further distinction by reviewing the current list of board members and reducing the number of individuals who also serve on its new Management Committee for each business unit. In addition, Sony will enhance its system of checks and balances by increasing the number of outside directors. To reinforce cooperation, the Management Committee will comprise top managers from its major business units.

11 Sony made Sony Music Entertainment (Japan), Sony Chemical Corporation (for printed circuit-board business), and Sony Precision Technology (for semiconductor inspection equipment and precision measuring devices) wholly owned subsidiary companies of Sony Corporation on January 1, 2000. In addition, Sony Computer Entertainment, which is currently owned by Sony Corporation (49.8 percent share) and Sony Music Entertainment Japan (49.8 percent share) will also become wholly owned subsidiary companies of Sony Corporation. This is part of Sony's effort to create a group structure that respects company autonomy while promoting coordination between businesses.

12 This story is based on interviews with Masao Maekawa about Maekawa's corporate history and management system, conducted by Ikujiro Nonaka and Kazuo Ichijo on November 11, 1994, and by Ikujiro Nonaka, Georg von Krogh, and Kazuo Ichijo on September 17, 1996; on an interview with Yoshio Iwasaki about Maekawa's corporate history and management system, conducted by Ikujiro Nonaka and Kazuo Ichijo on March 16, 1995; and on an interview with Shun Murakami, president of Maekawa's Food Processing corporation, conducted by Ikujiro Nonaka and Kazuo Ichijo on March 16, 1995.

13 The conversion of the yen amounts is based on an exchange rate of 118.10 yen to 1 U.S. dollar of March 31, 1999.

14 Before the current system based on independent corporations, Maekawa went through a number of more traditional organizational structures: craftsmen (from its opening to the end of the second world war); area-based management (the end of the second world war to the early fifties); functional divisions (the late fifties); and group-based management (the early seventies).

15 There are nine local blocs, one staff bloc, seven metropolitan blocs, four overseas blocs, one technology development bloc, and one service industry bloc.

16 From an interview with Shun Murakami, conducted by Ikujiro Nonaka and Kazuo Ichijo on March 16, 1995.

17 Ibid.

18 Masao Maekawa quoted in *Nikkei* Business, October 3, 1994, p. 69.

19 Ibid.

20 This story is based on an interview with senior vice president Souichiro Kage about AD-I, conducted by Kazuo Ichijo on December 14, 1995; an interview with deputy president of AD-I Oka Komiyama about AD-I, conducted by Kazuo Ichijo on May 30, 1996, and September 16, 1997; and an interview with senior vice president Akira Kuwahara about Toshiba's growth strategy, conducted by Kazuo Ichijo on May 30, 1996.

21 The Japanese names for these companies are Tanaka Seisaku-jo (Tanaka Engineering

Works), Shibaura Seisaku-jo (Shibaura Engineering Works), Tokyo Denki (Tokyo Electric Company), and Tokyo Shibaura Denki (Tokyo Shibaura Electric Company).

22　The conversion of the yen amounts is based on an exchange rate of 127.74 yen to 1 U.S. dollar by Toshibano.

23　From the *1997 Toshiba Annual Report.* Heavy electrical apparatus and consumer products fall into the mainstream category. Although some of these products still exhibit excellent growth potential, the growth rate and share of mainstream business at Toshiba has become smaller. Personal computers, peripherals, semiconductors, LCDs, and network-computing products are considered high-growth sectors, and here Toshiba intends to foster such growing businesses through direct investments as well as alliances with leading companies in Japan and overseas. At the same time, Toshiba is paying an increasing amount of attention to emerging businesses like interactive TVs using set-top boxes and DVD hardware and software.

24　From fiscal year 1999, the Advanced-I Group was replaced by a newly created Toshiba's corporate business development center. The reason for this integration is the introduction of a new "company system" by which Toshiba is divided into nine companies. The duties of the Advanced-I Group will be assumed by this center, which functions as an integration mechanism among the nine companies and pursues new business development involving different companies. According to an interview by Ikujiro Nonaka and Kazuo Ichijo on May 14, 1999, in Tokyo, with Toshiba's CEO Taizo Nishimuro, the function and mission of the Advanced -I Group is still important for Toshiba and is firmly reflected in the creation of the corporate business development center.

CHAPTER 9

1　For more information on globalization tendencies, see Dunning (1993).

2　For more on descriptions and language, see Russell's work (1956, 1959).

3　Leonard and Kraus (1985) were concerned with active resistance against new technologies transferred. The remedy they suggested is for top management in the receiving organization to take control and symbolically support technology transfer and technology implementation.

4　In making this assumption shift, we would be wise to recollect Maurice Merlau-Ponty's notion that absolute knowledge (that is, necessary for intellectual control) is impossible, because our experience of truth is inseparable from our being in a particular situation. See Merleau-Ponty (1961) and Langer (1989).

5　We find support of this view in Jain and Triandis (1997). These authors suggest that local acceptance of a technology coming from the outside is likely to increase when the local organization is allowed to experiment with, test, and incrementally improve the innovation. Similar arguments have been made with respect to early adopters in von Hippel (1978).

6　Although originating from a study of a different set of issues, Casson (1991) suggested that when transferring new concepts to a different location, face-to-face interactions need to be high.

7　This information is based on lectures in international management at the University of St. Gallen by Georg von Krogh in 1998.

8　In complexity studies, the assumption that simple principles generate complex patterns is well known. See, for example, Holland (1992) and Kauffmann (1993).

9　The idea of self-similarity in managerial processes is also associated with the "Fractal Company." Two pioneering companies in this area are Sencorp of Cincinnati (see von Krogh and Roos, 1995a) and Mettler-Toledo of Albstadt, Germany. Warnecke (1993) suggested that a fractal factory is based on the general principle of simplicity, and, more specifically, on self-organization of teams with similar or consistent goals, high transparency of organizational processes, motivation as the key design principle, cooperation rather than confrontation, the internalization of objectives among team members, quality-awareness as a matter of course, and an understanding of competition that is not limited to the immediate surroundings of the company. Several of these principles are similar to those underlying the process of knowledge creation, especially those of self-organization, internalization of consistent goals, motivation, and cooperation rather than confrontation.

10 This story is based on longitudinal ethnograhic field research conducted by Carla Kriwet, who, as part of our larger research program on knowledge, spent a year (1995 to 1996) working and living with Adtranz representatives in India; also see Kriwet (1997)

11 This information is based on http://www.abb.com (checked on Sept. 15, 1999).

12 This information is based on http://www.daimlerchrysler.com (checked on Sept. 15, 1999).

13 The current Adrantz information is based on http://www.adtranz.com (checked on Sept. 15, 1999).

14 This information bases on http://www.adtranz.com (checked on Sept. 15, 1999).

15 Statement of a CHTRA manager in Zurich, India Team Office, March 15, 1996, recorded by Carla Kriwet.

16 This information is based on a personal interview with one Indian manager conducted by Carla Kriwet.

17 Kogut and Zander (1992), p. 384.

CHAPTER 10

1 The story was compiled on the one hand on the basis of internal papers from Gemini: The Role and Career for Knowledge Specialists, August 21, 1998; Internal Knowledge Management Project, May 14, 1998; Gemini Internal Knowledge Management, February 24, 1998; Recommendations for Innovation Management, September 18, 1998; The Future of Gemini's Internal Knowledge Management, July 31, 1998. On the other hand it was compiled from dialogues and reviews by Bernd-Michael Rumpf with the chairman of the Gemini Consulting on August 21, 1998; with internal Knowledge Project Manager at Gemini Consulting on April 28, 1999: and with the worldwide manager responsible for Knowledge Management July 8, 1999. The views presented here, however, are those of the authors.

2 Knowledge sharing at consulting firms is never entirely open and unhindered; it takes place within the limits of confidentiality agreements.

3 In most cases straw model project teams have already been identified during the business development phase.

4 Gemini Consulting refers to our understanding of knowledge enabling as *knowledge management*. However, we use the term *knowledge enabling* here to distinguish the activities described in this chapter from more conventional knowledge-management concepts.

5 Some of the global service offerings are linked with their equivalent at Cap Gemini IT services, forming a groupwide pool of knowledge and expertise.

6 Beyond confronting its own barriers, Gemini applies a tool called "knowledge-barrier analysis" for clients in the initial phases of a project.

7 In many multinationals, the organizational structure within one country can also be a barrier—for example, when a company has a strong unit structure with no clearly separated target markets. However, this was never an issue at Gemini Consulting due to its discipline/global-market-team structure.

8 In this section, we describe only the potential effects of individual barriers. They are by definition individual and thus are difficult to generalize.

REFERENCES

Adtranz. 1996. *ABB Daimler-Benz Transportation*. Company Brochure, No. 1.

Andrews, K. 1971. *The concept of corporate strategy*. Homewood, Ill.: Dow Jones-Irwin.

Anderson, B. 1983. *Imagined communities: Reflections on the origin and spread of nationalism*. London: New Left Books.

Argyris, C. 1992. *On organizational learning*. Cambridge, Mass.: Blackwell.

Aronowitz, S. 1990. On intellectuals. In *Intellectuals*, ed. B. Robbins, 3–56. Minneapolis: University of Minnesota Press.

Asakawa, K. 1995. Managing knowledge conversion process borders: Towards a framework of international knowledge management. Working paper, INSEAD, No. 95/91/OB.

Banker, R. D., H. H. Chang, and S. K. Majumdar. 1996. A framework for analyzing changes in strategic performance. *Strategic Management Journal* 17, no. 9:693–713.

Banner, D. K., and T. E. Gagnè. 1995. *Designing effective organizations: Traditional and transformational views*. Thousand Oaks, Calif.: Sage.

Barnes, B. 1988. *The nature of power*. Cambridge, Mass.: Polity Press.

Barney, J. B. 1991. Firm resources and sustained competitive advantage. *Journal of Management* 17, no. 1:99–120.

Bartlett, C. A., and S. Ghoshal. 1992. *Transnational management*. Homewood, Ill.: Irwin.

———. 1990. Managing innovation in the transnational corporation. In *Managing the global firm*, ed. C. A. Bartlett, Y. Doz, and G. Hedlund, 215–55. London: Routledge.

———. 1986. Tap your subsidiaries for global reach. *Harvard Business Review* 64, no. 6: 87–94.

Bateson, G. 1979. *Mind and nature*. New York: Bantam Books.

———. 1973. *Steps to an aecology of mind*. London: Paladin.

Berger, P., and T. Luckmann. 1967. *The social construction of reality*. New York: Penguin.

Bettis, R., and C. K. Prahalad. 1995. The dominant logic: Retrospective and extension. *Strategic Management Journal* 16, no. 1:5–14.

Block, N. 1990. The computer model of mind. In *Thinking: An invitation to cognitive science*, ed. D. H. Osherson and E. E. Smith, Vol. 3. Cambridge, Mass.: MIT Press.

Boam, R., and Sparrow, P. 1992. *Designing and achieving competency*. London: McGraw Hill.

Boisot, M. H. 1998. *Knowledge assets: Securing competitive advantage in the information economy*. Oxford: Oxford University Press.

Boulding, K. E. 1995. *The future: Images and processes*. Thousand Oaks, Calif.: Sage.

Bourdieu, P. 1980. *Questions de sociologie*. Paris: Editions de Minuit.

Brand, A. 1998. Knowledge management and innovation at 3M. *Journal of Knowledge Management* 2, no. 1:17–22.

Brown, J. S., and P. Duguid. 1991. Organizational learning and communities of practice: Towards a unified view of working, learning, and innovating. *Organization Science* (February):40–57.

Buckman Laboratories. 1997. Presentation at RSO Forum Alta Professionalita, Milano, April 23.

Burns, T., and G. Stalker. 1961. *The management of innovation*. London: Tavistock.

Calhoun, J. 1991. Indirect relationships and imagined communities: Large-scale social integration and the transformation of everyday life. In *Social theory for a changing society*, ed. P. Bourdieu and J.S. Coleman, 95–121. Boulder, Col.: Westview Press.

Camman, C. 1988. Action usable knowledge. In *The self in social inquiry*, ed. D. N. Berg and K. K. Smith, 109–122. London: Sage.

Casson, M. 1991. A systems view of R&D. In *Global research strategy and international competitiveness*, ed. M. Casson, 99. London: Blackwell.

Castanias, R. P., and C. E. Helfat. 1991. Managerial resources and rents. *Journal of Management* 17, no. 1: 155–71.

Cave, T. 1995. Fictional Identities. In *Identity*, ed. H. Harris, 99–128. Oxford: Oxford University Press.

Chandler, A. D. 1994. The function of HQ unit in the multibusiness firm. In *Fundamental issues in strategy: A research agenda*, ed. R. P. Rumelt, D. E. Schendel, and D. J. Teece, 323–60. Boston: Harvard Business School Press.

Churchland, P. 1986. *Neurophilosophy: Towards a unified science of the mind/brain*. Cambridge, Mass.: MIT Press.

Clegg, S.R., C. Hardy, and W. R. Nord, eds. 1996. *Handbook of organization studies*. London: Sage.

Couldon, T. C., and T. Coe. 1991. *The flat organization: Philosophy and practice*. Corby: British Institute of Management Survey.

Cyert, R. M., and J. G. March. 1992. *A behavioural theory of the firm*, 1963. Reprint, London: Blackwell.

Darrah, C. N. 1995. Workplace training, workplace learning: A case study. *Human Organization* 54, no.1:31–41.

Davenport, T., and Prusak, L. 1997. *Working knowledge*. Boston: Harvard Business School Press.

de Geus, A. 1988. Planning as learning. *Harvard Business Review* (March-April):70–74.

Denison, D. R. 1997. Toward a process-based theory of organizational design: Can organizations be designed around value chains and networks. *Advances in Strategic Management* 14:1–44.

Dennet, D. 1988. Why everyone is a novelist. *Times Literary Supplement*, September, 16–22.

Dennet, D., and Humphrey, N. 1989. Speaking for ourselves. *Raritan: A quarterly review* 7, no. 9:69–98.

Deutsch, M. 1973. *The resolution of conflict*. New Haven, Conn.: Yale University Press.

Dreyfus, H. L., and S. E. Dreyfus. 1986. *Mind over machine*. New York: Macmillan.

Drucker, P. 1994. The age of social transformation. *Atlantic Monthly*, November, 53–80.

Dummet, M. 1993. *The seas of language*. Oxford: Oxford University Press.

Dunning, J. 1993. *The globalization of business*. London: Routledge.

Dyer, J. H. 1996. Specialized supplier networks as a source of competitive advantage: Evidence from the auto industry. *Strategic Management Journal* 17, no. 4:271–93.

Eco, U. 1992. The original and the copy. In *Understanding Origins*, ed. F. Varela and J. P. Dupuy, 273–305. Dodrecht, Netherlands: Kluwer Academic Publishers.

Eden, C., and Spender, J. C., eds. 1998. *Managerial and organization cognition: Theory, methods, and research*. London: Sage.

Edman, I., ed.1936. *The works of Plato*. New York: Tudor Publishing Company.

Edvinsson, L., and M. Malone. 1997. *Intellectual capital*. New York: HarperCollins.

Edvinsson, L., and P. Sullivan. 1996. Developing a model for managing intellectual capital. *European Management Journal* 14, no. 4:356–64.

Fajey, L., and V. K. Narayanan. 1986. *Macroenvironmental analysis for strategic management*. St. Paul. Minn.: West Publishing.

Feigenbaum, A., S. Hart, and D. Schendel. 1996. Strategic Reference Point Theory. *Strategic Management Journal* 17, no. 3:219–35.

Feyerabend, P. 1975. *Against method: Outline of an anarchistic theory of knowing.* London: New Left Books.

Fiol, C. M. 1991. Managing culture as a competitive resource: An identity-based view of sustainable competitive advantage. *Journal of Management* 17, no. 1: 191–211.

Flanagan, O. 1991. *The science of the mind.* Cambridge, Mass.: MIT Press.

Foucault, M. 1986. *The order of things: An archeology of the human sciences,* 1966. Reprint. London: Routledge.

——. 1972. *The care for the self.* New York: Vintage Books.

Galvin, R. 1996. Managing knowledge towards wisdom. *European Management Journal* 14, no. 4: 374–78.

Gardner, H. 1985. *The mind's new science: A history of the cognitive revolution.* New York: Basic Books.

General Electric. 1997. *Annual report.*

Gilligan, C. 1982. *In a different voice.* Cambridge, Mass.: Harvard University Press.

Gioia, D.A., and K. Chittipeddi. 1991. Sensemaking and sensegiving in strategic change initiation. *Strategic Management Journal* 12, no. 5:433–48.

Goldman, A. 1992. *Liasons: Philosophy meets cognitive science.* Cambridge, Mass.: MIT Press.

——. 1986. *Epistemology and cognition.* Boston, Mass.: Harvard University Press.

Goldman, S. L., R. N. Nagel, and K. Preiss. 1995. *Agile competitors and virtual organization: Strategies for enriching the customer.* New York: Van Nostrand Reinhold.

Govindarajan, V., and J. Fisher. 1990. Strategy, control systems, and resource sharing: Effects on business unit performance. *Academy of Management Journal* 33:259–85.

Grace Commission. 1980–1984. *Documents from the Grace Commission: President's private sector survey on cost control, 1980–1984.*

Grice, H. P. 1975. Logic and conversation. In *Syntax and semantics,* ed. P. Cole and J. L. Morgan, Vol. 3, 41–58. New York: Academic Press.

Guns, B. 1998. The chief knowledge oficer's role: Challenges and competencies. *Journal of Knowledge Management* 1, no. 4:315–19.

Gupta, A,. and V. Govindarajan. 1994. Organizing for knowledge flows within MNCs. *International Business Review* 3, no. 4:443–57.

——. 1991. Knowledge flows and the structure of control withing multinational corporations. *Academy of Management Review* 16, no. 4:768–92.

——. 1986. Resource sharing among SBUs: Strategic antecedents and administrative implications. *Academy of Management Journal* 29:695–714.

Gurevitch, Z. 1995. The possibility of conversion. *The Social Quarterly* 36, no. 1: 97–109.

Hackman, J.R. 1977. The designing work for individuals and groups. In *Perspectives on behaviour in organizations,* ed. J. R. Hackman, E. Lawlwer III, and L. Porter, 242–56. New York: McGraw-Hill.

Hamel, G. 1996. Strategy as revolution. *Harvard Business Review,* Jul/Aug., 69–71.

Hamel, G., and C. K. Prahalad. 1994. *Competing for the future.* Boston: Harvard Business School Press.

Hammer, M., and J. Champy. 1993. *Reengineering the corporation: A manifesto for business revolution.* New York: Harper Business.

Harris, D., and C. E. Helfat. 1997. Specificity of CEO human capital and compensation. *Strategic Management Journal* 18, no. 11:895–920.

Harvey, D. F., and D. R. Brown. 1992. *An experimental approach to organizational development.* Englewood Cliffs, N.J.: Prentice-Hall.

Hedberg, B., G. Dahlgren, J. Hansson, and N. G. Olve. 1997. *Virtual organizations and beyond.* New York: Wiley.

Hedlund, G. 1994. A model of knowledge management and the N-form corporation. *Strategic Management Journal* 15:73–90. Special Issue.

Hedlund, G., and I. Nonaka. 1993. Models of knowledge management in the West and Japan. In *Implementing strategic processes: Change, learning and cooperation*, ed. P. Lorange, et al., 117–44. Oxford: Blackwell.

Heidegger, M. 1962. *Being and time*. San Francisco, Calif.: Harper.

Helgesen, S. 1990. *The female advantage: Women's ways of leadership*. New York: Double-day/Currence.

Hill, C.W.L. 1994. Diversification and economic performance: Bringing structure and corporate management into pictures. In *Fundamental issues in strategy: A research agenda*, ed. R. P. Rumelt, D. E. Schendel, and D. J. Teece, 297–321. Boston: Harvard Business School Press.

Hof, R. D. 1995a. The Education of Andrew Groove. *Business Week*, 16 January, 50–52.

———. 1995b. How to kick the mainframe habit. *Business Week*, 26 June, 58–59

Holland, J. H. 1992. *Adaptation in natural and artificial systems*. Cambridge, Mass.: MIT Press.

Humphrey, R.H., and B. E. Ashford. 1994. Cognitive scripts and prototypes in service encounters. In *Advance in service marketing and management: Research and practice*, ed. T. A. Schwart, D. E. Bowen and S. W. Brown. Greenwich, Conn.: JAI Press.

Husserl, E. 1931. *Ideas: General introduction to pure phenomenology*. London: Collier Macmillan.

Hyman, J. 1992. *Training at work: A critical analysis of policy and practice*. London: Routledge.

ICBI. 1997. *Conference documentation to the first international congress on knowledge management*. London, 3–4 June.

Idei, N. 1996. Re-generation and strong headquarters will develop future in Japanese. *Diamond Harvard Business Review*, April/May, 1.

Jain, R. K., and H. C. Triandis. 1997. *Management of research and development organizations*. New York: Wiley.

Just, G. 1972. *Darstellung und Appell in der "Blechtrommel" von Günther Grass*. Frankfurt: Atheneum.

Kalthoff, O., I. Nonaka, and P. Ueno. 1997. *The Light and the shadow*. Oxford: Capstone.

Kauffmann, S. A. 1993. *The origins of order*. Oxford: Oxford University Press.

Kenyon, J. D. 1997. A framework for corporate knowledge. *Knowledge Management* 1 (October/November):21–25.

Knopf, M. 1996. Ein Mann spinnt—im Auftrag seiner Firma. *Süddeutsche Zeitung*, 16 November.

Knowledge Inc. 1997. *The executive report on knowledge, technology, and performance* 2, no. 8 (August).

Kogut, B., and U. Zander. 1992. Knowledge of the firm, combinative capabilities and the replication of technology. *Organization Science* 3, no. 3:383–397.

Kolb, D. A. 1984. *Experiental learning: Experience as a source of learning and development*. Englewood-Cliffs, N.J.: Prentice-Hall.

Kreps, G. 1989. Stories as repositories of organizational intelligence: Implications for organizational development. In *Communication Yearbook 13*, ed. J. Anderson. Newbury Park, Calif.: Sage.

Kriwet, C. 1997. *Inter- and intraorganizational knowledge transfer*. Ph.D. diss., University of St. Gallen.

Kurzweil, R. 1990. *Intelligent machines*. Boston: MIT Press.

Lakoff, G. 1987. *Woman, fire, and dangerous things: What categories reveal about the mind*. Chicago: The University of Chicago Press.

Lakoff, G., and M. Johnson, 1983. *Metaphors we live by*. Chicago.: University of Chicago Press.

Langer, M. M. 1989. *A guide and commentary to phenomenology of perception*. London: Macmillan.

Lave, J., and E. Wenger. 1991. *Situated learning: Legitimate peripheral participation*. Cambridge: Cambridge University Press.

Leonard, D. 1995. *Wellsprings of knowledge*. Boston Harvard Business School Press.

Leonard, D., and W. A. Kraus. 1985. Implementing new technology. *Harvard Business Review*, November-December, 102–10.

Levenhagen, M., J. F. Porac, and H. Thomas. 1993. The formation of emergent markets: Strategic investigations in the software industry. In *Implementing strategic processes*, ed. P. Lorange, x–xx. Oxford: Blackwell.

Liebig, J. E. 1993. *Merchants of Vision*. San Francisco: Berrett-Koehler Publishers.

Lyles, M., J. H. Aadne, and G. von Krogh. 1998. The making of high knowledge acquirers: Understanding the nature of knowledge enablers in international joint ventures. Paper presented at the INFORMS/College on Organization Science Conference, Seattle, Wash., 1998, and the Strategic Management Society Conference, Orlando, Fla., 1998.

Lyotard, J.F. 1984. *The postmodern condition: A report on knowledge*. Minneapolis: University of Minnesota Press.

MacKenzie, D., and G. Spinardi. 1995. Tacit knowledge, weapons design, and the uninvention of nuclear weapons. *American Journal of Sociology* 101, no. 1:44–100.

Maekawa, M. 1995. Energizing individuals through benchmarking (in Japanese). *Diamond Harvard Business Review*, March, 31–33.

—— 1994. Information and corporate activities in Japanese. *Forum Communication*, 10 August.

March, J .G. 1991. Exploration and exploitation in organizational learning. *Organization Science* 2, no. 1:71–85.

March, J. G., and J. P. Olsen. 1976. Ambiguity and choice. Oslo: Norwegian University Press.

March, J. G., and H. Simon. 1958. *Organizations*. New York: Wiley.

Matthews, P. 1997. Aqua Universitas. *Journal of Knowledge Management* 1, no. 2:105–13.

Maturana, H., and F. Varela. 1987. *The tree of knowledge*. Boston: New Science Library.

Mayeroff, M. 1971. *On caring*. New York: Harper and Row.

McCulloch, W., and W. Pitts. 1943. A logical calculus of the ideas imminent in nervous activity. *Bulletin of Mathematical Biophysics* 5:115–33.

Merleau-Ponty, M. 1961. *Phenomenology of perception*. London: Routledge & Keegan Paul.

Merton, R. K. 1957. *Social theory and social structure*. Revised edition. New York: Free Press.

Minsky, M. 1963. Steps toward artificial intelligence. In *Computers and thought*, ed. E. A. Feigenbaum and J. Feldman. New York: McGraw Hill.

Mintzberg, H. 1994. *The rise and fall of strategic planning*. New York: Prentice Hall.

——. 1975. The manager's job: Folklore and fact. *Harvard Business Review*, July-August, 49–61.

——. 1973. *The nature of managerial work*. New York: Harper & Row.

Moran, R. T., and J. R. Riesenberger. 1994. *The global challenge: Building the new worldwide enterprise*. London: McGraw-Hill.

Morgan, G. 1996. *Images of organization*. Thousand Oaks, Calif.: Sage.

Moss Kanter, R. 1977. *Men and women of the corporation*. New York: Basic Books.

Neumair, R. 1998. *A general model of corporate failure and survival: A complexity theory approach*. Ph.D. diss., University of St. Gallen.

Newell, A., and H. Simon. 1972. *Human problem solving*. Englewood Cliffs, N.J.: Prentice-Hall.

Nishida, K. 1990. *An inquiry into the good*, trans. M. Abe and C. Ives, 1921. Reprint. New Haven, Conn.: Yale University Press.

———. 1970. *Fundamental problems of philosophy: The world of action and the dialectical world*. Tokyo: Sophia University.

Nonaka, I. 1998. The concept of "Ba": Building a foundation for knowledge creation. *California Management Review*, Spring 1998, 40–54.

———. 1994. A dynamic theory of organizational knowledge creation. *Organizational Science* 5, no. 1:14–37.

———. 1991. The knowledge-creating company. *Harvard Business Review*, November-December, 14–37.

Nonaka, I., and T. Nishigushi, eds. Forthcoming. *Knowledge emergence*. New York: Oxford University Press.

Nonaka, I., and H. Takeuchi. 1995. *The knowledge-creating company: How Japanese companies create the dynamics of innovation*. New York: Oxford University Press.

Nonaka, I., and G. von Krogh. 1999. Wissens-Hysterie. *Managermagazin*, April, 164.

Osborne, H. 1986. What makes an experience aesthetic? In *Possibility of aesthetic experience*, ed. M. H. Mitias, 117–38. Dordrecht, Netherlands: M. Nijhoff Publishers.

Petrash, G. 1996. Dow's journey to a knowledge value management culture. *European Management Journal* 14, no. 4:365–73.

Pettigrew, A. M. 1992. On studying managerial elites. *Strategic Management Journal* 13: 163–82. Winter Special Issue.

Pfeffer, J. 1992. *Managing with power: Politics and influence in organizations*. Boston: Harvard Business School Press.

Piaget, J. 1960. *The psychology of intelligence*. Totowa, N.J.: Littlefield, Adams, & Co.

Polanyi, M. 1967. *The tacit dimension*. Garden City, N.Y.: Anchor Books.

———. 1958. *Personal knowledge: Towards a post-critical philosophy*. Chicago: University of Chicago Press.

Polanyi, M., and H. Prosch. 1975. *Meaning*. Chicago: University of Chicago Press.

Porter, M. E. 1990. *Competitive strategy*. New York: Free Press.

Prahalad, C. K., and R. Bettis. 1986. The dominant logic: A new linkage between diversity and performance. *Strategic Management Journal* 7, no. 6:485–501.

Radhakrishnan, R. 1990. Toward an effective intellectual. In *Intellectuals*, ed. B. Robbins, 57–101. Minneapolis: University of Minnesota Press.

Reich, R. B. 1998. The company of the future. *Fast Company*, no. 19:124–52.

Ricoeur, P. 1992. *Hermeneutics and human sciences*. Cambridge: Cambridge University Press.

Roos, J., G. Roos, L. Edvinsson, and N. C. Dragonetti. 1997. *Intellectual capital: Navigating in the new business landscape*. New York: Macmillan Business.

Rosenau, P. M. 1992. *Post-modernism and the social sciences*. Princeton, N.J.: Princeton University Press.

Rosener, J. 1995. *America's competitive secret: Utilizing women as a management strategy*. New York: Oxford University Press.

Ruggles, R. 1997. *Knowledge management tools*. Boston: Butterworth Heinemann.

Rumelt, R. 1980. The evaluation of business strategy. In *Business Policy and Strategic Management*, ed. W. F. Glueck. New York: McGraw Hill.

Russell, B. 1959. *Introduction to mathematical philosophy*. London: Allen and Unwin.

———. 1956. On denoting. In *Logic and knowledge*, ed. R.C. Marsh, 41–56. London: Allen and Unwin.

Sartre, J. P. 1978. The psychology of imagination. Westport, Conn.: Greenwood Publishing Group.

———. 1976. *Critique of dialectical reason*, New York: New Left Books.

Schiessl, M. 1996. Meine Chaos-Chance. *Der Spiegel* 20:121–27.

Schrage, M. 1997. Collaborative tools: A first look. In *Knowledge management tools*, ed. J. Ruggles, 167–86. Boston: Butterworth-Heineman.

Schutz, A. 1967. *The phenomenology of the social world*. Evanston, Ill.: Northwestern University Press.

Schwandt, D. 1997. Integrating strategy and organizational learning. In *Advances in strategic management*, ed. A. Huff and J. Walsh, Vol. 14, 337–60. Greenwich, Conn.: JAI Press.

Schwartz, P. 1996. *The art of the long view*. New York: Wiley.

Senge, P. 1990.The leader's new work: Building learning organizations. *Sloan Management Review* 32, no. 1:7–24.

Shanks, D. R., and T. Johnstone. 1998. Implicit knowledge in sequential learning tasks. In *Handbook of implicit learning*, ed. M. A. Stadler and P. A. French, 533–72. London: Sage.

Shimizu, H. 1995. Ba-Principle: New logic for the real-time emergence of information. *Holonics* 5, no. 1:67–79.

Shiseido. 1996. *Annual report*.

Simon, N. 1989. *Models of thought*. Vol. 2. New Haven, Conn.: Yale University Press.

Smith, K., and D. N. Berg 1987. *Paradoxes of group life*. San Francisco: Jossey-Bass.

Souder, W. 1987. *Managing new product innovations*. Lexington, Mass.: Lexington Press.

Sparrow, J. 1998. *Knowledge in organizations*. London: Sage.

Stchr, N. 1994. *Knowledge societies*. London: Sage.

Sveiby, K. E. 1996. Transfer of knowledge and the information processing professions. *European Management Journal* 14, no. 4: 379–88.

Szulanski, G. 1996. Exploring internal stickiness: impediments to the transfer of best practice within the firm. *Strategic Management Journal* 17:27–43. Special Issue.

Tannen, D. 1994. *Talking from 9 to 5*. New York: Avon Books.

Teece, D. J. 1981. The market of know-how and the efficient transfer of technology. *The Annals of the Academy of Political and Social Science*, 81–96.

Thomas, C. 1998. Scenario-based planning for technology investments. In *Learning from the future: Competitive foresight scenarios*, ed. L. Fahey and R. M. Randall, 246–63. New York: Wiley .

Thomas, R. J., ed. 1995. *New product success stories*. New York: Wiley.

Tilghman, B. R. 1991. *Wittgenstein, ethics, and aesthetics*. London: Macmillan.

Time Magazine. 1997/1998. Shape of things to come. *Time Magazine*, 28. Winter Special Issue.

Time Warner. 1996. *Annual report: Even better together*. New York: Time Warner.

Toffler, A. 1990. Powershift: Knowledge, wealth and violence at the edge of the twenty-first century. New York: Bantam Books.

Tolman, C. E. 1935. Psychology versus immediate experience. *Philosophy of Science* 2:356–80.

Tomrey, A. 1971. *The Concept of expression*. Princeton, N.J.: Princeton University Press.

Toshiba. 1997. *Annual report*.

Varela, F., E. Thompson, and E. Rosch. 1994. *The embodied mind: Cognitive science and human experience*. Cambridge, Mass.: MIT Press.

Venzin, M. 1997. Crafting the future: strategic conversations in the knowledge economy. Ph.D. diss., University of St. Gallen.

Volkmann, H. 1996. *Xenia, Stadt des Wissens und Stätte der Begegnung am Wege zur Infor-*

mationsgesellschaft. Documentation for the CeBit Home, August 28 to September 1. Hanover.

———. 1995. Wandel der Informationskultur mit der "Stadt des Wissens als Stätte der Begegnung." *Gabler Magazin* 3:25–29.

———. 1994. Über Datenautobahnen spricht man nicht—man benutzt sie. *Computerwoche,* November.

von Hippel, E. 1978. Users as innovators. *Technology Review,* January, 31–37.

von Krogh, G. 1998. Care in knowledge creation. *California Management Review* 40, no. 3:133–54.

von Krogh, G., K. Ichijo, and I. Nonaka. Forthcoming. Bringing care into knowledge creation of business organizations. In *Knowledge emergence,* ed. I. Nonaka and T. Nishigushi. New York: Oxford University Press.

von Krogh, G., I. Nonaka, and K. Ichijo. 1997. Develop knowledge activists! *European Management Journal* 15, no. 5:475–83.

von Krogh, G., and J. Roos. 1997. A phraseologic view of organizational learning. In *Advances in strategic management,* ed. by A. Huff and J. Walsh, Vol. 14, 53–74. Greenwich, Conn.: JAI Press.

———, eds. 1996a. *Managing knowledge: Perspectives on cooperation and competition.* London: Sage.

———. 1996b. A tale of the unfinished. *Strategic Management Journal* 17, no. 9:729–39.

———. 1996c. The new language lab—parts 1 and 2. *Financial Times* 21, no. 3:9–12.

———. 1996d. Conversation management for knowledge development. In *Managing knowledge: Perspectives on competition and cooperation,* ed. G. von Krogh and J. Roos, 218–25. London: Sage.

———. 1995a. *Organizational epistemology.* London: Macmillan.

———. 1995b. A perspective on knowledge, competence and strategy. *Personnel Review* 24, no. 3:56–76.

———. 1992. Figuring out your competence configuration. *European Management Journal,* December, 422–26.

von Krogh, G., J. Roos, and D. Kleine, eds. 1998a. Knowing in firms. London: Sage.

von Krogh, G., J. Roos, and K. Slocum. 1994. An essay on corporate epistemology. *Strategic Management Journal* 15:53–72. Special Issue.

Warnecke, H. J. 1993. *The fractal company: A revolution in corporate culture.* Berlin: Springer.

Weber, J. 1998. The global 1000: The year of the deal. *Business Week,* 13 July, 42–55.

Weick, K., and L. Browning. 1986. Arguments and narration in organizational communication. *Journal of Management* 12:243–59.

Weick, K., and F. Westley. 1996. Organizational learning: Affirming an oxymoron. In *Handbook of Organization Studies,* ed. S. R. Clegg, C. Hardy, and W. R. Nord, 440–58. London: Sage.

Wenger, E. 1998. *Communities of practice: Learning, meaning and identity.* Cambridge: Cambridge University Press.

Westley, F. 1990. Middle managers and strategy: Microdynamics of inclusion. *Strategic Management Journal* 11, no. 5:337–51.

Whitehead, A. N. 1954. *Dialogues of Alfred North Whitehead.* Recorded by L. Price. Boston: Little, Brown.

Wiig, K. 1995. *Knowledge management methods.* Arlington, Va.: Schema Press.

Wilson, I. 1998. Mental maps of the future: An intuitive logics approach to scenarios. In *Learning from the future: Competitive foresight scenarios,* ed. L. Fahey and R. M. Randall, 81–108. New York: Wiley.

Wittgenstein, L. 1958. *Philosophical investigations.* New York: Macmillan.

INDEX